TRADERS

TRADERS

*Risks, Decisions, and Management
in Financial Markets*

**Mark Fenton-O'Creevy
Nigel Nicholson
Emma Soane
Paul Willman**

OXFORD
UNIVERSITY PRESS

OXFORD

UNIVERSITY PRESS

Great Clarendon Street, Oxford OX2 6DP

Oxford University Press is a department of the University of Oxford.
It furthers the University's objective of excellence in research, scholarship,
and education by publishing worldwide in

Oxford New York

Auckland Bangkok Buenos Aires Cape Town Chennai
Dar es Salaam Delhi Hong Kong Istanbul Karachi Kolkata
Kuala Lumpur Madrid Melbourne Mexico City Mumbai Nairobi
São Paulo Shanghai Taipei Tokyo Toronto

Oxford is a registered trade mark of Oxford University Press
in the UK and in certain other countries

Published in the United States
by Oxford University Press Inc., New York

© Oxford University Press 2005

The moral rights of the author have been asserted
Database right Oxford University Press (maker)

First published 2005
First published in paperback 2007

British Library Cataloguing in Publication Data
Data available

Library of Congress Cataloging in Publication Data
Data available

Typeset by SPI Publisher Services, Pondicherry, India
Printed in Great Britain
by Ashford Colour Press Ltd.,
Gosport, Hampshire
ISBN 978–0–19–926948–8 (Hbk.)
      978–0–19–922645–0 (Pbk.)

1 3 5 7 9 10 8 6 4 2

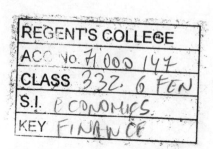

Acknowledgements

We gratefully acknowledge the help of the investment banks which cooperated in this research and provided financial support, and the Economic and Social Research Council which provided funding as part of the Risk and Human Behaviour Programme (grant number L211252056). We are especially grateful to the traders and managers who gave us their time and shared their understanding.

Contents

List of Figures

List of Tables

Chapter 1

INTRODUCTION
Traders, Markets, and Social Science

I grew up in a small town in Florida and none of this stuff really exists like stocks and bonds and things like that. No one I ever knew growing up did this sort of thing and to me it all seems like a fantasy world sometimes and it's very abstract. You know, I explain to my mother what I do and I can't, you can't put it into words, it just doesn't make any sense. I am so removed from the daily life of the average person that I think at some point this has got to come to an end. Whether I really believe that or not I don't know but in my head I kind of think this is all fantasy land and one day I'm going to wake up and I'm going to say I had the most amazing dream, I've been working on some place called Wall Street, that paid me lots of money and I just sat around and looked at computers all day and put these pieces together and everything worked out and it was all a lot of fun. So in my mind that's kind of what I think.

Derivatives Trader, firm B

We live in a world that is shaped by financial markets and we are all profoundly affected by their operation. Our employment prospects, our financial security, our pensions, the stability of political systems and nature of the society we live in are all greatly influenced by the operation of these markets.

The role and importance of international financial markets and the traders who inhabit them has grown dramatically in the past few decades. The level of financial flows in these markets can rise to quite staggering levels. For example, in the day before the setting of entry exchange rates to the Euro, trades in currencies entering the Euro totalled about ten times World gross domestic product (GDP). At any one time, outstanding derivatives contracts have a total value of around four times World GDP.

Professional traders figure prominently in media accounts of the workings of financial markets and the economy. Television news bulletins on the economy or stock market frequently include interviews with senior traders, or footage of a trading floor. Stories about 'rogue' traders are big news. The decisions of individual traders are often seen as having the potential to move markets and affect national economies. Yet, the role of the professional trader is largely absent from mainstream financial economic accounts of markets.

Professional traders, we argue, inhabit a borderland in markets where some of the orthodox assumptions of efficient, instantaneously adjusting prices break-down. They are often well placed to exploit market imperfections, by virtue of lower transaction costs, access to privileged information, critical mass, or proprietary knowledge and models. However, at the same time, they work in a fast-moving landscape of noise, rumour, unreliable information, and uncertainty. Thus, it is often difficult to tell whether an opportunity is real or illusory.

This is a book about professional traders in this noisy borderland: what they do, the kind of people they are, how they perceive the world they inhabit, how they make decisions and take risks. This is also a book about how traders are managed and the institutions they inhabit: firms, markets, cultures, and theories of how the world works. Our approach to writing this book is explicitly interdisciplinary. We draw on psychology, sociology, and economics in order to illuminate the work of traders and their world. Our focus is traders and the firms they work in.

It is not the purpose of this book to mount an extensive critique of the dominant rational–economic account of financial markets, nor is 'markets' our central focus. We are concerned principally with understanding the world of the professional trader. However, we do believe our work is relevant to an understanding of financial markets.

First, in order to understand the role and work of the trader, it is important to understand that the neoclassical paradigm of efficient markets and rational pricing breaks down at the margins and that professional traders both benefit from and contribute to this departure from orthodox financial economic theory. Second, the efficient markets paradigm rests on the assumption that in the absence of uniformly rational investors, there is a sufficient group of rational investors who are able to drive out pricing anomalies through arbitrage.[1] Professional traders in investment banks seem good candidates to play this role. Hence, the evidence that we present on the ways in which traders can deviate significantly from rational–economic norms of behaviour may be fruitful in helping to explain market phenomena.

1.1 Our Work and How It Informs the Book

This book is based on a study of traders in financial instruments in four large investment banks operating in the City of London. Over the course of 1997 and 1998, we carried out interviews with 118 traders and trader managers in four large City of London investment banks and collected qualitative and quantitative data on their roles, behaviour, performance, and psychological profiles. We carried out follow-up interviews in 2002.[2] We use detailed quotations from the interviews throughout the book. Where we use these quotes they are presented verbatim. We had three main concerns.

First, we came to the study with a strong interest in decision-making and risk. While all business is concerned to some extent with risk, investment banks and financial traders are almost unique in the extent to which their work is founded on the management of risk and the extent to which they must make decisions about risk.

Second, in the vast literature on financial markets relatively little attention has been paid to the role of finance professionals in these markets and we wanted to redress this.

Third, we observed that the large literature on markets and the (somewhat slimmer) literature on traders are marked by very different approaches and paradigms in three branches of the social sciences: economics, sociology, and cognitive and social psychology. We wanted to bring together the insights of these different disciplines.

Throughout the book we draw both on the data we gathered in this study and on the insights of prior research and literature in financial economics, psychology, and the sociology of markets. We turn now to those literatures.

1.2 Traders in the Social Science Literature

Neoclassical Financial Economics

Financial economics is a relatively young discipline. The origins of modern (neoclassical) financial economics are often located in the early 1950s in the work by Markowitz (1952) on portfolio theory. During this period, finance moved from a concern with describing the activities of actors in financial markets to the construction of parsimonious models of markets founded on assumptions of rational investor behaviour. The central organizing idea of neoclassical financial economics is the efficient markets hypothesis, which holds that price changes are essentially a random walk. All new information relevant to prices is incorporated into prices instantaneously (Fama, 1970). This central proposition and much of the theory which springs from it is founded on the idea that any asset which is not 'rationally priced' provides opportunities for profit, which will be instantly taken up and cause prices to converge to the 'rational' level (i.e. arbitrage). This assumption is both illustrated and lampooned in the finance joke about two efficient market theorists who pass a $50 bill lying in the street. They leave it untouched and congratulate each other on realizing that if it presented an opportunity for profit someone else would have picked it up already.

Even the strongest proponents of the efficient markets hypothesis do not claim that it represents a good description of the behaviour of individuals in markets. Rather it is claimed to be a good enough description, which should be judged on its predictions rather than its assumptions.

Fama (1970), who set out an early comprehensive account of the efficient markets paradigm, has more recently suggested that:

> Like all models, market efficiency (the hypothesis that prices fully reflect available information) is a faulty description of price formation. Following the standard scientific rule, however, market efficiency can only be replaced by a better specific model of price formation, itself potentially rejectable by empirical tests. (Fama, 1998: 284)

The finance professional is largely absent from orthodox financial economic accounts of markets. The assumption of efficient markets, with no privileged information held by any investor, leaves little room for an account of how professional investors might make better than market returns. However, more recently, there has been an increasing interest within financial economics in explaining empirically observed departures from the predictions of the efficient markets hypothesis and rational–economic pricing theories. Many of these fall in the emerging field of behavioural finance.

What has allowed consideration of the role different types of investor might play in markets is the growing recognition that perfectly efficient markets are not an automatic consequence of the existence of arbitragers: an idea that has been captured eloquently by Lee (2001: 284).

> I submit that moving from the mechanics of arbitrage to the [efficient markets hypothesis] involves an enormous leap of faith. It is akin to believing that the ocean is flat, simply because we have observed the forces of gravity at work on a glass of water. No one questions the effect of gravity, or the fact that water is always seeking its own level. But it is a stretch to infer from this observation that oceans should look like millponds on a still summer night. If oceans were flat, how do we explain predictable patterns, such as tides and currents? How can we account for the existence of waves, and of surfers? More to the point, if we are in the business of training surfers, does it make sense to begin by assuming that waves, in theory, do not exist?

A more measured, and more descriptive, statement is that the ocean is constantly trying to become flat. In reality, market prices are buffeted by a continuous flow of information, or rumours and innuendos disguised as information. Individuals reacting to these signals, or pseudo-signals, cannot fully calibrate the extent to which their own signal is already reflected in price. Prices move as they trade on the basis of their imperfect informational endowments. Eventually, through trial and error, the aggregation process is completed and prices adjust to fully reveal the impact of a particular signal. But by that time, many new signals have arrived, causing new turbulence. As a result, the ocean is in a constant state of restlessness. The market is in a continuous state of adjustment.

Lee argues that the relationship between inefficient pricing and arbitragers may be like predator–prey dynamics. In equilibrium there must be both predator and prey. Similarly, in equilibrium there will be both arbitragers and arbitrage opportunities in the market place.

There is another important way in which financial markets are widely accepted as departing from the efficient markets paradigm. Investors trade much more often than the theory suggests they should. More recent financial economics accounts often distinguish two types of investors: 'noise traders' and 'smart traders' (a recent example is Daniel, Hirshleifer, and Teoh, 2002). Noise trading is trading on the basis of information that is either irrelevant to price or has already been discounted by the market. 'Smart' traders are those who act rationally, trading only on the basis of genuinely new and relevant information. This distinction is sometimes taken to map on to the difference between naïve investors and trained professional investors (e.g. Ross, 1999; Shapira and Venezia, 2001).

Behavioural Finance

There has been increasing interest within the field of financial economics in using what is known about persistent biases in human cognition to explain departures of market behaviour from the predictions of efficient markets theory. Collectively known as behavioural finance, these models and empirical studies generally seek to explain market behaviour that departs from the predictions of orthodox financial economics by reference to systematic cognitive bias among investors or important subgroups of investors.[3] Behavioural finance draws heavily on work from behavioural decision-making, a branch of psychology concerned with modelling human decision-making processes. While, in the main, this literature does not distinguish between professional traders and other investors, there have been some attempts to compare the susceptibility to biases of finance professionals to that of the wider population.

For example, Shapira and Venezia (2001) found professional brokers less susceptible than independent investors to one common bias, the disposition effect (a bias towards selling stocks more readily to realize gains than to realize losses), although they were not immune to the bias. In an experimental study Anderson and Sunder (1995) compared the behaviour of laboratory markets populated by experienced commodity and stock traders with the behaviour of markets populated by MBA student traders. They found the amount of trading experience to be an important determinant of how well market outcomes approximated (efficient market) equilibrium predictions. Student traders' markets exhibited departures from rational prices founded in common cognitive biases while bias levels in markets with experienced traders were substantially lower. However, as we explore in Chapter 5, our own research offers evidence that professional traders are just as susceptible as other groups to some forms of bias, with important consequences for their behaviour and performance.

Sociology of Markets

Sociologists interested in markets have paid rather more attention to the role of professionals than have financial economists. Unlike financial economists who take markets to be naturally occurring, sociologists tend to stress the 'social embeddedness' of markets and the ways in which they are sustained as social institutions through active intervention and regulation. One important strand of work is concerned with the social networks that operate within markets and in particular the ways in which professionals within markets act through these social networks and exercise informal sanctions over participants departing from accepted norms of behaviour (e.g. Baker, 1984a; Abolafia, 1996). Research by financial economists also demonstrates the significant effect the detailed structure and organisation of markets[4] can have on the flow of information, liquidity, and prices (e.g. Amihud, Mendelson, and Lauterback, 1997; Lipson, 2003).

Others have been concerned with the nature and consequences of financial economic theory. Traders, from this perspective, do not simply inhabit markets; they enact them. That is, the beliefs they hold

Introduction

about the nature of markets affect those markets in non-trivial ways. MacKenzie (2002), for example, describes how the adoption of the Black–Scholes equation for option pricing by traders did not simply enable more effective pricing of options, but helped to bring about conditions that better fitted the assumptions on which it was based. The close empirical fit between the predictions of the equation and options prices was bought about, at least in part, by the use of the equation to identify arbitrage opportunities. The empirical fit has deteriorated subsequently as beliefs have changed to incorporate, *inter alia*, changed beliefs about the likelihood of market crashes. We pick up this theme of the reflexive relationship between beliefs and markets in Chapter 4.

1.3   Overview of Book

Chapters 2 and 3 set the context for our study and exploration of the role of traders. Chapter 2, 'The Growth of Financial Markets and The Role of Traders', considers the growth of international financial markets in a historical context and outlines the role investment banks and professional traders have come to play. In Chapter 3, 'Economic, Psychological, and Social Explanations of Market Behaviour', we take a more detailed look at differing economic, psychological, and social explanations of market behaviour.

Chapter 4, 'Traders and Their Theories', considers the nature of traders' knowledge and the interplay between their subscriptions to theories of the 'way the world works' founded in neoclassical financial economics and their more particularist and idiosyncratic theories of 'how to work the world'.

Chapter 5, 'A Framework for Understanding Trader Psychology', starts by outlining a psychological model of the trader founded in a self-regulation framework. It draws on the qualitative and quantitative evidence that we have about trader decision-making and bias. It challenges the financial economics dichotomy between rational and non-rational and explains the different rationalities that arise as a consequence of internal goal states. We also present evidence on the vulnerability of traders to control illusions and the consequences for their performance.

Chapter 6, 'Risk Takers: Profiling Traders' presents a new model of risk taking that shows how trader behaviour emerges from a web of circumstantial and individual causes. The remainder of the chapter explores these individual differences in greater depth, especially how personality impacts different kinds of risk taking and decision-making. The chapter explores what kinds of people traders are, focusing particularly on personality and risk propensity, but also drawing on what we know about their demographics and background.

Chapter 7, 'Becoming a Trader', uses a career transitions framework and a model of social learning to frame trader development and entry into a community of trading practice. We examine the ways in which they both learn and construct knowledge about the process of trading.

In Chapter 8, 'Managing Traders', we explore the ways in which traders are monitored and managed within investment banks. We highlight the fact that traders are often not 'managed' at all, so much as monitored.

Our concluding chapter (Chapter 9) draws together the implications of our findings for traders, their management and regulation, and for further research.

Notes

1. Arbitrage: purchasing currencies, securities, or commodities in one market for resale in others in order to profit from price differences. The effect of arbitrage is to act as a mechanism to bring about convergence of prices in different locations and markets or between equivalent securities.
2. A more detailed account of the sample and methods is given in the appendix.
3. We give a more detailed treatment of behavioural finance arguments in Chapter 3.
4. Often referred to as the institutional microstructure.

Chapter 2

THE GROWTH OF FINANCIAL MARKETS AND THE ROLE OF TRADERS

Hardly a day passes without newspapers and television carrying a story about financial markets and their impact on our lives. Even a casual perusal of these news stories makes it apparent that the activities of financial institutions and markets have come to play a central role in our economic well-being and security: whether through their direct impact on individual investments and pensions or through their pervasive impact on the level of economic activity within nations and across the globe.

The last decade of the twentieth century was marked by a series of international financial crises. These underlined both the interdependence of national economies and financial markets and the global scope of those markets. Financial crises in Latin America, the Asian Tiger economies, and Russia highlighted the speed at which capital can flee countries in which investors have lost confidence and the impotence of national governments to control such outflows. The impact around the world of these crises on economies and financial institutions demonstrated the highly interconnected nature of financial markets.

In the same period a number of financial institutions suffered very significant financial losses as a consequence of the actions of single traders. One of the best publicized of these was Nick Leeson's role in bringing about the collapse of Barings Brothers, in 1995. The collapse of Barings caused Alan Greenspan of the US Federal Reserve to comment that

It is probably fair to say that the very efficiency of global financial markets, engendered by the rapid proliferation of financial products, also has the capability of transmitting mistakes at a far faster pace throughout the financial system in ways that were unknown a generation ago . . . Certainly, the recent Barings Brothers episode shows that large losses can be created quite efficiently. Today's technology enables single individuals to initiate massive transactions with very rapid execution. Clearly, not only has the productivity of global finance increased markedly, but so, obviously, has the ability to generate losses at a previously inconceivable rate. Moreover, increasing global financial efficiency, by creating the mechanisms for mistakes to ricochet throughout the global financial system, has patently increased the potential for systemic risk. (Greenspan, 1995)

While the behaviour of individual traders has at times seriously damaged the firms they work for, individual financial institutions have also shown the capacity to endanger the stability and operation of financial markets around the world. In 1998, the collapse of Long Term Capital Management, a hedge fund holding positions in financial derivatives with a notional value of $1,250 billion seriously endangered the stability of the world's financial systems.

How could a single trader bring down a bank? How could a single hedge fund threaten the stability of the world's financial systems? The answer lies in the way in which 'derivatives' allow for the multiplication of market risks (and returns). The very features that make derivatives[1] so useful as a tool for managing risk provide for the possibility of massively increasing risks.

In this chapter, we argue that the role of financial markets, in both world and national economies, has increased dramatically.

The potential, and sometimes actual, impact of individual traders on firms, markets, and economies is enormous. In the following chapters we show that financial markets are neither as rational nor as natural as financial economists paint them and that we need to bring a wider range of social science theory to bear on understanding traders, their firms, and the markets they operate in.

As we show below, the current globalization of financial markets is not new but simply the latest of several cycles of international financial integration over two millennia. In particular, the recent growth in international financial markets could be seen as a return to levels of international financial integration seen at the end of the nineteenth century and interrupted by a period, which included two world wars and the Great Depression. However, the depth and scale of these markets does seem to be different this time and the emergence of new forms of financial instruments, derivatives, capable of massively multiplying possible risks and returns has led to a qualitative difference in the potential impact of individual actions on institutions, markets, and economies.

2.1   A Brief History of Financial Markets

International financial markets are not a purely modern phenomenon. Basic forms of financial exchange can be found throughout recorded history and international financial systems are known to have existed two millennia ago. Historical evidence suggests that there have been a series of cycles of international financial integration (Lothian, 2002). In the three centuries following the collapse of the Roman Empire, currencies were very unstable and constantly debased. However, in the fourth-century AD, the Emperor Constantine introduced a stable gold coinage, the bezant (also known as the nomisa or solidus). This became widely used throughout the Mediterranean region. It was produced in Byzantium till the thirteenth century and kept more or less the same gold content through till the eleventh century. Until the introduction of the dinar in the Muslim world in the seventh century, it had no competitors as an international medium of exchange. While records are patchy, it is clear that the existence of a stable medium of international exchange during the period between the fourth and eleventh centuries allowed quite sophisticated financial transactions to take place (Lopez, 1986; Lothian, 2002).

The thirteenth century was another period of growth in international trade, both within Europe and between Europe and other parts of the world. Much of this was organized around regular international trade fairs (most notably at Champagne and Brie). This period was marked by the growth of an extensive and sophisticated banking system and by the development of financial instruments such as bills of exchange (which acted jointly as a credit and foreign exchange transaction). It is clear from the records of the dominant northern Italian banks of the time that not only were there quite sophisticated foreign exchange markets, but also that arbitrage was a common activity (Lothian, 2002).

During the fourteenth century the importance of these trade fairs and the Italian banks declined. By the fifteenth century, Amsterdam was the more important centre of financial activity. The sixteenth century saw the development, in Amsterdam, of negotiable financial instruments such as discounting commercial paper and, by the seventeenth century, the development of perpetual bonds, futures contracts, selling short, and other such financial instruments and techniques that would be easily recognized in modern financial markets (Homer and Sylla, 1996; Lothian, 2002). By the start of the eighteenth century, the Amsterdam Exchange, the centre of Dutch trading, had become a world market in which a wide range of commodities and securities were traded. During this period, London took on increasing importance as a centre for international financial trade. With the establishment of the Bank of England and the London Stock Exchange and the intervention of the Napoleonic wars, London came to eclipse Amsterdam as a financial centre by the start of the nineteenth century.

The nineteenth century saw a marked expansion of international trade and further development of financial markets. The growth of the US economy drove much of this expansion. The New York Stock Exchange was established in 1817 and by the end of 1886 it hit its first day on which more than a million shares were traded. By the late 1920s New York had overtaken London as a world financial centre. However, the early twentieth century, a period that included two world wars and the Great Depression, saw the collapse of international

Growth of Financial Markets

trade and the rise of national regulation and controls on international flows of capital, which effectively unwound the integration of international financial markets. Rajan and Zingales (2003) show that on a range of indicators of financial development including stock market capitalization as a proportion of GDP, world financial markets did not regain their pre-war (1913) levels until the late 1980s.

The second half of the twentieth century once again saw a very substantial increase in international financial integration. As we have seen, there is historical evidence that the current period of globalization of financial markets is not a new phenomenon. Rather there have been cycles of high international integration of markets interspersed with periods of low integration throughout the last two millennia. However, it is also clear that with each new cycle the nature and depth of those markets has been changing. Changes in the sophistication of financial instruments and technologies, and changes in communications and information technologies have all been important factors influencing the scale and complexity of financial markets.

The period since the 1970s has seen a very substantial increase in the size of financial markets. Figure 2.1[2] shows the increase in annual

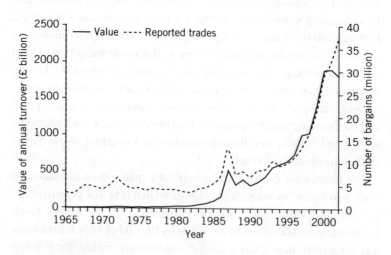

Fig. 2.1 Post-war UK equity market growth—UK equity turnover 1965–2002

Source: London Stock Exchange.

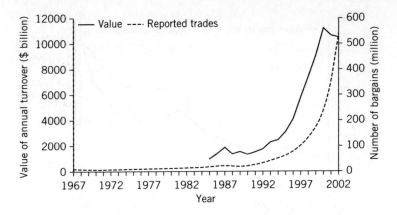

Fig. 2.2   Post-war US equity market growth—New York Stock Exchange equity turnover 1967–2002

Source: New York Stock Exchange.

value of shares traded on the London Stock Exchange between 1965 and 2002. Figure 2.2 shows the change in annual number of shares traded on the New York Stock Exchange between 1960 and 2002 and the annual value of shares traded from 1985.

Both markets show exponential growth over the period, but the real story over the last decade is the growth in derivatives trading. By 2002, outstanding over-the-counter derivatives[3] (OTC) contracts had a notional value of $128 trillion, around four times greater than total world GDP. Figure 2.3 shows the growth in number of active contracts between 1992 and 2002.

Much of the recent concern about systemic risks in markets has centred on the role of derivatives. All financial investments carry risk. However, there is a difference of degree with derivative trading. They involve contracts which are contingent on the price of underlying assets and because of the way in which trades are regulated, derivatives[4] enable investors to speculate on the price of an asset while only depositing a small proportion of the underlying asset price (margin requirements) (Zhang, 1995). In other words, the financial risk borne in an options trade may be many times the money actually deposited to make the trade. Financial firms which do not have sophisticated control mechanisms to manage their exposure to derivatives risk may

15

Growth of Financial Markets

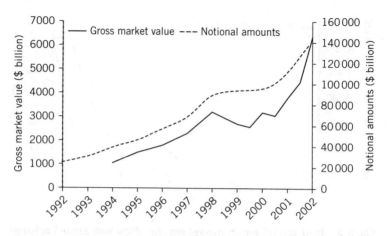

Fig. 2.3   Global growth in OTC derivatives—global value of outstanding contracts

Source: 2000–2, Bank for International Settlements; 1994–9, Swaps Monitor publications Inc.

unwittingly find themselves exposed to potential losses greater than the total firm assets. Such risks can emerge very rapidly in the course of trading and require analysis of the whole firm's current portfolio of trading assets in real time to identify potential overexposure to market risk. Of course, the leveraging effect of derivatives does not only affect market risk but also amplifies risk in the other categories. For example, since derivatives typically have greater volatility than the underlying asset, even a short period in which a firm is unable to trade (say due to computer failure) could result in significant risk exposure. The complexity of some derivatives may mean that managers are ill-equipped to understand the trades dealers are engaging in, increasing behavioural risk (Chorafas, 1995: 16).

In evidence given to the US House of Representatives, George Soros, a highly successful financial speculator, said of derivative instruments:

> There are many of them, and some of them are so esoteric, that the risks involved may not be properly understood by even the most sophisticated of investors. Some of these instruments appear to be

specifically designed to enable institutional investors to take gambles which they would otherwise not be permitted to take. For example, some bond funds have invested in synthetic bond issues that carry a 10 or 20-fold multiple of the risk within defined limits. And some other instruments offer exceptional returns because they carry the seeds of a total wipe out. (Soros, 1995: 312)

2.2   The Role of Investment Banks in Financial Markets

To understand the role of modern investment banks it is necessary to understand how world financial markets have come to be dominated by an American model of finance. Much as Byzantium, Lombardy, Amsterdam, and London have been the dominant centres of financial innovation and power in previous eras, US financial markets and institutions are today. The central feature of the US model that emerged in the post-war years was the decline of relationship banking and the increasing commoditization of financial products and services. The roots of this system lie in the unintended consequences of anti-trust and banking legislation passed in the United States during the 1930s. The segregation of commercial and investment banking in the United States laid the foundation for the development of a strong investment-banking sector. The fragmentation of the banking industry, imposed by legislation, created conditions in which financial transactions were more readily managed through markets than within large banks. The elimination of fixed commissions for broking financial instruments in 1975 provided a further impetus for competition. More and more, firms seeking to raise finance looked to impersonal markets rather than relationships with banking institutions. Progressively more transparent and liquid markets in both corporate debt and equity and the corresponding increased competition in these markets served as a significant stimulus to financial innovation.

As these markets developed it became apparent to market participants and to the government that effective market operation could only be maintained through active intervention and regulation. A series of waves of external and self-regulation, often in response to market crises, led to the development of regulations and supervisory arrangements designed to contain insider manipulation of markets and ensure free flow of information. On the demand side, the expansion of institutional investment (insurance, pensions, and mutual funds) stimulated and was stimulated by the growth of these financial markets.

The slower growth of financial markets and institutions in other parts of the world meant that, as other countries began to follow the United States in opening up competition, US financial institutions were well placed to play a major role. In the wake of the major changes in market regulation in 1986, the long-established London merchant banks were swept away by the US-based investment banks and non-US owned European investment banks have increasingly adopted US approaches.

The principal competitive advantage of American firms lay in their expertise in managing risk (Steinherr, 2000: 49). Investment banks manage risk in four main ways: they absorb risk for clients, they act as intermediaries for the diversification of risk, they advise on the management of risk and they engage in proprietary trading—taking risk on their own account in the pursuit of returns (Casserley, 1991).

Absorbing Risk

Investment banks absorb risk for clients in a number of different ways. For example, when they act on behalf of a client they absorb credit risk (the risk the client will default on payment for the transaction and they are unable to unwind the transaction at a favourable price). They underwrite issues of securities (e.g. commercial paper[5] to cover short-term financing needs), guaranteeing to buy from the client at a fixed price should the security fail to achieve its expected price in the open market. They also play an important risk absorption role in trading markets. In some of these the bank will act as a market-maker,[6] providing liquidity in a particular financial instrument. The bank fixes prices at which it will buy or sell a financial instrument and stands ready to buy or sell at those prices even if there is no party to pass the transaction on to immediately. In return for the spread between these prices the bank absorbs the risk of the market moving against them.

Risk Intermediation

In other cases the bank will act as an intermediary for the diversification of clients' risk. This may be by acting as an intermediary in trading markets or by putting together complex OTC deals that rely on aggregating (or disaggregating) financial instruments provided by third parties. The banks benefit from this intermediation work in two principal ways. First, they charge commission and second, they have access via their customers to information about order flows in the markets in which they operate. Such flow information provides opportunities to exploit temporary market imperfections and profit through trading on their own account.

Risk Advice

The risk advice role overlays risk absorption and risk intermediation. For example, the bank may play an important advisory role related to underwriting activities or in putting together a complex OTC deal. The role of the bank in providing risk advice to clients rests not just on technical skills and experience in managing risk, but also in a (sometimes) greater overview of the markets in which they operate. An important issue here is the tension between the bank's desire to make profits on its own account and to earn a return through providing effective advice and services to customers. This tension is reflected to some extent in tensions which emerge in most banks between trading and sales desks. As we will see later in the book, banks vary in the priority they give to serving customer needs versus seeking opportunities for returns through trading on their own account.[7]

Proprietary Trading

In providing services to customers, investment banks build up information on order flows, they develop expertise in valuing particular securities or in economic fundamentals in particular sectors or countries, they build proprietary models of price behaviour and they build up data on historic behaviour of prices and relationships between them. This can place them in a better position to judge risks and returns than other market participants and opens up the possibility of earning good returns on their own account. This activity typically takes two forms: short-term (often intra-day) trades designed to exploit knowledge of temporary price fluctuations linked to flows of orders in the market and longer-term trades, often based on arbitrage (exploiting pricing inconsistencies between different securities, markets, or time periods).

2.3   The Role Played by Traders

The work of traders can be divided into three broad categories: trading on behalf of customers, market-making, and proprietary trading.[8] Traders acting on behalf of customers take the least risk on behalf of the bank, while proprietary trading potentially involves the greatest risk. However, in practice, the three spheres of activity often overlap. For example, a trading desk acting on behalf of clients may also have authority to take intra-day positions to benefit from short-term price movements in the markets they operate in. Alternatively, in some circumstances, while not strictly acting as a market-maker, they may stand ready to create liquidity for important clients by buying or selling to those clients when they cannot find a counterparty for their trades. As one senior trader told us:

> We are paid to be on the wrong side of the market for our customers. If we have an institution that pays us thirty million dollars a year in commissions, we will, on occasion at their request, be a buyer for them when there are only sellers on the market or be a seller for them when there are only buyers. When they're in a more normal market environment where there is plenty of liquidity and good two-way flow, they don't necessarily need our capital. In fact they prefer not to use our capital because all that does then is create another buyer or another seller in the market with them. But when the market is heavily tilted in one direction than the other, even the market's selling off, there are much more sellers than buyers or a very strong market where there are much more buyers than sellers. That's when they need us to step in and serve as that intermediary to facilitate the execution of their order.[9]

Alternatively, a trading desk operating as a market-maker may combine this with some proprietary trading. One trader described the activity of his desk:

> We have a P&L [profit and loss], budget of about $20m a year through plain vanilla market making with customers. However, we make about half the money in proprietary trading using the flow and information from customers—putting it on our book instead of putting it back into the market. For the first half of this year we were number one for turnover in our niche with between 10% and 15% of the market. The

more that number increases, the better information we would have for proprietary trading, but we would probably start losing money from the market making function because prices would have to be so keen, so there is a balance.

Equally, traders mostly engaged in proprietary trading will seek opportunities to generate customer business:

> I do proprietary business and I'm supposed to be doing proprietary but I interface with the flow desk so I would be looking at customer business trying to generate customer business. My slant is proprietary but I'm always trying to emphasise customer business using my positions.

2.4   How do Traders Make Profits?

If, in efficient markets, price changes are essentially a random walk and all new information relevant to prices is incorporated into prices instantaneously (Fama, 1970), then how do traders make money? The first answer is that they charge commission for their intermediation and advisory role. By aggregating customer orders they can reduce transaction costs.

However, as we will explore in Chapter 3, in practice, markets are not completely efficient and information asymmetries exist. Traders essentially earn economic rents[10] by exploiting information advantages. These may come from a number of sources, including information on asset flows within markets (e.g. from having a large customer base); privileged information on the economic basis for an asset price; proprietary databases allowing more accurate calculation of probabilities (e.g. historical asset volatility for pricing options); models of the relationship between prices and economic fundamentals; models for extracting the information inherent in historical price changes of an asset and other related assets; and effective understanding of the 'sentiment' and likely behaviour of other market actors.

All of these information advantages are potentially short-lived. The very act of trading may reveal information to other parties. Others may emulate models. Others may access the same sources of information. New information may wipe out the utility of earlier information. At the same time markets are in practice very 'noisy'. That is to say, there is a lot of trading going on that is not based on information genuinely relevant to the underlying value of an asset. Black (1986) noted in his presidential address to the American Finance Association that

> Traders can never be sure that they are trading on information rather than noise. What if the information they have is already reflected in prices? Trading on that kind of information will be just like trading on noise.

Traders can only earn above market returns, on average, over time, if they are genuinely trading on new and relevant information. However, on any individual trade it will be difficult to tell whether a positive outcome is the result of trading on information or of essentially unpredictable market movements (as a result of noise trading in the market, changes in sentiment, or new unexpected events). Similarly, for any individual trade it is difficult to determine whether a negative outcome is the result of trading on noise rather than information or the result of unforeseeable market movements.

So it will often be the case that trading outcomes are not contingent on the trader's strategy or information. Further, it will often be difficult to determine once an outcome is achieved whether the outcome was indeed contingent on a trader's information and skill. While trading is a skilful activity, many trading outcomes are not contingent on skill. At the same time traders are highly motivated to establish causal relationships between information they hold and prices, since a significant source of rent for any trader is the capacity to establish contingent relationships before others observe them. This problem of determining the links between behaviour and outcome for traders is one we will return to repeatedly in the book.

While the detail of different trading strategies is not our principal focus, we describe some common trading approaches to set the stage for our later discussions. In order for traders to achieve better than average market returns, it is not sufficient that markets are imperfect; it is also necessary they have some competitive advantage relative to others who seek to exploit those imperfections. Within this fast-moving and uncertain world, traders adopt a variety of strategies to exploit the information and expertise to which they have access. These can be divided into four main categories: insider strategies, technical strategies, fundamental strategies, and flow strategies.

Insider Strategies

Insider strategies involve achieving advantage by exploiting privileged access to information (Casserley, 1991). Of course, some such strategies are illegal. It is, for example, illegal to exploit privileged access to advanced knowledge of company earnings news or potential takeovers. However, most of these strategies are concerned with perfectly legitimate attempts to build an information advantage over rivals. The extent to which it is possible to achieve such information advantages varies significantly from market to market. For example, in relatively undeveloped markets such as the 'emerging markets' there may be frequent and persistent information asymmetries. In these circumstances, traders who are able to establish good personal networks may build an advantage, which enables them to anticipate price movements. However, in mainstream equities markets, the speed and efficiency of information dissemination may make such advantages difficult to achieve. Insider strategies can improve a trader's ability to anticipate market movements. However, as we noted earlier, it is often difficult or impossible for a trader to determine whether they have a genuine information advantage or whether their information is simply noise, already discounted by the market.

Technical Strategies

If markets are perfectly efficient, then historic prices contain no information that can be used to infer future price movements. However, many traders claim to do just that. They seek to exploit market imperfections through the analysis of past price information. One form of technical trade concerns using patterns in price data to identify likely turning points in price trends (charting). Traders seek to identify trends early, buy into those trends and exit before the trend breaks. Many traders consider these patterns and trends in market prices to be driven by underlying investor sentiment. While there is some evidence that supports the existence of exploitable patterns in market prices (e.g. Kwon and Kish, 2002), many financial economists are sceptical of their existence. Fama (1970) dismissed technical analysis as a futile undertaking on the grounds that historical prices have no predictive validity. However, more recent arguments against technical trading strategies take a weaker position: that while there is some predictability in market movements, exploiting these does not, on average, make returns in excess of transaction costs (e.g. Allen and Karjalainen, 1999).

A second important technical strategy requires the analysis of historical price relationships between different financial instruments. Traders scan markets looking for discrepancies in pricing relative to these relationships on the assumption that they will move back to the historical pattern.

Often the gains on technical trades will be small and over short time periods, thus these trades often depend on an ability to identify opportunities rapidly and frequently. This allows the trader to make large numbers of such trades each making a small profit. To benefit from such trading strategies requires the ability to trade at low transaction costs, frequently, with considerable IT support.

Many traders use technical strategies to supplement other approaches. For example, a trader having established a trade on the basis of customer flow information may use technical information on trend behaviour to determine the precise point at which to take profits or cut losses. Others, while fundamentally sceptical about strategies relying on historical trend data, assume prices will be driven to some extent by investors using such models. For example, one trader told us:

> A lot of traders are chartists and a lot of people here don't like you looking at charts, they don't believe in them. However, I look at a chart if I am putting on a large position, or looking for something to trade because if there are people out there who use charts as a model to trade, this will affect how things trade in the markets whether I believe in it or not.

Fundamental Strategies

Technical strategies are purely concerned with anticipating trends and pay no attention to the underlying economic basis for evaluation of the security being traded. By contrast, fundamental strategies are concerned with the fundamental relationship between economic value of the underlying asset and market price. Traders following these strategies essentially seek to use expertise and information in the accurate valuation of securities, on the assumption that market values will converge to theoretical values. To the extent that traders can establish an advantage in valuation of securities, they may be able to earn profits from identifying securities that are undervalued or overvalued by the market. One highly successful trader told us:

> I tend to take positions that depend a lot on central bank decisions e.g. interest rates, so depend on macro economic position of the country, the judgement about how the Bank of England is going to behave and how the market is going to proceed. I try to put myself in Eddie George's[11] feet and try to understand. We have been building a model of Bank of England reactions to economic events. I have lunches with people who decide our interest rates and try to understand how they think . . . It all comes down to focus and completely immersing myself in an area.

However, as with insider strategies it can be genuinely difficult for a trader to understand whether they have a genuine advantage in valuation. Further, as we will see in Chapter 3, trading on valuation advantage depends on the market converging to a value in a time scale over which you can finance a trade.

Flow Strategies

This strategy predicts prices as a function of demand and supply for securities in the market. Particularly for securities in which there is not much liquidity,[12] large trades can shift prices significantly.

Where a bank has a large customer base in a particular niche, this can give them access to valuable market information, in particular, information on trading flows. These kinds of advantage are more readily achieved in OTC markets, which lack the transparency of trades organized through exchanges. However, in any given market niche, there will be a very limited number of firms that can capture sufficient order flow information to give them a genuine advantage. Feldman and Stephenson (1988) studied the use of flow information in the US treasury bonds market. They suggest that through the use of informal information trading with customers, a firm with a 3–4 per cent share in trading may have a good sense of what is going on in 30 per cent or more of the market. However, they also show that medium sized players in these markets are often unable to exploit their customer relationships effectively. They argue that large players systematically shut medium sized players out of information networks while providing good market information to smaller players who they mostly relate to as customers rather than competitors.

As we have seen, financial markets have a long history and have been through multiple cycles of global financial integration over the last two millennia, but their development into domains of such immense complexity and global influence has occurred only within the last 50 years. The volume of trading and of traders has no historical precedent, nor has the complexity and variety of the instruments traded. Within this context, the activities of traders within investment banks are important not just to their customers, but also at the level of national and international economies. Naturally, these phenomena have attracted the attention of academics and commentators, from a variety of disciplines, who have, as we shall show in the next chapter, different and sometimes competing explanations of what influences and explains behaviour within global financial markets.

Notes

1. Derivatives are financial products, which depend on or derive from other assets.
2. Values in all figures are nominal (non-inflation-adjusted).
3. OTC derivatives are not traded in an exchange but are contracted directly between the two contracting parties.
4. Exchange requirements generally only require traders selling options to deposit a proportion of the potential claim. Further, speculation using derivatives is often highly leveraged (funded through borrowed funds).
5. Market traded short-term corporate debt.
6. Market-makers stand ready to buy or sell an asset or class of assets. Typically a market-maker quotes a buy (bid) and sell (offer) price to a client before the client declares whether they wish to buy or sell. The spread between bid and offer both provides a return and some protection against market movements in the time taken for the market-maker to readjust their holdings after a trade.
7. There are also important differences between the United States and the United Kingdom in how this tension is regulated. UK banks face fewer constraints on the relationship between customer business and proprietary trading.

8. The types of financial instruments dealt in by traders cut across these categories. Some traders specialize by a particular type of instrument (e.g. equities or bonds in a particular sector), others deal in a range of instruments related to a particular geographical region or sector.

9. See also Abolafia (1996) for a description of such market stabilizing behaviour by market-makers.

10. Returns in excess of the market risk premium.

11. Eddie George was Governor of the Bank of England at the time of interview.

12. Liquidity: the availability of parties willing to buy or sell a security at any given time.

Chapter 3

ECONOMIC, PSYCHOLOGICAL, AND SOCIAL EXPLANATIONS OF MARKET BEHAVIOUR

For at least forty years psychologists have amassed evidence that economic man is very unlike a real man and that reason—for now, defined by the principles that underlie expected utility theory, Bayesian learning and rational expectations—is not an adequate basis for a descriptive theory of decision making.

De Bondt, 1998

I am in fundamental disagreement with the prevailing wisdom. The generally accepted theory is that financial markets tend towards equilibrium and, on the whole, discount the future correctly. I operate using a different theory, according to which financial markets cannot possibly discount the future correctly because they do not merely discount the future; they help to shape it.

Soros, 1995: 111

If we are to understand traders, we have to first understand the markets they inhabit. Neoclassical economics has been extraordinarily successful in explaining most market behaviour in the aggregate. However, it has two principal weaknesses for our purposes. The first concerns what it does not address and the second concerns some important failures at the margins.

Neoclassical financial economics treats markets as a given, or naturally arising. Investor preferences and risk appetites are treated as external to the model but predictably ordered and distributed. Markets are modelled as adjusting instantaneously with little attention to the detail of how such adjustments come about.

While neoclassical financial economic models effectively explain a great deal of market behaviour, there are some important failures at the margins. There is a wide range of anomalies which are difficult to explain within this paradigm.

If markets instantaneously adjust and are perfectly efficient, then the only role for professional traders is as intermediaries who cannot earn above market returns, but essentially earn commission as intermediaries. There is nothing to be earned by arbitrage activities or speculation. Indeed, it is not even clear within neoclassical accounts of markets that there is a role for intermediation.

However, if we assume markets to be only nearly perfect and 'sticky', the trader's role as someone with privileged expertise, tacit knowledge, and access to private information (within limits) makes more sense. Here, traders are the oil in the market machine; they are one of the processes by which the market adjusts. Hence, rent-earning possibilities exist (albeit only fleetingly). At this point we begin to see the limitations of neoclassical economic models in understanding and interpreting the trader's world.

If we are to understand traders and the role they play in markets we need to step outside the boundaries of what is modelled by the neoclassical economic model and examine the marginal deviations from the theory, the reflexive relationships between market 'events' and investor 'sentiment' and the ways in which markets are constructed and enacted through institutional process, and active agency.

3.1 Strengths and Weaknesses of the Efficient Market Paradigm

The dominant financial economic approach to understanding markets rests on the fundamental principle that markets are efficient. By efficient, economists mean that the price of any asset reflects all available information about that asset. As new information becomes available then investors instantaneously (and in consistent and predictable ways) take the information into account and the price at which they are prepared to buy or sell the asset adjusts accordingly. Generally, financial economists treat markets as part of the natural order and their existence and properties as givens. There are three different forms of the efficient market hypothesis (Fama, 1970):

1. The weak form states that present prices reflect all information contained in the record of past prices. In other words, past prices are no guide to the future.
2. The semi-strong form states that current prices incorporate not only all information from past prices but also all other published information.
3. The strong form states that current prices incorporate all information that could be acquired by a painstaking fundamental analysis of the asset and economic circumstances.

Another fundamental plank of the classical approach is a set of assumptions about how individual investors approach risk and the relationship between risk and return. These assumptions are expressed through expected utility theory. Expected utility theory assumes all that matters to an investor is the price of an asset, the expected stream of returns from that investment and the risk (or expected variability) attaching to those returns. Preferences are assumed to be well ordered. By this we mean that if an investor prefers A to B and B to C, then the investor also prefers A to C. Finally, expected utility theory assumes that for any investor, as their wealth increases, the value to them (utility) of adding a further unit of wealth decreases: £100 is worth less to a rich man than a poor man. In consequence, no investor will be interested in a fair bet: a bet with equal odds of gain and loss. The anticipated loss of utility consequent on a loss of £100 is greater than the anticipated utility of a gain of £100. In consequence, investors are risk averse; they will always prefer to avoid risk unless there is a premium to be gained by accepting it. Prices of assets will then reflect the premium investors require for accepting the risk[1] of the asset. While individual risk preferences vary, in the aggregate they produce a market price for risk. This is the foundation of the capital asset pricing model. A notable feature of the efficient markets hypothesis is that it must necessarily be treated as a joint hypothesis with a pricing theory (usually the capital asset pricing model). Hence data, which may potentially disconfirm the efficient markets hypothesis, may in many cases equally well be explained by failure of a pricing model.

There is a considerable body of empirical evidence that, broadly, supports both expected utility and the efficient market hypothesis (Fama, 1991). Market prices are generally consistent with risk profiles of assets in a way that supports expected utility theory. Statistical analysis of stock prices reveals them (mostly) to follow a random walk: past prices do not predict how future prices will change. Studies of investor reaction to new information generally show such information to be rapidly incorporated into prices. Studies of fund managers show that on average they do not outperform the market, as you would expect them to if market prices did not incorporate all information that could be acquired.

In order for a market to be (weak form) efficient it is not necessary that all investors make rational[2] decisions on the basis of all available information. It is only necessary that such rational investors exist in the market with sufficient funds to buy and sell assets where they perceive differences between market price and the 'rational' value. However, we should note that the operation of this adjustment mechanism implies the existence of (albeit fleeting) deviations of prices from the 'efficient' value. At the margin the markets are not efficient and while the actions of these rational investors will bring prices back into line, in the process they have the opportunity to earn super-normal profits.

There are two forms of trading that can bring about a convergence between market prices and efficient prices. First, some investors, by engaging in sustained analysis of economic fundamentals can spot opportunities to profit from irrational differences in the price of two assets or the same asset at different times. Second, other investors by analysing patterns or cycles in historic prices can exploit those patterns. However, by doing so, they generally cause those patterns to disappear.

Markets are not perfectly efficient because there are imperfections for these traders to exploit, but their activities cause market imperfections to disappear, if not instantaneously then certainly very quickly. Such arbitrage trading both benefits from and eliminates market anomalies. In consequence, for most investors, all available information about the value and future performance of an asset is already incorporated in the price of that asset. There is no value for an individual investor in researching an asset. Anything they can find out has already been incorporated in the price (although the market in aggregate does depend for efficiency on some number of investors researching assets).

Who might these 'rational investors' be? It seems plausible that a good candidate group are professional traders in investment banks, who are selected, trained, managed, and rewarded for investment success and who have superior and rapid access to timely, high quality information on markets in comparison to many investors.

As we noted earlier, the evidence broadly suggests that the neoclassical financial economics approach to understanding the operation of financial markets is a good basis for understanding aggregate market behaviour. However, there are some important problems that neoclassical theory is insufficient to explain. In the next section we look at some important examples of deviations from the predictions of the efficient market hypothesis.

3.2   Failures of the Efficient Markets Paradigm

There is little doubt that the efficient markets paradigm successfully explains a large proportion of aggregate market behaviour. However, there is an increasing body of empirical evidence that market phenomena exist which cannot be explained within this model. We set out some examples below.

Noise Trading

Classical models of market behaviour predict that market participants will trade very little. The reasoning goes as follows. If all traders are rational and if you are offering to sell me an asset at a price at which I want to buy, then I will suspect that you know something I do not. Of course, all investors will, from time to time, need to rebalance their portfolios or realize assets but nonetheless the model would predict low trading. Actual trading is many times higher than could be predicted. For example, the daily trading volume in all currencies is roughly one quarter of the annual value of world trade. Approximately 75 per cent of this trade is made up of inter-bank transactions (Dow and Gorton, 1997). In other words the vast bulk of this trading is not on behalf of a customer. It is a zero-sum game. For every winner in these deals there is a loser.

Excess Volatility

In an efficient market peopled by rational investors, prices should change only when genuinely new information arrives. Work by Schiller (1981), among others, has shown that prices are more volatile than the theory would predict.

Equity Premium

Historically, the return on investment is much higher for equities than for government bonds. This is, of course, partially explained by differences in risk. However, work by Mehra and Prescott (1985), among others, has shown that the difference in returns is much greater than can be explained by differences in risk alone.

Overreaction to News

An increasing body of evidence suggests that in some circumstances investors overreact to news in ways that systematically distort market prices. For example De Bondt and Thaler (1985, 1987) showed that stocks which had experienced extreme losses tended subsequently, over several years, to outperform stocks which had experienced extreme gains. If markets are efficient then this should not happen since historical prices should be no guide to future price movements. De Bondt and Thaler interpreted this finding to mean that the market had overreacted in response to the news that had led to the initial extreme price. Prices had increased (or decreased) more than was justified by the news, and subsequently the readjustment led to underperformance (or overperformance). Interestingly they found that the overreaction effect was greater for losses of value than gains in value. Although their research was controversial, subsequent work has confirmed their findings (e.g. Chopra, Lakonishok, and Ritter, 1992).

Speculative Bubbles and Crashes

Speculative bubbles are an enduring feature of financial markets. One of the earliest recorded examples is the market for tulip bulbs in seventeenth-century Holland; the prices of contracts for future crops of bulbs reached extraordinary heights before crashing. Other examples include the 1980 crisis in the silver futures market where prices soared from $10 per ounce to $50 per ounce and fell back to $10 per ounce in 7 months, and the stock market crash of October 1987 where prices fell by 20 per cent in a day. More recently, we have experienced a period in which stocks in Internet and technology related companies were highly overvalued, even based on extremely optimistic estimates of the cash flows the companies might generate in future and of the risk associated with the stocks. Many of these stocks subsequently dramatically collapsed in price.

It is possible (as some economists do) to preserve the efficient markets paradigm in the face of such market phenomena. Since any full test of the efficient markets hypothesis must be a joint test with a pricing model, it is always possible to argue that the market is still setting an efficient price and that the changes in price can be explained as a consequence of 'external shocks' to investor risk preferences and tastes. In other words the market is simply adjusting to factors that are outside the scope of the model. However, this seems to stretch the theory to the point of tautology and to rule out the possibility of effectively studying such phenomena.

3.3 Alternative Approaches

The efficient markets paradigm is effective in explaining much market behaviour in the aggregate most of the time. However, there is ample evidence of persistent anomalies and market failures to suggest other approaches may add explanatory power to our understanding of markets. More importantly, for our purposes, many of the points at which the efficient markets paradigm fails or has nothing to say are important to an understanding of the role played by professional financial traders.

Tetlock (1991) identifies three competing metaphors employed for understanding human decision-making: people as naïve economists, as naïve psychologists, and as naive politicians. Financial economics rests on the first approach. People are seen as making rational judgements in pursuit of maximum expected utility. In some variants people are modelled as making such judgements effectively; more pessimistic versions assume limited capabilities. While this approach has met with great success, not least because it is easy to model mathematically, there is abundant evidence that it is a poor description of individual behaviour.

The second approach sees people as driven to achieve cognitive mastery of their environment. Again there are more optimistic and more pessimistic versions. The more optimistic describe people who make effective use of lay versions of formal logical and statistical procedures to arrive at conclusions about the physical world and the behaviour of others (Kelley, 1967). The more pessimistic depict us as cognitive misers, prone to a wide range of systematic judgemental failings and biases (Nisbett and Ross, 1980). There is increasing evidence that we move between the two extremes, switching from simple heuristics to more complex cognitive strategies in response to the importance of the situation and desired outcomes (Fiske and Taylor, 1991).

Both the economic and psychological perspectives tend to converge around a notion of people as limited capacity information processors and have in common the concept of 'bounded rationality'. There are limits to the cognitive and information processing capacity we can devote to any judgement. Both perspectives also share a common gap;

people are largely understood in isolation from their social milieu. This is the starting point for the third perspective identified by Tetlock: people as politicians. In this approach people are seen as acting to manage the social world they inhabit. A key goal in decision-making is satisfying the constituencies to which the individual feels accountable. The key question from this perspective is 'what strategies do people use in managing accountability to social groups and norms?' This is the domain of sociology and of neo-institutional theory in particular.

So having discussed the rational economic approach to understanding markets and the people who inhabit them, we turn to consider the psychological paradigm and people as politicians.

3.4 Behavioural Finance

There is a steadily increasing body of theory and research drawing on the psychological paradigm, which offers explanations of departures of market behaviour from the predictions of neoclassical market economics. Collectively known as behavioural finance, this work draws on behavioural decision-making research and has begun to explore how an understanding of investor psychology might explain departures from the joint predictions of the efficient markets hypothesis and rational economic pricing models.

The first challenge that behavioural finance has to meet is to explain why, if market phenomena arise as a result of individual departures from economically rational expected utility maximization, these effects do not simply disappear as more rational traders identify opportunities for arbitrage. The answer is that exploiting arbitrage opportunities is not costless, there may be significant risks attached. In order to profit from a perceived anomaly, an arbitrageur must be confident that there are sufficient other 'rational' investors in the market to force discrepant prices to converge within a manageable time scale.

Thaler cites the example of the Royal Dutch /Shell Group (Froot and Dabora, 1999; Thaler, 1999). Royal Dutch Petroleum and Shell Transport are separately incorporated in the Netherlands and the United Kingdom. In 1907 an alliance led to the two companies merging their interests in a 60 : 40 ratio. Royal Dutch trades mainly in the

United States and the Netherlands. Shell Transport trades mainly on the London Stock Exchange. In an efficient market the prices of these two stocks should trade in a 60 : 40 ratio. They do not. The actual ratio has deviated from the theoretical by as much as 35 per cent.

Arbitrageurs seek to profit from such discrepancies. However, they are not always successful. Indeed, Royal Dutch Shell was one of the arbitrage opportunities that a hedge fund known as Long Term Capital Management (LTCM) was seeking to exploit when it collapsed in the summer of 1998. The problems of LTCM are highly relevant to the issues we consider in this chapter so the story of the fund's collapse is set out below.

Long Term Capital Management[3]

In August 1998, the collapse of LTCM came close to doing serious damage to the world economy. LTCM was a hedge fund set up in 1994 to exploit arbitrage opportunities. The fund was set up by a team which included some of the most highly respected theorists in the world of finance and highly experienced traders. The partners included Robert Merton and Myron Scholes, who had won the Nobel Prize for their work on hedging derivative risk. Around half the LTCM partners had finance doctorates. John Meriwether, a trader who had built up a near legendary status in the Salomon Brothers' arbitrage group, led the team.

In the first 2 years of trading, investors in the fund earned staggering returns (45 per cent in 1995 and 41 per cent in 1996). The fund did less well in 1997 and returns dropped to 17 per cent. By the beginning of 1998 the fund was operating with funds of $4.7 billion. Loans brought the value of the fund to about $125 billion.

Essentially, the fund operated by looking for assets whose prices they believed should be closely related. For example, shares in Royal Dutch and Shell Transport. If they believed that assets X and Y should be priced at the same level, and Y was priced higher than X, they would buy X and sell Y short.[4] Their strategy depended on the prices of the two assets converging within a time scale over which they could afford to maintain the trading position.

Because the fund was careful to spread investments across a wide range of unrelated markets, their different positions were uncorrelated.

That is, movements in prices on one trading position were unrelated to movements in prices on another.

On 17 August 1998, Russia defaulted on its public debt. This event sent shock waves through the markets as investors panicked and sought 'safe' homes for their investments. Many of LTCM's positions became untenable and they sought to move out of a series of their positions. It became apparent that it would be difficult or impossible to unwind many of these positions for two reasons.

First, there was a crisis of liquidity in the market, there were very few buyers; hence they could not sell their sizeable investments without driving down the price substantially. Second, their investments had become strongly correlated. In theory their very diverse investments should have had completely unrelated values. However, LTCM had built up a strong 'fan club'. Noting their success, other investors had sought to emulate their trading positions. The assets they held had become correlated by virtue of having a common set of owners. LTCM had become the leader of a herd. The prices of assets held by LTCM became a function of what the market thought LTCM would do. As LTCM tried to unwind its positions, so did the fan club, driving prices down further. The strenuous efforts by LTCM to hedge risk by investing in uncorrelated assets were defeated by the effect of so many other investors holding the same portfolio of assets.

Long Term Capital Management was bailed out by a group of fourteen major banks organized by the US Federal Reserve. Had this not happened the series of defaults triggered by allowing the fund to collapse would have caused a wave of financial collapses among banks around the world.

There are two main lessons to be learnt from the LTCM story. First, there are barriers to arbitrage in financial markets. The main mechanism, by which 'rational investors' are theorised to eliminate the effects of 'irrational' or 'quasi-rational' behaviour, does not always work. If the 'irrational' sentiment behind an anomaly persists in a market for long enough and there are enough investors sharing that perception of value then betting against the herd carries a high risk. A trader making such a bet can make substantial losses if the anomaly is not corrected in a suitable time scale. Internet stocks at the turn of the millennium were another good example of this. Most analysts agreed that many Internet stocks were overpriced. However, a major shake-out of prices took some time to happen. The number of investors willing to bet on a correction in the market and 'short' these stocks was limited and consequently they remained high for a significant period.

Second, market movements cannot be properly understood without understanding the social processes behind phenomena such as herding, the formation of 'fan clubs' and the generation and amplification of market sentiment. In particular, as reflected in the quote from George Soros with which we started this chapter, markets are highly reflexive. The behaviour of markets influences economic conditions rather than simply reflecting them, and the beliefs of market participants affect the object of their beliefs. Mackenzie, a sociologist who has studied the LTCM crisis in detail, emphasizes this reflexivity (Mackenzie, 2002). He points out that theories of arbitrage do not just describe but also help to bring about market conditions. On the one hand the acceptance of theories which identify arbitrage opportunities led to arbitrage becoming more widely practised. On the other hand, the success of arbitrage leads to the number of arbitrageurs outstripping arbitrage opportunities and generates increased risks for this activity. Much as in the dynamics of predator–prey populations, over-predation can lead to a sudden collapse in both populations.

Understanding Market Anomalies from Within the Psychological Paradigm

Psychologists have long been interested in the limits to human rationality. More recently, behavioural finance theorists have started to use what we know about cognitive processes to explain market anomalies.

Recency and Availability Biases

People have an innate tendency to overweight recent and other easily available or retrievable information. In their study of market over-reaction, De Bondt and Thaler (1985, 1987) argued that overreaction to news could be explained by a recency bias. Their argument goes as follows: when news relevant to the price of an asset becomes available to the market, investors give more weight to this recent news than to existing information relevant to the value of the asset. Consequently, they overreact. Subsequently, as the news becomes less recent, the weight attached to it falls, causing prices to move back somewhat. While the evidence is that overreaction effects are largest among stocks in small firms, which are held mostly by individual investors not institutional investors, De Bondt and Thaler found in a separate study that professional security analysts also suffer from recency biases and associated overreaction to recent news (De Bondt and Thaler, 1990).

Prospect Theory

Classical economic ideas of investor risk behaviour are founded on expected utility theory. Expected utility theory predicts that investors will always be risk averse. The shape of the utility curve (utility plotted against increasing wealth) is convex. This is founded on the common sense notion that I will value £100 less if I am very wealthy than if I am poor. Figure 3.1 illustrates that (at any point x) the utility of an increase (+a) in wealth is less than the disutility of a decrease (−a) in wealth. This is used to explain why investors can be assumed to be risk averse. In a 50/50 gamble the disutility of the possible loss is greater than the utility of the potential win, so they will require a premium to engage in the gamble. However, we know that individuals are not always risk averse; rather, they tend to be loss averse. They may be prepared to take considerable risk to avoid or recover from a loss.

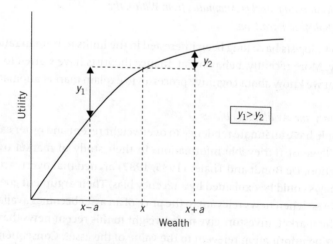

Fig. 3.1 Expected utility theory

Prospect theory (Kahneman and Tversky, 1979) suggests that whether an individual is risk seeking or risk averse will depend where they are in relation to a personal reference point. The reference point divides the area where they feel as if they are in loss from the area where they feel they are in gain. This point is not usually zero, and will change over time. For example, a professional financial trader who is paid a bonus of £100,000 may experience this as gain if he[5] had been expecting a lower bonus. But say that he had expected £200,000 and had committed to a house purchase on that assumption. In these circumstances he will experience the bonus as taking him into the domain of losses. In the first instance, the reference point was somewhere between current wealth and current wealth plus £100,000. In the second case the reference point is at current wealth plus £200,000. Prospect theory suggests that because people are loss averse, they are risk averse above the reference point and risk seeking below. Figure 3.2 illustrates this.

Prospect theory suggests that reference points are central to understanding decisions about risk. An important feature of reference points is that they differ according to how a situation is 'framed'. The form in which information is presented can shift reference points.

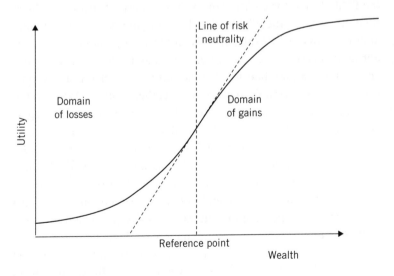

Fig. 3.2 Prospect theory

For example, doctors presented with mortality rates as a basis for choosing between two medical procedures make different decisions depending on whether information is presented in the form of lives lost or lives saved. The framing of information affects the point at which they see outcomes as in the domain of losses or gains.

Another feature of prospect theory is the idea that reference points may arise out of internal rules to establish self-control. For example, standard utility theory would suggest that no rational investor would put money into savings at one rate of interest (say to save for a wedding) and at the same time borrow at a higher rate of interest (say to buy a car). Yet, such behaviour is commonplace. Kahneman and Tversky (1982) describe this as mental accounting. The function of such behaviour is self-regulatory.[6] We commonly set ourselves rules such as: never touch the children's college fund; put one spouse's salary into savings and only spend from the other salary; pay a fixed sum into a pension every month regardless of other financial circumstances; only spend from current income not capital. These self-imposed rules protect us from the occasional inability to sacrifice immediate satisfaction for long-term goals.

Prospect theory has been applied to a whole series of problems in the field of investor choice. For example, prospect theory has been used to explain the dividend behaviour anomaly[7] (Shefrin and Statman, 1984). One explanation is simply that investors apply different mental accounting rules to dividends and capital gains. Shefrin and Statman argue that investors account for dividends and capital gains or losses separately at times and together at others. When in the domain of gains the investor will wish to 'savour' both gains separately. However, in the event of a small fall in the price of the shares the investor considers the capital loss and dividend together in order to offset the capital loss by the dividend. Finally, in the event of a large fall in price the investor will once again consider them separately in order to still savour the dividend rather than simply offset it against the fall in price. Shefrin and Statman show that as a result investors gain greater utility from a combination of dividends and capital growth than from capital growth alone. They also note that prospect theory would predict that investors will be more affected by falls in dividends than by rises in dividends. Their empirical evidence shows that market prices do indeed seem to be more affected by dividend falls than dividend rises.

While the disposition to the framing biases underlying prospect theory varies between individuals, they are sufficiently prevalent to account for the observed market effects.

Regret Aversion

People are generally more affected by regret about adverse consequences of actions they chose to take than by regret about adverse consequences of not taking an action. We can more readily imagine deleting an action from a remembered chain of events than inserting an action that did not happen. Further, when thinking about the future we imagine and account for the regret we may feel if our actions go amiss. We do this less readily for our imagined failure to act. For example, consumers will often choose known brands rather than anticipate the regret of making a bad choice (e.g. Simonson, 1992).

Regret aversion has been used to account for a number of market phenomena. One commonly observed aspect of investor behaviour is the tendency to ride losers and sell winners. For most investors, it is more tax efficient to sell stocks that realize losses than to sell stocks that realize capital gains. Nonetheless, there is a demonstrable tendency for investors to sell winning stocks in preference to losing stocks (Shapira and Venezia, 2001). As we have noted before, in an efficient market, previous price movements should tell us nothing about future price movements.

The explanation of this effect relies on another form of 'mental accounting' Shefrin and Statman (1984) argue that many investors treat 'paper losses' and realized losses differently. If the price of a stock they own falls, they can tell themselves that it may well go back up. However, if they realize the loss they have to accept it as a loss. It is only when realizing the loss that they experience the regret. This is compounded by having to admit the loss to others (e.g. tax authorities, a spouse, etc.). The avoidance of regret causes investors to be less willing to realize losses than to realize gains. Professional traders exercise a number of self-control mechanisms to avoid this bias: chief among these being the 'stop-loss', where they pre-commit to get out of a trade at a particular price point.

In drawing on the behavioural finance literature there are a number of cautions we should observe. First, behavioural finance does not, in aggregate, amount to an alternative theory of market behaviour. Rather, it amounts to a theory of departures from the neoclassical model. It may be best regarded less as a challenge to neoclassical market economics than as a useful supplement to it. This is not least because as such anomalies are identified and explained, they tend to be exploited by market actors and disappear. Second, thus far, the behavioural finance literature rests on a relatively unsophisticated set of models of human cognition. In part, this is due to the need of financial economists to extract models that are simple enough to model mathematically. In part, it is also due to the current state of the 'cognitive bias' literature in psychology, which tends towards taxonomy rather than elaborating an overarching theory of human cognition.

3.5   Markets as Institutions (People as Politicians)

Neoclassical financial economics tends to treat markets as naturally occurring. However, there is a paradox. The existence of markets which approximate the perfect competition of neoclassical economics requires active regulation and intervention. Market participants are not only concerned with utility maximization but also with legitimacy maximization. The ability of an individual to continue trading depends on their legitimacy within the norms of the market and the ability of the market to continue to exist depends on its legitimacy within the norms of wider society. As Coase notes, these conditions require an authority structure to secure the market 'involving an intricate system of rules and regulations to prevent malfeasance' (Coase, 1988: 7).

Within this institutional paradigm, markets are understood to be socially constructed. Economic actors jointly create their social environment in ways that shape their future transactions. They are not simply passive recipients of a market environment but also engage in creating that environment. Every market participant is part of a community with social relationships, institutional structures, and cultural norms which shape economic activity. Rather than being impersonal arenas defined by the invisible hand of the market and driven by the single-minded pursuit of self-interest, markets exhibit a complex mix of the pursuit of self-interest and mutual restraint in pursuit of legitimacy (Abolafia, 1996). Market actors are, of course, concerned to maximize profits, but they are also concerned to maintain the legitimacy and viability of the markets in which they operate. Consequently, markets exhibit considerable self-regulation. Some of this is formal as in the operation of regulations, but much is informal and tacit.

What do we mean when we say markets are socially constructed? We inhabit a social world. Many of the 'facts' of our lives which we take for granted are 'facts' only insofar as we hold common mental models about them: for example money, contracts, marriage, the rules of the road, democracy, to name just a few. To understand the nature of social influences on decision-making we need to start from this idea that the environment within which we exist and the meanings which we attribute to that environment, even to a large extent the categories available to us to think about that environment, are socially constructed.

Of course, the extent of agreement about meaning can be highly variable. From the ephemeral (a certain style of clothing may come to stand for a shared attitude among a small group of teenagers for a short period) to the more profound (such as the idea of 'a market'). Sociologists refer to these more profound shared meanings as institutions. In this sense, an institution is a persistently reproduced social pattern that is relatively self-sustaining. However, to say that institutions are relatively self-sustaining is not to say they cannot change. In recent decades, to take one example, the shared understanding of the meaning and rules of the institution of marriage have changed considerably.

These shared social meanings powerfully influence and constrain the way in which we reason and decide. They provide categories within which we think. Again to return to the example of marriage, the socially shared categories of fidelity, housework, childcare, separation, divorce, and so on, provide a framework within which we think about such relationships. These shared social meanings are tacit, implicit, and taken for granted. We understand them as 'facts' and they quite literally shape how we see the world. Social institutions powerfully affect how we perceive the world and exercise judgement.

Market Behaviour

If we are to negotiate our social environments and to collaborate with others, our success depends on our understanding and mastery of social institutions; so too in the world of business. Economists have typically explained firm behaviour in terms of the search for economic advantage. Many sociologists (while not denying the role of economic forces) have looked to the importance to firm survival of establishing legitimacy in terms of relevant social institutions.

What does this all imply for the way in which people make decisions in the world of finance? First, it leads us to emphasize the notion that financial decision-makers do not simply seek to reach economically optimal decisions on the basis of (albeit imperfect) rationality. Rather, they try to make decisions that are seen to be legitimate. Of course, in many situations profit maximization is one (though not usually the only) criterion for legitimacy. A second implication is that the conceptual frameworks and notions of cause and effect that are available to decision-makers to reason with are largely socially determined. This can operate at different levels, national, industry, firm, team, etc. For example, at the industry level, some researchers have looked at the way in which cognitive communities develop. That is networks of firms whose managers share core ideas about how the industry works, cause and effect relationships, and what constitutes reasonable conduct. These ideas simplify and constrain the ways in which managers within a group identify competitors and customers, and reason about competitive strategy (Porac, Thomas, and Baden-Fuller, 1989).

Social Structure of Financial Markets

There is evidence of similar processes in financial markets. In a series of studies of US securities markets, Abolafia noted that to understand the operation of financial markets, it is important to understand their social structure, and in particular the social rules which influence and constrain behaviour within them. On the one hand, market participants are expected to act opportunistically in pursuit of their own interests. On the other hand, markets cannot operate without some degree of institutional restraint on individual opportunism; since otherwise there is insufficient basis for trust between the parties to any exchange. Shared conventions and social norms form a basis on which exchange can take place in the market. Some of these social rules are embodied in law or formal self-regulation and some in broadly shared ideas of appropriate behaviour.

Such shared understandings may be specific to a market or a firm. Lewis gives an example of a clash between two different understandings of appropriate market behaviour early in the development of the US mortgage bond market. A customer of a savings and loan corporation, Salomon Brothers reneged on a commitment to purchase bonds from Salomon Brothers. The agreement had been made orally over the phone. The customer claimed that the appropriate rules to govern the mortgage bond transactions were not those of the bond market (which emphasized oral contracts) but those governing real estate, where an oral contract was not binding. Although Salomon Brothers eventually won the case it took years to resolve (Lewis, 1989: 118).

To give another example, in our own research in the City of London, we saw that the tacit norms about the extent to which it is permissible to exploit the information asymmetry between traders and bank customers opportunistically varied significantly between firms.

Abolafia (1996) combined a social constructionist approach with detailed ethnographic research in a variety of Wall Street markets. These markets are seen by Abolafia, not as neoclassical, naturally occurring phenomena but as socially produced and reproduced by market actors.

Abolafia suggests that there are three different levels at which institutional effects in markets can be understood: individual, transactional, and regulatory. First, individual traders conduct themselves within a set of formal and informal rules and social arrangements. Second, trading transactions are carried out within a context of norms of exchange and reputations for trustworthiness. Trading opportunities are shaped by the trader's reputation in a network of market actors. Traders who break formal or informal norms are likely to be sanctioned by other network members and find themselves excluded from trading opportunities. Norms that start as informal practices arising through interactions in networks come to take on an external and objective character. Third, markets are not only subject to self-regulation, but also, increasingly, to regulation by the state. The interaction between market insiders and state regulators is an important arena in which tensions between opportunism and market restraint are played out (Abolafia, 1996: 174–175).

Socially determined shared mental frameworks do not only apply to the 'rules of the game', but they also concern such things as what may be considered a legitimate commodity to trade or a legitimate trading partner. For example, there has been enormous variation over history in whether children fall into the socially defined category of goods that may be legitimately traded, as slaves and bonded workers, and there remains some international variation today. More recently, we have seen changes in the social legitimacy of junk bonds and emerging market debt as commodities that may be traded. At the time of writing, atmospheric carbon is in the process of being socially redefined as a tradable commodity.

This perspective, of people as legitimacy seekers who inhabit a socially constructed world, allows us to understand some market phenomena that are not well addressed by neoclassical economics. Two good examples of this approach are the work done by Zuckerman (1999) on the 'illegitimacy discount' and by Baker (1984a) on the relationship between social networks in markets and price volatility.

Zuckerman argued that, in any product market, products are legitimate to the extent that they fit existing socially defined categories. Products that do not easily fit pre-existing categories are difficult to compare with other products and are consequently often ignored in the initial screening phase of purchasing decisions. In the market for equities an important legitimacy-bestowing group are stock-market analysts working for investment banks. Analysts frequently specialize by industry group. Zuckerman was able to show that equities that do not readily fit within the groups defined by this specialization trade at a discount.

Baker studied floor trading at an options exchange. He found that the effectiveness with which traders and market-makers could informally police norms of reciprocity (and hence ensure an orderly market) were related to the size of a market in any particular security. In larger markets opportunism became less visible and less easily restrained through informal sanctions. Were markets efficient, larger markets should decrease price volatility, since the number of potential trading partners increases. However, Baker found, consistent with his observations of the social network structure of this market, that volatility was higher for larger markets because of the greater opportunities for opportunism, given larger and more diffuse networks and the greater problems of information flow as large social networks fragment into sub-networks.

Another key strand of work is that on herding; mutually aware actors engage in mimetic, irrational behaviour (Adler and Adler, 1984). Abolafia and Kilduff (1988), following Kindleberger (1978) have described panics in which investment manias followed by panic selling imply that market actors both create and are influenced by their trading environments (see also Warner and Molotch, 1993).

3.6 Implications

In this chapter, we have briefly surveyed three different approaches to understanding markets and the role traders occupy within them: the economic, the psychological, and the sociological paradigms. We have accepted that the economic paradigm has had remarkable success in explaining market behaviour at the aggregate level. However, we have also argued that the other two paradigms offer complementary insights, first in understanding deviations from neoclassical models at the margins, and second in helping us to understand what the economic paradigm fails to address.

We have argued that professional financial traders operate to a large extent in the territory where neoclassical financial models break down. Where traders are able to make above market returns, it will often be through exploiting opportunities which the efficient markets paradigm suggests cannot exist. This suggests that while formal financial theory will be important to traders, much of their intellectual effort will go into constructing and acting on practical theories concerned with how to identify and exploit deviations from efficient market behaviour. We return to this theme in more detail in Chapter 4.

Of course, correctly identifying opportunities is not straightforward. We have noted that traders live in a fast-moving world of noise, rumour, unreliable information, and uncertainty. Thus, it is often difficult to tell whether an opportunity is real or illusory. At the same time, they are driven by more than simple economic rationality. Being human, traders are also driven by social and personal goals that imply very different forms of reasoning.

This picture of the trader searching for hard to identify opportunities, in a shifting and highly uncertain world, subject to social pressures and prone to biases and illusions has significant implications for how traders are selected, how they learn, how they work, and how they are managed and regulated.

The research on which we report in the remainder of this book explores these themes in more detail. To effectively illuminate the trader's world and the role traders play our research draws on all three paradigms: economic, psychological, and sociological. We have sought to understand how traders use financial theories to make markets work. We have attempted to understand the psychology of trading by applying a number of well-validated measures of personality and bias. We have, above all, tried to understand how traders construct their own understanding of the complex and volatile markets in which they work. We turn directly to this in the next chapter.

Notes

1. This is the unavoidable or 'market' risk of the asset which relates to market movements. Portfolio theory (Markowitz, 1952) shows that by investing in a suitable portfolio of assets investors can 'hedge' away any risk that is unique to a particular asset.
2. 'Rational' is used here in the sense of the normative rationality of neo-classical financial economics.
3. Our account of events in LTCM draws on Stulz (2001).
4. To sell an asset short is to borrow the asset and sell it against a promise to buy it in the open market later to return it to the lender. Hence, if the price of the asset falls in the interim, the investor profits. If the price rises in the interim the investor makes a loss.
5. We have most often used the masculine form throughout the book rather than 'he or she' in recognition that almost all our study sample were male.
6. We say more about self-regulation as a basis for framing effects in Chapter 5.
7. The preference of investors for dividends over pure capital growth, despite tax disincentives.

Chapter 4

TRADERS AND THEIR THEORIES

We have seen that finance theory uses some of the most powerful analytical tools available in social science to model the operation of financial markets, usually on the basis of strong assumptions about the rationality of actors and the availability of information. There are also practitioner theories, which often put less emphasis on rationality; books by and about traders describe trading strategies that may generate large rewards. Trading in financial markets sustains heroes and myths; it sustains movies and television shows.

People who trade professionally in financial markets are generally aware of both sets of theories. They are trained to understand the academic theories of the market, but also immersed in the folklore of the practitioner theorists. These two sets provide, by the nature of the markets they govern, two rather different frameworks. The first is a theory of how the world of financial markets works. The second is a theory or set of theories which act as guidelines for successful action within markets: theories of 'how to work the world'.

As Giddens (1990) notes, financial markets are very specific types of domain. They are institutionally structured risk environments. Risk is not incidental to their activities; the activities themselves involve the measured pursuit of risk. They are also domains of sophisticated reflexivity in which behaviour is influenced by the type of theory preferred by the actor. In such markets, traders trade according to one or more theories, knowing that others act similarly.

In this chapter, we are primarily concerned with the theories that guide trader behaviour. Specifically, we explore the relationship between the general theories of the market and the specific theories that traders use. Building on the previous chapter, Section 4.1 looks at the ways in which economic theories try to explain both the behaviour of individuals in the market and the aggregate effects of that behaviour. Section 4.2 looks at some essential properties of individual theories in action in this context. Section 4.3 uses our data to explore traders' individual theories; three features are selected for closer examination—intuition ('flair'), the role of reflexivity and the emergence of contrarian beliefs. In Section 4.4 we look in particular at the phenomenon of noise trading. Section 4.5 looks at the relationship between formal theories and theories in action, attempting an assessment of performance implications.

4.1 Academic Work on Financial Markets

As Coase (1988: 9) notes, financial markets are often cited as examples of perfect competition. As such, they have three features. First, they are assumed to be efficient in one of the Fama senses noted in Chapter 3. Second, they are characterized by perfect information, such that all actors have the information necessary to trade both costlessly and immediately; transaction costs are low. Third, multiple sellers cannot fix prices (Swedberg, 1994: 274). Paradoxically, as Coase also notes, these conditions require an authority structure to maintain the market 'involving an intricate system of rules and regulations to prevent malfeasance' (1988: 7). Swedberg (1994: 259–261) and Coase (1988: 1–27) also argue that, in financial economics, markets are often assumed to exist rather than empirically analysed.

However, this is a rather incomplete picture. Financial economics has a rather rigid neoclassical structure in which individuals are seen to maximize utility under the assumption of a close correlation between risk and return (Markowitz, 1952; Bernstein, 1996: 248–259). In the aggregate, these actions determine asset prices. However, as we have noted, financial economists do not generally assert that financial markets are perfect and informationally efficient; only that this is a sufficiently good approximation to explain most aggregate market behaviour. If financial markets were fully efficient, then there would be no profit opportunities (defined as a return in excess of the risk). As Bernstein puts it (1996: 297) 'at any level of risk, all investors would earn the same rate of return'.

Much work on market microstructure has been concerned to understand the process through which prices are set and thus how opportunities for profit may arise. Two broad conventional approaches can be identified. The first focuses on inventory, looking at the flow of trades and how temporal imbalances between supply and demand may arise. The second looks at informational differences between traders. Together, they imply that profits may emerge from the existence of transaction costs and private information (for a review, see O'Hara, 1995). There is empirical work on financial markets which supports both approaches (Lyons, 1998; Ito, Lyons, and Melvin, 1998) that remains fully within the neoclassical tradition in assuming rational, utility maximizing actors.

As we showed in Chapter 2, risk–return relationships emerge in the aggregate in financial markets.[1] But it is not necessary to assume that all individuals have the same risk–return preferences; indeed, we show in Chapter 6 that this is not the case. As we discussed in Chapter 3, both utility theory and prospect theory suggest that the behaviour of individual actors in relation to risk is determined by the shape of their utility functions above and below current wealth. It is, though, possible to distinguish the market price for risk from the variable risk preferences of individuals in the market. Expected utility theorists can acknowledge evidence, for example, from experimental economics, that individuals do not always behave according to the predictions of expected utility theory. They rely on the weaker proposition that investors behave, on average, consistent with the prediction, and expected utility theory can be shown to be consistent with most aggregate market behaviour most of the time (Bernstein, 1996: 296).

Close attention to irrationality, the possible benefits from irrational action and its aggregate consequences are central to the project of 'behavioural finance' discussed in Chapter 3. In practice, the focus is on 'quasi-rationality' (Thaler, 1991), which Bernstein describes as analysing how market actors 'struggle to find their way between the give and take between risk and return, one moment engaging in cool calculation and the next yielding to emotional impulses' (1996: 287).

Sociological work on financial markets has tended either to examine the empirical pattern of market transactions or to examine social and non-rational influences on decision-making. The former is the concern of the microstructural work carried out by Baker and colleagues (Baker, 1984a, b; Baker and Iyer, 1992). As we discussed in the previous chapter, Baker identified systematic relationships between network size and density on the one hand and price volatility on the other. His central finding that increased network size is associated with increased volatility challenges economic assumptions about perfect markets.

Each of these theories has different implications for the behaviour of traders in markets. The efficient markets hypothesis assumes irrational behaviour is driven out; since wealth accrues to the rational. In behavioural finance, market outcomes are influenced by deviations from rationality whose origins do not lie within the market. In sociological approaches, there is variance in the primacy accorded to structure and action but in all cases individual action occurs within a socially produced market context.

We argue that all these approaches imply that, in addition to an understanding of financial theory, individuals in the market need a set of theories and heuristics to guide their own profit-seeking behaviour. We also argue that these individual theories have social dimensions. We detail the argument in the next section.

4.2 Individual and General Theories

The key distinction is between general theories of how the market works and the personal theories guiding specific individuals working in the market. Markets may be (approximately) perfect, rational, and governed by expected utility theory, but individuals trade within differentiated networks, more frequently than necessary and with variable risk–return trade-offs. Their behaviour is reflexive in two senses. First, they learn idiosyncratic trading strategies based on their market experience. Second, they factor predictions of others' behaviour into their own trading strategies. In the following section, we use data from our trader interviews to examine the following propositions.

Proposition (i) Traders believe that the market as a whole works in accordance with general finance theory; this is 'how the world works'.

Proposition (ii) Theories that guide individual action in the market involve a belief in the existence of exceptions to the general theories; this is 'how to work the world'.

An example of the former from our own research would be the use made by a Gilts trader we interviewed of macroeconomic theories and financial economic models of yield curve behaviour. An example of the latter would be the same trader's use of networks and contacts to build models of the thinking of the Governor of the Bank of England and the Monetary Policy Committee.

Consider Fig. 4.1. It is a simple representation of an aggregate risk–return relationship in the market. Traders in the market wish to succeed; that is, they wish to trade in the area above the trend line, but

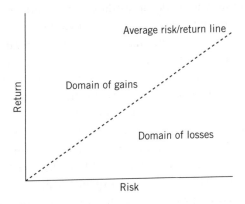

Fig. 4.1 The relationship between risk and return

Source: Adapted from Figure 2 in Willman, P., Fenton-O'Creevy, M. P., Nicholson, N. and Soane, E. (2001) 'Knowing the risks: theory and practice in financial markets', *Human Relations*, 54(7): 887–910.

without moving the trend line up. A market in which there is perfect information about risk–return relationships will, other things being equal, offer few such opportunities.[2] The strategy of the successful trader is thus, from one perspective, an attempt to identify or create and then subsequently use and protect the market imperfections that allow the majority of trades to occur above the line.

Traders' theories of how to work the world differ from the prevailing theory of how the world works in the following respects:

1. They seek anomalies in the operation of the general theory; they are often contrarian in nature.
2. However, they depend logically on a belief in the general validity of the theory of the world; they involve plays around the efficient price line which require a general belief in its existence.
3. Traders deploy these theories consciously and instrumentally; this may be to the advantage of the principal,[3] or the trading agent, or both.
4. There are clear incentives to render the individual theory in use inappropriable both by others operating competitively in the market and by principals.
5. Individual differences between theories of how to work the world are likely.

Theories of how to work the world generate variance around the trend line. We do not assume at this point that they are rational. Such a theory may, as we show in Chapter 5, simply be founded on optimistic bias or illusion of control, and may be associated with poor trading performance. They may involve beliefs about fundamental properties of the stock or instrument being traded or beliefs about patterned movements in the market, accessed by analysis of historic data; we examined these differing trading styles in Chapter 2. They may involve more intuitive responses, based on 'feel' for the market. They may, thus, also vary in their degrees of formality. Such theories are recipes for action based on the need to generate purposeful action in a world governed by probabilistic rules; they function to generate a sense of control over the environment.[4] They are reflexive in the sense that individuals are aware of the development of their own theories. They are heuristic in the sense that they reduce complicated tasks on the assessment of probability and value to simple judgement operations (Bazerman, 1997). They have symbolic functions in at least two, slightly contradictory, senses. First, they are used to render actions accountable; they must fit within a broader vocabulary of trading motives (Wright-Mills, 1963) to assist presentation of self. Second, they may be used to articulate a distinctive trading strategy and identity; they may function to generate self-esteem. As we discuss below, these two senses may relate to accountability in the domains of loss and gain, respectively.

Work the world theories are thus similar in many respects to lay theories, particularly in terms of their functions (Hewstone, 1983). However, they differ from 'pure' lay theories in several respects. They are the product of experience in a specific expert context, not pure 'common sense' (Furnham, 1988: 22–46). They are theories of process rather than content (i.e. how to trade not what to trade), often deductive rather than inductive, situational rather than individualistic; that is, based on trades not people (Furnham, 1988: 2–7). However, this is not to say that such theories about the market do not contain pure 'lay' elements in their characterization of the psychology of other traders.

Of necessity, such theories are different from general knowledge. If trading behaviour is routinized application of general rules then, as many have argued, it can be automated. Routines imply fatalistic trading behaviour which can, incidentally, be exploited by others in the market. By contrast, popular accounts stress the existence of 'wizards' and 'heroes' who 'beat the market' (Insana, 1996); our research shows not fatalism but unrealistic optimism and illusion of control among traders. Traders routinely display optimistic bias in assigning low probabilities of loss to trades based on their work the world theories. They interpret the aggregate theories as defining an action space rather than providing behavioural rules; we explore the implications of this in more detail below.

4.3 Working the World

In this empirical section, we explore the content of working the world theories. Three elements are important. The first is a belief in the importance of flair and intuition; traders believe technical knowledge is not enough. We argue that this belief sustains the generation of tacit and inappropriable knowledge. The second is a belief in the importance of reflexivity; we argue that this belief sustains learning by doing. The third involves contrarian strategies. These are counterintuitive beliefs that generate divergent behaviour. We argue that these generate intractable management problems. They cannot easily be articulated and their pursuit often involves dissimulation.

It is important at this point to describe the social world of traders in our sample. All traded electronically with counterparties all over the globe. There were no traditional open outcry markets such as those described by Baker or Abolafia. Rapid, truncated electronic conversations were the medium of exchange. Knorr Cetina and Bruegger (2002: 910) have used the term 'global microstructure' to describe this environment, in which '. . . traders perform market transactions through conversations. . . . These sequences of utterances do not just convey information, but perform economic action'.

Electronic exchanges, though brief and formalized, are the prime means of knowledge exchange in financial markets—whether a trade is completed or not. Personal conversations within institutions are often ways of rehearsing, rationalizing, or accounting for trading behaviour or positions. In what follows we seek to build up a picture of how traders see and make accountable the markets they inhabit.

Flair and Intuition

The following exchange took place between one of the authors and a senior trading manager on an equities desk.

What happens to new entrants?
'People join as juniors, answering phones and monitoring positions . . . they sit with traders and move around the desks . . . if they show flair, they try out in trading. We are recruiting MBA's but you need flair; flair plus a good technical base.'
What is flair?
'Flair is anticipating the market, showing intuition, having a contrary, different view of events; not going with the herd, not following the market trend.'

Traders also had views on flair. Here are five, from traders in different institutions and markets:

> Having a feeling is not the same as experience, it's like having whiskers, like being a deer . . . you need a certain type of intelligence, but it's more about intuition.

> Knowledge and experience do count for a lot; but there are some people you could never teach trading to in your life. Some people are just too academic.

> There is an instinct that you have and you build on that.

> You just feel right, that this is the one at the bottom or it's the one at the top and that it's a good bargain. Why? I don't know!

> People who have done well with this are those that are very street smart rather than book smart, although there are a lot of exceptions to that. Some book-smart learned people are very instinctual traders, but by and large, it's the guy that has always used his wits. I think I am like that. Sometimes it can be an emotional type thing, other times it is a feel type thing.

Intuition was seen by many to be something to do with learning from experience, and with learning about information processing. One trader manager put it as follows:

> [Flair] comes with experience in terms of learning by putting trades on, which you think will make money, and you end up losing money. And this is a process where you learn the quickest because it is not a pleasant process and you think what have I done wrong, what did I think at the time when I put the trade on, what caused me to lose money. These might be external factors, but sometimes, there are things that you learn about what the models are not taking into account. You could argue that there are some traders who have been trading for 5 years and still do not pick this up.

Another spoke about 'subjectivity':

> The subjective part of trading strategy is the assessment of the quality of information and how prepared you are to rely on it to assess your risk . . . you have to tell the difference between probabilities and possibilities.

A recent entrant to one firm spoke about the learning process.

> No-one has told me how to trade since I have been here. I sit next to the guy that runs the desk, so they're always asking 'what's the P&L how's the desk doing, what's the desk doing?'

Intuition is particularly difficult to justify before the event and particularly glamorous after. Our trader interviews nonetheless abounded with assertions of the importance of intuition and, conversely, the failure of purely technical ability to explain success. This differed by market, being more likely in 'vanilla' equities trading than in more complicated derivatives trading; however, it was not absent in the latter. One derivatives trader remarked: 'It is very difficult in my experience to articulate why you get into a trade and what you do when you're in a trade'.

The importance of intuition was expressed in a variety of contexts. Most generally, trader managers would note that some people 'get it'[5] and some do not, referring to the performance of trainees. Those who did not 'get it' went to sales or research. At the most fundamental level, then, displaying some form of intuition was a ticket of entry to the trading floor. As we explore in Chapter 7, new traders go through a period of apprenticeship, gradually earning an identity as a trader. Those who are seen to have the required qualities continue on to become fully fledged traders. Their managers and mentors are particularly concerned to know if they 'get it', if they have 'flair'. Often managers found it hard to articulate what they were looking for.

> Spotting it [flair] takes a massive amount of gut feeling. What I am trying to spot is the internal energy so you can have them very quiet on the outside, people who don't shout when they talk so on and so forth, but you feel that they have power inside them and they have internal energy and they're naturally strong and they're not going to be moved away by something happening. This has to be balanced with the way they—the way they criticise themselves, the humility if you want, within themselves, their self criticism. And then all kinds of things which have to do with the product we are dealing with which in some cases could be complex which in some cases can be a bit maths, market ability, financial knowledge, be of quick mind, that's it. In some cases, it's not—we know that every time we are making an investment and every time you probably have different background, you can be a good trader, you can have exactly the same background and you can be an awful trader. It's not—I don't know what kind of people they look for in other companies but for us, we have not found a formula yet.

Finally, individuals noted changes in their behaviour over time. Traders remarked on times when they were 'on a roll', 'seeing the ball really well', 'going for it', when the intuitive feel for the market had to be exploited to the full. They reported being more likely to trade frequently in such circumstances. Use of intuition may be associated with noise trading and, conceivably, with risk taking. As one put it, 'I think one of the keys to successful trading is to know when you're hot and there's no better feeling than when you're trading from strength.'

Once this tacit skill was developed, not only was it difficult to articulate, there were few incentives for many to do so. Several traders remarked on the individualistic[6] and secretive strategies necessary for market success.

> Everyone has the right to know arbitrage information, but people do not necessarily think it is their duty to share the information.
>
> This business is not about team spirit. We should be better at trading as a group . . . but in reality people get very parochial and very protective of what they're doing.
>
> If I didn't know something and went and asked someone, this gives them bargaining power.
>
> Systems are not set up to be able to see what other people are doing. Information is not shared enough and there is too much Chinese whispers about position taking.

In short, traders believe both that they have private information and that they develop tacit knowledge. Our findings are thus consistent with those of Abolafia, who examined trading floors in New York and Chicago. He refers to the 'hyperationality' employed by traders involving 'context dependent versions of vigilance and intuitive judgement' (1996: 23). It is the balance which is important, rather than the rational and the intuitive being in competition. As we shall see in the next chapter, this reflects the nature of human cognitive functioning.

Reflexivity

Keynes described stock market behaviour as 'anticipating what average opinion expects average opinion to be' (1936: 156) manifesting the concern with reflexivity which is characteristic of many who focus on the social construction of financial markets. Financial markets are, in fact, highly reflexive domains in which traders 'colonize the future' in terms of models from the past (Soros, 1986; Giddens, 1990). There is awareness of the general theories, awareness of one's personal theory in use and awareness of the existence of variance between one's own and others' theories.

Traders are trying to construct models of how others behave using the limited signals about others' behaviour they gain electronically. This is a very different social milieu from the traditional open outcry market (cf. Knorr Cetina and Bruegger, 2002). For example, one trader specializing in Japanese markets told us:

> It is a market that will do things that are totally unexplained. It would do things that are not based on fundamentals. It would do things that have no logic at all and this comes down to what has always been termed 'the herd mentality of the Japanese' who tend to all be buyers at one stage and all be sellers the next time. Sentiment and emotion have a huge part to play in the market because invariably it is a market that you buy in expectation of what potentially could happen as opposed to buying it on the basis of what has happened. So yes, certainly a sentiment and emotion driven market.

The manager of a foreign exchange derivatives desk told us:

> I would actually say that making money is about understanding as much as you can about people and their honesty, and I generally work on the basis that I am quite courageous in various ways—business or, you know, spare time activities, whatever. I sometimes get very afraid, so I work on the basis that if I'm fairly brave and I get very afraid sometimes, that means the rest of them must be terrified, so I kind of use that as a measuring stick, and if I know people are terrified, I know I can take money off them.

A senior trader manager explained:

> What I ask the trader to do is look at each one of those stocks and try to judge the emotional conditions, the sentiment regarding each of those stocks individually, thinking what is the momentum, has it gone too far, is it just starting to turn. If you are an experienced trader, you look at a chart and you can watch it for a week or a couple of weeks, but you watch it everyday, not just look in the morning and see whether it's trading more on the offer side or the bid side, whether there's more time going up or going down, how's it trading when the overall index or benchmark is moving in one direction or another, whether it seems jittery, whether there are a lot of bids building up so even if it's not trading, is there a lot of

demand underneath?. Those kinds of things. Then you can put that in the context of, what was it doing yesterday and a week and a month ago and then it forms a pattern and try to relate that pattern to patterns you have seen in other stocks and think do I have a sense of which direction it seems to be heading in.

Some traders reflected on the contradictions involved.

When we make a lot of money, I tend to worry about it. I think we can't be making all that money, something is wrong. Our systems are not all that good.

Once you've entered a position, you realise no rule book prepares you for it. And we've all read the world's best trader books. Every person has a different approach.

One way to approach this issue is to examine three of the theories about loss and gain which pass the membership test (i.e. traders talk in these terms). They are depicted in Fig. 4.2. Figure 4.2(a) depicts risk neutrality in the face of loss and gain as generally assumed in finance theory. Whatever the wealth or performance position of the trader, each trade is dealt with according to its own risk level, analytically and rationally. In interviews, traders would acknowledge the need to behave in this way but would also point to the experience of losses, the progress towards bonus targets and their mood as influences on trading behaviour. Figure 4.2(b) presents the prospect-theoretic pattern of

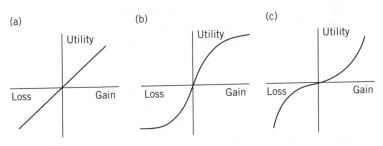

Fig. 4.2 Idealized trader risk profiles (a) risk neutrality, (b) prospect theoretic, and (c) trader ideal

Source: Adapted from Figure 3 in Willman, P., Fenton O'Creevy, M. P., Nicholson, N. and Soane, E. (2001) 'Knowing the risks: theory and practice in financial markets', *Human Relations*, 54(7): 887–910.

risk aversion in the domain of gains and loss aversion in the domain of losses. This was to be avoided; many traders quoted the maxim 'you don't cut profits and you don't chase losses'. Figure 4.2(c) illustrates the traders' ideal; chase profits, cut losses. That is, risk aversion in the domain of losses and risk seeking in the domain of gains. Figure 4.2(a) represents what traders know they should do, Fig. 4.2(b) what they should not do (but apparently—on occasion—do), and Fig. 4.2(c) what they would like to have done *ex post*. They are simultaneously aware of the rules, the need to break the rules and the risks involved in so doing. They know the risks in a fairly sophisticated way, but not in the way predicted by finance theorists.

Finding out about the risks involved learning by doing. Experience was seen to be important. Here are some sample views:

> To trade anything well, you need at least a year's experience of trading that stock.

> The more experience you have, the more certain you are of some things and the more importance you give to small details. Experience is knowing about the full range of information, which things you have to care about. When you start, you care about most of the information; you don't know what is important. You learn through trial and error and watching more experienced people how they make their decisions, how they run their portfolios etc.

> I would let [an inexperienced trader] take a position. Not a large position for obvious reasons. And by letting them take a position they learn something and that to a certain extent shapes their experience and without allowing people to take positions on the back of their judgement then they're not going to learn.

Reflexivity, thus, has two important implications for trading. First, the reflexive nature of markets means that as particular theories become more widely adopted, market behaviour changes in consequence. Theories of how to work the world are thus often both dynamic and provisional. Effective trading is less about the adoption of particular theories than developing the capacity to create and modify theories in response to changing conditions. Second, the ability to draw conclusions about other market actors' motivations and models of the world is an important trading skill.

Contrarian Beliefs[7]

Behaviour manifesting flair was often seen as the opposite of herding. Good traders must be better than average. As several noted, this involved *believing* you were better than average.

> A lot of people in the market are trend followers and that's where opportunities are created for those who are not.

> I think that to get to the top you would have to adopt a higher risk strategy because otherwise it is a risk-return trade off. If you're happy to take bigger risks then you might end up getting fired or getting to the top.

Contrarian beliefs use the language of the general theory to articulate vocabularies of motive. The general laws of the market are interpreted in idiosyncratic ways as part of the vocabularies of motive used to justify situated action by traders (Wright-Mills, 1963). A trading manager in equities told us the following story:

> Six weeks ago [i.e. mid-October 1998] I woke up on Sunday, read the papers and decided that the market was going to turn. On the Monday, I told the traders 'you can be level or long but don't come back short'. We made a lot of money . . . it's been the best six months in a while. When everyone tells you something, don't be with the crowd. It was a bad market . . . we decided it was better to do something than do nothing.

Another trader manager remarked: 'I ask my team what they are doing and then I do the opposite.'

Of course, by definition, everybody cannot be contrarian. A trading cliché is 'the trend is my friend'. However, individuals 'on a roll' may have the confidence to buck the trend. Managers may use contrarians or deliberately encourage a contrarian position on their desks in order to hedge against the trend. If all traders on a desk are trading with the herd, the manager may see benefit in having some contrarian positions which 'question existing wisdom'.

We asked traders about their best experiences and about their best trades. Some responded by talking about the times they had made a great deal of money, or made a big trade. However, several responded to this open ended question by talking in explicitly contrarian terms; the best trade was seen as the one which proved their theory right, in the face of arguments to the contrary, irrespective of profitability. As one put it:

> My best experiences have been where I was very active in the market when I felt that a lot of people were positioned incorrectly. There has been one recent experience where the market moved very quickly in my favour because the market was the wrong way round. So I used this movement to make money and then get out of my positions.

> I was bored and going through the French newspapers when the political crisis was on and there was a privatisation of a company coming up which was big enough to go straight into the index. However, I thought if the government went left wing and was anti-privatisation, this thing won't go into the index, then something else would because there was a merger coming up. I worked out which stock was going to go into the index . . . we all looked great to managers. It was not my biggest ever gain, but I did feel great.

The context in which these beliefs are expressed is important. Traders often have to justify their trading positions to managers. Trader managers in this sample were predominantly ex-traders who continued to run their own books. They had fairly wide spans of control and could not monitor the trading of individuals directly; they simply knew inputs (i.e. trading strategies) and outcomes (profit or loss). Because they do not wish to rely solely on retrospective outcome data, they frequently resort to monitoring the logic of the trading position. In one interview, a manager reported firing a trader because of deficiencies in his explanation of his position, rather than on the basis of outcome data. This episode epitomizes the social aspects of 'work the world' theories. There may be strong incentives for traders to offer 'herding' representations of contrarian positions, or simply to conceal such positions from managers, until the hypothesis prompted by the theory in use has been tested. After the event, a successful contrarian strategy may be publicized as the basis for reputation building.

Consequently, the contrarian views expressed in the interviews involve retrospection and are thus likely at best to be a biased sample of the contrarian positions actually taken. The failed ones will not form part of the folklore of trading, while the successful ones achieve a cachet perhaps out of proportion to their significance. Successes that arise simply from luck may be retrofitted to a contrarian argument.

Traders who strongly believe in their own efficacy may be subject to fundamental attribution error. In short, there may be strong incentives, after the event, for traders to emphasize the use of flair for the purposes of reputation building.[8] As Frankfurter and McGoun (1999) note, those who work in financial markets may be predisposed to interpret beneficial outcomes, which are the result of chance events, as the result of deployment of tacit skill.

4.4 Noise

As Dow and Gorton (1997: 1025) point out 'there appears to be a consensus that trading volume or turnover (trading volume as a fraction of total market value) is inexplicably high'; Black originated the term 'noise' to describe this excess. He remarked:

> People who trade on noise are willing to trade even though from an objective point of view they would be better off not trading. Perhaps they think the noise they are trading on is information. Or perhaps they just like to trade. (1986: 531)

Noise traders may be acting rationally for liquidity or hedging reasons, or they may be acting rationally as agents in ways that differ systematically from the behaviour of those acting in markets as principals. For example, Dow and Gorton (1997) argue that noise trading exists because investors (principals) force traders (agents) to trade rather than be idle. Other approaches take a more radical view. De Long et al. (1990) argue, first, that noise traders are irrational, having 'erroneous stochastic beliefs'. Second, 'irrationality' in this sense helps, in that it may generate higher expected returns than those accruing to rational traders. Third, the rational traders' reaction to irrationality may cause prices to diverge from fundamental values.

Why would traders trade 'too much'? Our data suggest several possibilities, not all irrational. First, we have seen both the importance of intuition and its relationship to learning by doing; traders may pursue the rational strategy of exposure to short-term risk in the pursuit of long-term learning benefits. It may also be mimetic, trading because others trade, which would be a risk-averse strategy in general and perhaps rational also for one of Dow and Gorton's monitored agents.

Irrational noise trading may follow from enthusiasm, of which there was considerable evidence. Traders were likely to report trading more frequently when making money and less frequently when losing. There were several examples:

> When I make money I think it shows I'm doing something right. If I'm right, I will try and do more of them, to increase the size of my position to make more money.

> I think if you are on a roll, that is when you are prepared to put more money at risk. When you are not sure what is going on and you have a few losses that is when you pull back.

> I think it is a good idea when you lose money, especially a lot of money, to sit back, take it easy and maybe stop trading for a while.

> On average, people will trade more often when they are making money compared with when they are losing money because their risk aversion and loss tolerance change.

As Black put it, maybe for many, particularly where profits are being made, the trading activity itself enters the utility function (1986: 533). He goes on to remark that if things like enjoyment go into the utility function very little of expected utility theory can be salvaged.

Alternatively, it might be that excessive trading emerges from either boredom, or unjustified beliefs about the market. One of our respondents described how boredom trades are generated.

> You do boredom trades because you can be sitting up there doing nothing and you think, well I'll do that because it gives me something to do. The next thing you know you are wrong and you've lost money on it. Or you're right and you're inclined to do it again in bigger volumes.

Others had belief about relationships between trading volume and success:

> '. . . turnover is usually important in my business. The more trades I do the better. If I do 1000 trades I'll make more money than if I did 500 trades'.

Noise is interesting because it is such a pervasive market phenomenon. It is not a low probability high impact event but a feature of most markets most of the time. But finance theory has a hard time with it. Even from the interdisciplinary perspective employed here, it has severe implications. What has been termed 'the essential contribution of economics in the performing of the economy' (Callon, 1998: 23) is very evident in financial markets. We are arguing that the use of finance theory by traders who know other traders are using it helps to create the markets the theory predicts. There is other evidence for this. MacKenzie and Millo show how the use of 'Black–Scholes–Merton' theory in arbitrage in Chicago futures markets pushed prices towards Black–Scholes values and 'helped make one of its own key assumptions—that stocks could be purchased entirely on credit—true' (2001: 54).

Traders also know about noise and yet on a daily basis traders who know that much trading is noise apparently do not sit on their hands, but partake. One reason may be that there can be higher returns to noise trading. As De Long *et al.* put it:

> Because the un-predictability of noise traders' future opinions deters arbitrage, prices can diverge significantly from fundamental values even when there is no fundamental risk. Noise traders thus create their own space. [. . .] arbitrage does not eliminate the effects of noise because noise itself creates risk.
>
> The risk resulting from stochastic changes in noise traders' opinions raises the possibility that noise traders who are on average bullish earn a higher expected return than rational, sophisticated investors engaged in arbitrage against noise trading. This result obtains because noise trader risk makes assets less attractive to risk-averse arbitrageurs and so drives down prices. If noise traders on average overestimate returns or underestimate risk, they invest more in the risky asset on average than sophisticated investors and may earn higher average returns. [. . .] our point is that noise traders can earn higher expected returns solely by bearing more of the risk that they themselves create. Noise traders can earn higher expected returns from their own destabilizing influence, not because they perform the useful social function of bearing funda-mental risk. (De Long *et al.*, 1990: 705–706)

In the screen-based markets we have studied, it may be difficult to identify who the noise traders are, particularly if sophisticates are tempted to imitate them.[9] But if wealth accrues to the irrational, we are some way from even the weaker versions of the efficient market hypothesis.

While our data are not sufficient to examine theories of noise trading in depth, they do point in some interesting directions. The notion that there is a clear dichotomy between 'rational' professional traders and 'irrational' investors trading on noise is clearly erroneous. Further, our findings suggest that learning processes, the nature of work the world theories and erroneous beliefs may all lead to professional traders contributing to the volume of noise trading.

4.5 Knowing the Risks

Our central argument has been that the knowledge deployed by traders in financial markets consists of general, quasi-scientific knowledge about markets and tradable instruments on the one hand and, on the other, specific and idiosyncratic recipes for trading success. Perfect markets and rational decision-making in the aggregate models may be set against the local interest in the generation of imperfections, the use of heuristics and learning by doing at the individual level.

It is beyond the scope of this chapter to argue that these differences between, on the one hand, aggregate theories and, on the other, individual ones serve to undermine the former.[10] It may be that, as in the philosophy of science literature, one regards individual decision-making by traders as involving the critical and reflexive process of 'depending on ideas while assessing their dependability' (Sabel, 1994). From this perspective, overcoming what we have termed the actuarial fallacy,[11] (i.e. believing aggregate probabilities apply to specific actions) is similar to maintaining Feyerabend's (1970) notion of the 'principle of tenacity' under which scientists maintain a belief despite acknowledging its infirmity. The fundamental belief here is that one can beat the market and its infirmity lies in the fact that many traders hold it and they cannot all be right.

We conclude this chapter by examining three issues. The first is the pursuit of the perfect market particularly by regulators. The second is the pursuit of learning by doing by traders. The third is the generation of contrarian strategies by traders. All three have both theoretical and policy implications.

Financial markets are not perfect and traders do not have perfect information. Moreover, their actions keep things that way. Imperfections are essential to making money but are intrinsically unknowable to the majority of traders at any time. The markets are, in fact, a complicated mixture of formal, publicly available knowledge and knowledge which is tacit in one of two senses (Willman, 1997).

It may be necessarily tacit, based in intuition about market change. This knowledge is typically generated in learning-focused noise trading which results in experientially grounded 'feelings' about the market which provide a basis for risk exposure. It may be conceptualized as a deeply embedded heuristic which traders describe as flair, the precise content of which cannot easily be articulated. We refer to this as Type 1 inappropriability.

It may be contingently tacit—kept so for profit by the originating trader or traders in order to be locally rather than generally appropriable. This knowledge may contain facts about arbitrage possibilities or market-maker reactions that are in principle easily articulated but which will be protected by individuals as the basis for continued trading success. This private information is Type 2 inappropriability.

As Hayek points out, markets are highly decentralized in information terms. Relevant knowledge 'never exists in concentrated or integrated form, but solely as the dispersed bits of incomplete and frequently contradictory knowledge which all separate individuals possess' (Hayek, 1945: 519). Winning strategies in such markets may not last long and individuals have incentives to prevent others from smothering the advantage their strategy creates (Bernstein, 1996: 299).

Both forms of knowledge are used by traders to make money. Use of know how which is Type 1 inappropriable is not fully rational, but it may generate profit. Use of know how which is Type 2 inappropriable is rational for traders but may cause problems for managers or regulators; it will often be covert. Before the event, traders may misrepresent or dissimulate the bases of their trades in both cases. In the first case, because of the irrationality, it would be very difficult to explain to managers and peers. In the second, because of appropriability issues, if everybody follows the strategy, it may yield no advantages. The vocabulary of motives which traders use to describe their trades to managers or other position monitors is that underlying Fig. 4.2(c).[12]

This relates to both noise trading and contrarian strategies. Our approach to noise trading is that a significant amount of it (within investment banks) consists of learning by doing. Traders are experimenting with their work the world theories. Since managers may not condone these trades, often the basis of the trade will be couched in language which conceals intent. Similar considerations affect contrarian strategies, but to a rather more compounded extent. Before the event, I will wish to conceal my contrarian strategy not only because my manager will not necessarily endorse a risk-seeking contrarian trade but also because it can only succeed to the extent that it does not too quickly induce mimetic herding. After the event, it may be the basis for reputation building. Not only do these motives underpin the dual symbolic role for work the world theories outlined above, they also suggest a link between trader learning, contrarian strategies, and noise trading. In short, the structure of the knowledge base which sustains trader success generates covert behaviour which also sustains the occasions of trader malfeasance which attract great publicity.

Notes

1. This is not necessarily the case for other markets; see Wiseman and Bromiley (1991), McNamara and Bromiley (1999).
2. Traders can of course profit simply by making markets; using liquidity to benefit from bid-offer spreads. Again though, in the case of perfect competition, competition between market-makers will reduce spreads to the point where profit opportunities disappear.
3. The firm owner, shareholders or customer on whose behalf the trader is doing business.
4. We argue in Chapter 5 that the need for a sense of control may at times lead to self-protective illusions.
5. We return to this theme of 'getting it' in our discussion of learning in Chapter 7.
6. In firm D, there was a greater emphasis on teamwork, associated with the customer service culture. In all the firms, by the time of our follow up interviews in 2002, there was greater rhetoric about teamwork, although the extent to which this was achieved in practice is not clear.
7. Abolafia (1996: 121) uses this term very specifically to describe the market stabilizing strategies of 'specialists' on the NYSE who sell on the up and buy on a fall as a matter of rule. Here, we use the term more generally to describe dissent from the prevailing view.

8. The drive to do this is founded in the psychology of self-regulation—the need to maintain self-serving and internally consistent cognitive schema, even when contrary to logic or evidence. We explore this theme further in Chapter 6.

9. In particular it will often be difficult to distinguish between noise traders as understood by De Long *et al.* (trading on the basis of erroneous stochastic beliefs) and flow traders (trading on an understanding of market sentiment and trend behaviour).

10. For a view of financial economics as wholly ideological, see Frankfurter and McGoun (1999).

11. We discuss this further in Chapter 6.

12. We discuss this further in Chapter 8.

Chapter 5

A FRAMEWORK FOR UNDERSTANDING TRADER PSYCHOLOGY

The core of a trader's role is making decisions under conditions of uncertainty and risk. Our purpose is to arrive at a deeper understanding of the demands this makes on the trader, in terms of capabilities, tolerances, and challenges to adjustment. It is widely recognized that trading is a difficult job that places enormous pressures on individuals—in terms of the complexity and flow of information, the major consequences that can flow from decisions, and the limited time frame and resources they have to make decisions. This is recognized in the extreme value investment banks place upon selecting people with high intellectual capabilities and personal qualities that will enable them to survive and prosper. As we shall see in later chapters, this is not generally approached through rigorous profiling, but rather by taking the brightest and best from the top of the higher education labour pool, and testing them on the job to see if they will make it as traders.[1]

There are two sets of issues we explore in this chapter and the next. First, are what might be called general cognitive and motivational variables that are likely to affect all traders, though to differing degrees according to their individual circumstances and characteristics. The second set of issues concerns important individual differences and how they affect trader style and performance. This second question we discuss at length in the next chapter. Here, we are concerned with the first question—what are the general forces at work in the trading environment (inside and outside the individual trader) that help to hold a trader to a line of effective performance, or which blow them off course.

Our interest in this question brings together theory and practice. How traders think, feel, and act in their decision environment is an important exemplar of human adaptive functioning in complex tasks. Particular demands of the trader role make it a uniquely valuable and interesting context for examining human decision-making. We shall be looking at the behavioural decision-making literature with a view to illustrating and illuminating some of its main themes and ideas. In doing so we seek a practical understanding of the snares and traps traders may be especially vulnerable to. From this flow insights about how best to apply appropriate supports, guidance and controls via management systems, incentives, and ancillary structures.

To address these questions we draw on arguments and ideas that concern rationality, control, and the regulatory processes through which perception, judgement, and action are formed.[2] Our starting point is not that humans are fundamentally irrational but that our rationality has a logic that is unlike the mechanics of formal mathematics but one which serves the goals of our biological identity (Calne, 1999). The most constant feature that has dominated human psychology, and continues to do so, is the need to anticipate, understand, influence, and adjust to the intentions of other humans within complex social groups (Nicholson, 2000). This is what has been called everyday 'mind-reading' (Whiten, 1991) and is an essential skill in order to do deals, detect cheats, form alliances, and advance our interests (Miller, 2000). More broadly, our cognitive capacities are also geared towards a range of planful behaviours to achieve our goals under conditions of potential adversity and scarcity. These include a range of simplifying and confidence sustaining heuristics that make us smart, when stopping the flow of action to undertake an exhaustive analysis would be foolish (Gigerenzer, Todd, and The ABC Research Group, 1999). As we shall see, these features militate against rigorous logic or straight-line reasoning, but are admirably suited to fast-paced intuitive judgements and actions (Nicholson, 2000). We will explore in theory and from the evidence of our research, how this profile that makes us supremely gifted in all kinds of trading behaviour is, on closer examination, deeply flawed when it comes to specifics of formally rational calculus, reasoning, and decision-making.

The most coherent account we find of how these paradoxical talents and disabilities cohere is contained in the ideas of self-regulation theory (Karoly, 1993). This does not, as yet, constitute a unitary body of knowledge and theory, but a collection of ideas running in parallel from a shared core insight. This insight is that the self is the psychological agency that exists in order to coordinate human thought, feeling, and action (Lord and Levy, 1994). People's sense of self can be fragile and quite often deluded. The reason for this is that the self's principal tasks are to maintain whatever is important to the person—especially mood, purpose, sense of efficacy, consistency, and identity (Tice, Bratslavsky, and Baumeister, 2002).

Writers have observed how self-regulation alternates between states of goal-directedness and internal adjustment (Kuhl, 1992), and a major theme is how individuals differ in orientation and what can induce them to change the amount they monitor their internal states versus the external world (Snyder, 1987). For much of the time our mental functioning is deeply concerned with maintaining emotional control and mood via the screening of inner thoughts, so that behaviour does not become unstable through continual shifts in affect[3] (Macrae, Bodenhausen, and Milne, 1998). Feedback and the formulation of cognitive strategies for adjusting to discrepancies between expectation and environmental change are central to this process (Carver and Scheier, 1998). Processes of self-regulation—modulation of thought, affect, action, and attention—are initiated when a routine is impeded or when goal-directedness is made salient, for example, by a new challenge or a failure (Karoly, 1993).

At the core of self-regulation processes is the maintenance of goal-directedness and functional integrity. For this reason, it is generally perceptions that shift to adapt to goals, rather than the reverse (Powers, 1973; Cziko, 1995). The point here is that self-regulation processes are capable of inducing attitudes, attentional focus, beliefs, and judgements that are inconsistent with the external world, for the sake of the imperative demands of psychological well-being, self-motivation, and feelings of integrity (Tomarken and Kirschenbaum, 1982). Within this framework, we can see that behaviour which appears irrational in terms of a financial–economic calculus, may yet be understood as rational in terms of goals concerned with maintenance of self-image and self-control.

This framework can help us to make sense of how traders see the world and act upon it. It is important for them to respond to the real world and its signals with a high degree of formal rationality, but not at the expense of self-control. The question this raises, somewhat philosophically perhaps, is whether rational action, in the narrow financial–economic sense, is possible in this world, given the demands it makes and the constraints on judgement that human psychology imposes. More practically, our aim in this chapter is to assess where the chief areas of trader vulnerability to bias and poor economic performance are likely to be found, and what one can recommend in order to facilitate increased effectiveness.

5.1 The Bounded Rationality of Trader Decision-Making

If we consider the definition of the trader role with which we started this chapter—financial decision-making under conditions of uncertainty and risk—it can be seen to have a commonplace and an extraordinary aspect. The commonplace is that trading is an extension of everyday human capacities and actions. Every time we cross a street, buy a product or join a club, we are engaging in decision-making under uncertainty and risk. The chances that we will get hit by a truck, buy something that breaks down the first time we use it, or join a club that fails to deliver what we expected, are typically low but not negligible.

Trader Psychology

Consciously—more often unconsciously—we factor in the risks and uncertainty by instinct rather than calculus. The risk and uncertainty are factored out or taken for granted in a flow of decision-making that has a high degree of automaticity to it (Bargh and Chartrand, 1999).

In this context we often only become aware of having made a choice under conditions of risk and uncertainty when an expected outcome fails to occur. We are reminded of the hazards of crossing streets only after a surprise encounter with a road user. This kind of decision-making by exception is, of course, an efficient solution to the challenge of maintaining operational control over multiple sequential actions in a complex and rapidly changing environment. Too much thought, and we grind to a halt. In fact, the times when we actually stop and make significant choices, weighing up the pros and cons of alternative courses of action, are quite rare.

It is this perspective that makes the trader's role so extraordinary, since their task is to continuously bring actions into the realm of the conscious, that in our day-to-day experience are highly automatic. It is a refined challenge to have to sit at a computer terminal and continually weigh the benefits of momentary changes in a current situation— whether to buy, sell, or hold a position; which of various options to select to fulfil a customer order; whether to put a proposition about a new decision to a client or another agent. To this extent automaticity is the trader's enemy. Coasting spells complacency. Neglect and occluded vision are hazards that managers are on the look out for and that traders are often aware of. As one derivatives trader told us in firm B:

> Ninety eight percent of good trading is hard work, attention to detail, making sure there are no surprises, paying attention to the huge amount of information and very valuable and accurate information that you, as a trader, have access to as quickly as anybody else in the world.

The following, not unusual, story was told to us by another trader in the same firm:

> We have an automatic trading system now which enables us as traders to work the orders ourselves whereas before, we used to have to rely on traders in the respective countries. You used to have to phone them up, get the order in and a delay meant you missed prices basically. So now we have our own system. . . . I had a sell order and I pressed the sell

button, it didn't flip from one stock to another and I sold not 400 000 shares of something that is normally very liquid but something that is not very liquid at all. I sold it down 15% and suspended it on the stock exchange. That wasn't pleasant. Attention to detail, no matter how busy you are—if I had checked that and noticed that it was still on F rather than C, I would have noticed that I was selling the wrong stock, but in the heat of the moment, you are so busy, you have got people shouting at you left, right and centre and I just pressed that go and it went.

Not all the decisions on a trading floor are alike. There are wide differences, for example, between 'flow traders'—engaged in numerous rapid judgement calls, often on the basis of patchy information about demand and supply, and 'fundamentalists', who pour long and hard over data on the economic value of financial instruments before taking a position; subsequently requiring substantive new information before they will unwind or alter the investment profile. Customer demands add another dimension to a trader's decision-making.

What unifies these different types of trading decision is that they all have a formally rational component. They obey the classical formula of steps for decision rationality:

1. Determine your objective—in trading environments typically this is to make money, avoid loss, and satisfy customers.
2. Consider alternative courses of action—for example, buy, sell, hold, or hedge.
3. Compute the likely outcomes of each course of action and the risks of each, for example, using mathematical pricing models and state of the world models.
4. Enact the outcome that optimizes risk and return according to predetermined decision criteria.

Financial economic theory dictates that all effective decision-making should be based upon this kind of rationality. Even the traders who are operating on 'gut feel' should, according to this account, be guided by a superior mental calculus of which their intuitions and feelings are no more than the palpable indicators. The highly experienced and effective trader is in effect expected to be saying to him or herself: 'I trust this feeling I have about this deal, because it is based upon thousands of similar decisions where my expectations were tested by the real world'. This viewpoint was reflected by many of the traders we interviewed. For example, a trader on firm A's arbitrage desk told us:

[Intuition] is more about assimilation, recognising patterns of how markets have moved in the past, than emotional feeling. For example: when I was a proprietary trader and I and my boss had opposing views. I thought the stock market was going down and my boss thought it was going up in the short term because, while mine was based on historical analysis, his view was based on the fact that the short term interest rates had come under a lot of pressure, rates had been going up and the stock market had not been selling off and generally speaking if the interest rates go up, the stock market should suffer; so he was saying that was a sign of the underlying strength of the stock market. He watched and then he thought the interest rates had got to the bottom, instead of buying them, he bought the stock market instead which he thought would out perform and it did, it went up and thereafter, it went down a long way, but he took that short term view and made money out of it whereas I hadn't refined the process enough to take this into account. I should have overlaid price action with a view based on the historical analysis.

A bond trader in firm B took a similar view:

I think many people do say they're gut feel traders but perhaps they're not analysing what they're actually thinking and they're seeing a lot of customer flow and a lot of buyers and they're probably don't necessarily realise the reasons why they want to buy but there are very good traders that say they're trading off gut feel that I believe actually have probably reasonable information, reasonable thoughts behind it—they wouldn't literally toss a coin.

However, others took a different view. An equities trader in firm D told us:

Gut feeling I think is a huge part of our day to day business. Gut feeling is like my sixth sense. I think it is telling me somehow, for some reason that it is the right or wrong thing to be doing and I will go with it. I would rather go with it and be wrong than not go with it and be right . . . I think it is very important for traders to go with their gut feeling at times. Almost as much, if not more, than any type of analytical report that they're reading.

While other traders distrust intuition as a basis for decision-making. For example a derivatives trader in firm B argued that

If someone says I'm doing it because it feels right and can provide no other explanation than that, I would say it is horse shit because gut feeling to me is the amalgamation of a complex set of variables that are hard to quantify but lead you to believe something. I think intuition is a very good thing and oftentimes it's correct, but gut feeling in the absence of rational decision making and thinking is ludicrous. I don't make decisions based on gut feeling. I may examine opportunities based on intuition that something is going to happen, but the decision is based on something I think is rational.

So what actually happens? What kind of rationality operates on the trading floor? Our data help to answer the question, and we shall put our observations about traders through the lens of behavioural decision theory (Bazerman, 1997).

When one of our senior manager informants expressed the view that 'only machines are rational', what was he actually saying about trader behaviour? The underlying thought is double edged. If by the term 'rational' one means ability to compute and reason without error, clearly humans are quite deficient in this respect. Despite having the most complexly wired system in the known world—a trillion neural connections in 1.4 l of cranial capacity in the human brain— we cannot keep pace with the computations of the most rudimentary pocket calculator, and we get confused when presented with more than a few negatives and inversions in a chain of logic. Yet, it took about two decades of development of all the computing power IBM could muster to create a genuine championship chess-playing computer. Chess is perhaps the ultimate challenge for rational decision-making, because its rules consist entirely of the bounded logic of a mathematical system. However, to play it well requires attributes that are rational, but until recently have not really been programmable— the ability to lay traps, see patterns and volunteer short-term losses for long-term gains. These are elements of strategic logic. It is these skills that give traders their value—they are playing a highly sophisticated rational game at a level that no machine will be able to simulate for a long time to come.

The double-edged nature of the manager's comment has on one side a respect for the extraordinary feats of memory, fast calculation, intuitive gifts, and far-sighted judgement that the best traders exhibit.

On the other side, also implied by the manager's comment, lie a forest of errors, emotional reactions, and self-delusions that can swiftly derail the performance of the decision-maker. As our analytical framework suggests, these are not failures in the human cognitive design, but attributes that help us to get by in situations for which evolution designed us: a social milieu of fellow-humans trying to develop collaborative action plans that enable us to survive and prosper in a dangerous world (Nicholson, 1998a, 2000). But these same attributes can trip us up when we try to apply this non-linear human intelligence to the apparently rational demands of the world of finance.

In the remainder of the chapter we examine what traders do in the light of what we know about human decision-making from experimental and field research.

It is a well-known trap in trading environments for traders to be reluctant to take the plunge of making a decision until they have 'sufficient' information, and employers hope to weed these out in the induction process, for perfectionists who are unable to be swiftly decisive cannot make money, and cannot survive. As the saying goes 'the best is the enemy of the good'. Effective decision-makers often have to 'satisfice': the necessity under conditions of uncertainty and insufficient data to reduce the costs of decision-making by letting a 'good enough' threshold trigger choice. Inexperienced traders need the help of experienced seniors to lower the threshold. One strategy is for managers to help them to take the perspective of a funnelled focus.

> Traders need to be quite assiduous at ferreting out information from multiple sources, looking at multiple overlays, what's happening in the industry, what's going on with company management, what's the strategy of the company, what's the regulatory environment in which the company is operating and things like that. The pure trader would just sit there all day. I discourage the trader from knowing anything about the companies. That's extreme, but knowing just the barest essentials about the companies whose shares they trade. I don't want them to know research, earnings expectations, none of that . . . A trader's job is to figure out what someone else will pay for it which is completely different from what it's worth. If your job is to determine what something is worth, you can have a time horizon of 6 months or 6 years. But a trader needs to have a shorter time horizon, not 5 minutes, but a day or a week.[4]

5.2   Cognitive Biases[5]

Human cognitive design does incorporate an impressive ability to scan fast and précis—mastering complexity by simplifying—plus a range of other mental devices that get us to our goals by the fastest and most effective route possible. These are traps for the unwary; since misapplied or applied in contexts for which other skills are needed, they lead to incorrect or ineffective outcomes. Problems can occur at all stages of the decision-making process. We shall review the major themes in human judgement and decision-making, considering how they operate and what hazards they bring at four stages of the process:

Diagnosis. This is the period of information search activities, when the decision-maker first scans, appraises, and questions the array of data to make a first assessment. For traders this amounts to judging what is the nature of the challenge or opportunity of the moment.

Assessment. At this juncture, various options are assessed, and the potential costs, risks, and benefits of various courses of action. For traders this is how they assess the merits of contracts, positions, or trades.

Action. This is committing to a course of action and seeing it through to its conclusion or outcome. Various contextual factors can impinge on and influence the actions of traders in implementing strategies.

Adjustment. This is how the decision-maker appraises the consequences of decision-making. Attribution processes are important here, especially for traders; how they account for outcomes.

We shall examine each in turn.

The Diagnosis Challenge

Cognitive science has been much preoccupied with how difficult it is to make impartial and detached assessments of information. Our skill at fast intuitive appraisals of complex arrays is only possible because of the pre-tuning of perceptual equipment. Our sensory equipment is designed to filter and structure information _before_ it is apprehended, and our cognitions are framed by a host of, mainly unconscious, expectations. A central part of a trader's training and learning is for this pattern recognition ability to be attuned to appropriate stimuli—so that in an array of data the 'important' information stands out. Analogous skills are developed in many occupations—for example, radiographers can read much more from X-ray charts than the layperson, or indeed many doctors.

Several things can go wrong in this diagnostic phase.

Retrievability Bias

Our cognitive equipment is designed to make instinctive discriminations between what is worth paying attention to and what can be ignored. Retrievability refers to the role memory plays in attuning expectations and awareness (Gigerenzer, Todd, and The ABC Research Group, 1999). What stands out will be what is familiar or surprising. Personal relevance or its vividness gives experiences a mental 'tag'. This means what each trader pays attention to will differ, since each has a unique stock of significant memories:

> I remember in my first few weeks at my previous firm I made a horrendous mistake. I lost millions of dollars. The MD came over and congratulated me on making one of the biggest mistakes he'd ever seen. In the end it wasn't such a big problem because the decision was a reasonable one. But I'll never forget it.

In our research, we tested for a number of biases by means of a short series of exercises adapted from some of the classic experimental tests of cognitive bias. Retrievability bias was one that we assessed by this means. The exercise asked participants to estimate the number of words in two pages of a novel that take the form of four letters followed by 'ing', and then to estimate the number of words in two pages of a novel that are seven letters long with 'n' as the sixth letter. Logic dictates that there will be more words of the second form, since the 'ing' words are a subset of seven letter words with 'n' as the penultimate letter. However, examples of words ending 'ing' are more easily retrievable than those with n as the penultimate letter. We found that 77.6 per cent of the traders (wrongly) gave a higher answer for '__ing' words than '__n_' words; just about the same as a sample of 173 MBA students and executives, 74 per cent of whom gave the erroneous response. The result shows that traders by virtue of their training and experience are not gifted with superior reasoning or defended against this kind of bias.

Base-Rate Insensitivity and Mistaken Frequency Estimates ⊕
This is a trap well known to statisticians, and people who deal in everyday actuarial computations—or at least it should be. The most familiar form of this error is to be overimpressed by percentages while overlooking absolute values (Kahneman and Tversky, 1972). For example, it occurs when anyone draws attention to a large percentage increase (or decrease) in some factor when the absolute level of change is negligible. An everyday example of the idea would be the logic that standing under a tree during a storm radically increases your chances of being struck by lightning, though the actual probability of the occurrence under either circumstance is vanishingly small. Politicians and sales people are especially adept at influencing by this misuse of statistics.

Traders, who deal in numbers are mainly well aware of this trap and avoid it in its more obvious forms. They may not do so, however, when it is more disguised. Major improbable events, such as in the quote above, stand out and may shape behaviour far more than they should (Bazerman, 1997). It only takes two or three bad experiences, for example, for traders, like the rest of us, to believe that they are the victims of a trend, and judge future risks to be greater than they are.

> There's times if I lose money like two or three days on the spin and I lose, you know, what I consider, you know, I didn't really need to lose that money—two or three days on the spin, perhaps I'll just stop trading for a day, two days, concentrate on my agency orders, sit back, have a look at it again.

A dysfunctional aspect of our sensitivities is that we tend to be very poor at evaluating frequencies. Rare events not only stand out, but they are often subjectively perceived to be more frequent than they actually are, especially negative events and major risks. We also suffer the opposite error of undervaluing the frequency of common events. Hence, people engage routinely in dangerous activities such as car driving, and are excessively nervous about relatively safe activities like flying, especially after some high profile airline calamity. In effect these are instances of failure to apply sampling theory, especially to small numbers (Tversky and Kahneman, 1971), which holds that any given percentage variation is much more likely be a chance event in a small than a large population. A 10 per cent change in the value of a thinly traded security, for example, is much more likely to be a chance occurrence than it would be for a highly liquid (frequently traded) security.

In our research we tested for the prevalence of sample size errors of reasoning using a familiar behavioural decision research problem. This asked respondents to estimate the likelihood of variations in the live birth ratio recorded, respectively, at a large and a small hospital. The incorrect response—that more variation is likely in the large hospital—was given by 55.5 per cent of the traders; even higher than the 47.7 per cent of our business school sample presented with the same question (though, because of sample size, this is not a statistically significant margin of difference). This result is rather more worrying than the previous test, since an elementary acquaintance with sampling theory would seem to be indispensable to people making financial decisions based upon changing market values. At the very least one would hope traders could outperform a student population (Anderson and Sunder, 1995).

Expectancy Effects

Perhaps the most obvious yet difficult trap to avoid in the diagnostic phase is the powerfully guiding influence of prior *expectations*. This problem is amplified by strong personal goal orientations (Milburn, 1978). The starving man is more prone to food mirages than the person with the sated appetite. One of the most pervasive forms this takes is the confirmation bias. Trained scientists—the people one might expect to be most immune to the bias—are highly prone to seeking evidence that is in line with their cherished theories rather than seeking to disprove their hypotheses by rigorous tests (Dunbar, 1995). Politicians, marketers, and strategists are all vulnerable to this kind of wish fulfilment. Are traders immune? The following quote from an arbitrage trader suggests that they are not.

> You have to build a framework on how you believe the world is working. You have your mental picture of what is going on. When you are making money, this mental picture is being reinforced; by definition your decisions are correct.

Another trader explained his approach to gathering information:

> I spend time talking to a lot of people; consultants, other traders on the desk, in the markets, finding out what people are doing. I am always absorbing information. . . . I like to find people who have the same thought processes as me.

Many traders, who reported that successful trades were rarely analysed *post hoc*, shared this point of view. Yet, there are many factors that mediate between a decision and its consequences, and success does not necessarily indicate correct thought processes.

A few traders might be more guarded and balanced in how they assess data, but they are also in a sense trained to be vulnerable to the bias. As we noted in Chapter 4, managers often say that the greatest sin for a trader is not to know why they hold a position. The compulsion to have a strong rationale for your trades means that you may unconsciously screen out evidence that is contradictory to your strategy and reasoning.

Another kind of expectancy trap is the *conjunction fallacy*—the assumption that contiguous phenomena are linked causally (Kahneman and Tversky, 1983). This can take many forms. The crudest is superstition. One might expect traders would be shielded against this kind of magical thinking, but this is not the case.

> There's lots of superstition. If they had a bad day they'll not wear the same suit or tie again, or not drive to work by a particular route. If I had a new suit on a bad trading day, I wouldn't wear it again, even if it was brand new. I'd still do that now.

It is disturbing, but only human, to find traders as full of *superstitions* as the rest of us, but at the same time most are aware of this irrationality enough to engage in some healthy discounting. However, less obvious forms of the conjunction fallacy are more difficult to deal with. One example is the perception of a trend or a cause between events that are in fact random or unrelated, such as the simultaneous movement of values in two separate markets, or those that are adjacent in time, but unconnected.

Finally, we turn to those factors in the environmental context that shape expectations, called framing effects. Framing effects are pervasive and powerful influences on decision-making (Kühberger, 1998), and occur at every stage of the process. In the diagnostic phase it is the colouring that is given to any perception by its current backdrop. Times and places supply frames. There is, for example, evidence that the weather has a significant framing influence on trading decisions. Hirshleifer and Shumway (2003) showed that market returns on the New York Stock Exchange are significantly higher when the New York weather is sunny. Other key framing influences for traders include where they are in the bonus cycle and their recent history of gains and losses. We discuss these further in Chapter 8.

The Assessment Challenge

Effective decision-makers do not trust their initial instinctive diagnosis. Even if it is based upon powerful and correct intuitions they still need to be checked, and the themes we have been considering could be taken as a checklist for the purpose. Following fast on the heels of this assessment comes the analytical phase at which one figures out the costs and benefits of different responses. In fact it is a feature of the dynamism of trading environments that these phases are separated more in theory than in practice, for the appraisal and the analytical process overlap in time, which constitutes an additional snare to decision-making.

One of the most important sources of non-linear biases in assessment, which we have already considered in Chapter 3 is summarized by *prospect theory* (Kahneman and Tversky, 1979). This is the asymmetrical appraisal of risk in the context of loss and gain. *Framing* is intimately connected with this phenomenon, since the context within which an event takes place can shape whether or how strongly it is apprehended as a loss or a gain. Rather like plunging one's hand into a bowl of tepid water after emptying the freezer, a neutral outcome can feel 'hot'—that is, a gain, after a sequence of losses, and be framed as a gain in the midst of losses. Loss and gain are notoriously subject to this kind of appraisal, despite injunctions to the contrary to take each trade and position afresh, as if one had 'a flat book' (i.e. from a position of neutral value, without a cushion of prior gains or a burden of prior losses).

The chief element of prospect theory in the context of assessing alternatives is the fact that we are more willing to take risks and exert effort to avoid loss than to seek gain (Tversky and Kahneman, 1991). The danger for traders and managers is that they become overly fixated on avoiding the downside in their actions. As a trader in firm C told us:

> Here, there is a tendency that when you make a million dollars, people don't question that much really what you are doing. But when you lose a million dollars, you get much more questions than when you make money. So, fundamentally, I am obviously very influenced by that. Personally I think I could feel more comfortable than I do losing money; because, at the end of the day, it's very hard to judge a good trader and a bad trader. Model arbitrage is a bit different because its quite technical, but if you look at the so called example—whether it's Nick Leeson, or Bob Citron in Orange County, at the end of the day, these guys had the right view and if they had waited 6 months more they would have been stars. In a sense their position was quite big—it should have been the right size if they could have had the patience to wait. They would have been stars if they had been able to wait 6 months. So you get quite influenced by that, by where you need to cut, by where you get into trouble.

A manager in firm A described the danger of a bias to *loss aversion* in traders he managed:

> The best thing to do is not to be over the top. The guys who shout about making money are the ones who shout a lot when they are losing money, throw the phones, smash the screens. They like to sing about it when they have made it. They get into a downward spiral and they think they can double the bet when something goes against them and they make desperate trades. The decision needs to be made to stop the trade or halve it rather than double it, maybe give the position to someone else and ask their advice.

Traders have to be inured to losses so that they are not lured into the action strategy of loss chasing—the ruin of many a gambler. One way of avoiding loss chasing is by framing even moderately large losses as being in the domain of neutrality. Many of the traders we interviewed described this as coming with experience. The manager of a bond trading department told us:

> I've been doing this for 8 years and when you first start and you make £50k, you think 'I'm a god' and then you lose £50k and think 'I'm going

to be fired tomorrow'. Eventually when you are up you say, 'that's fine I'm doing my job' and when you are down, 'it's the job'.... After a while, apart from the major swings (above $five million, which would affect me), it really doesn't bother me at all. This is to do with experience.

The positive and negative emotions associated with success and failure, while commonplace experiences for some traders, are, in theory, banished in the trading room, and indeed at their extremes both pose major challenges for traders and managers. Probably the most commonplace negative is stress (Broadbent, 1971). The ingredients of this are well known, but the most pernicious combination is high load plus low control (Karasek and Theorell, 1990), and research has shown that stress symptoms do run high in trading room, especially in the form of free-floating anxiety (Kahn and Cooper, 1993). As this manager in firm D describes, the effects of stress can be damaging to performance:

> There's one particular guy that works for me now who for probably two years he really was in the wilderness. His confidence was totally shattered. In just the last year he's been with a youngster who's got a bit of enthusiasm and he's started to get his confidence back and it's quite nice to see, because he was always a good trader but he got to a stage where he was just frightened of shadows and didn't want a position.

The trader who starts to pile up losses in an environment where the bad news keeps coming may be apt to feel loss of control. In most markets, with the exception of small illiquid markets or where block trades are made that are big enough to affect markets, no one trader has any control over events—one's role is to react to the market. Given that markets do (within limits) follow a random walk, trader judgements about them are especially vulnerable to misperceptions. Later in this chapter we shall look at one misperception that we devoted particular attention to: the *illusion of control*.

The fundamental attribution error is a related phenomenon, identified by psychologists as the tendency for events that were actually caused by impersonal forces to be attributed to human agency and intention (Ross, 1977). If a trader believes, as some do, that all winning trades are due to their good judgement and all losing trades are due to market factors, then they are only a whisker away from megalomania (on a winning streak) and depression (on a losing run).

In the phase of assessing options, emotions play a crucial part. One major amplifier of any perceptions and reactions is *ego-involvement*— the tendency to identify with one's actions (Dweck and Leggett, 1988). Traders and their managers will freely admit that the people who are most prone to this kind of bondage are among the most difficult to deal with—obsessive, emotionally reactive, and often living unbalanced lives because of their inability to shut off at the end of the day, weekends and vacations. One trader from firm B told us:

> I live my positions, I love them, I dream about them. I think about all my positions. I love my positions. I love them, I hate them, I sleep with them. I have breakfast with them. I am constipated with them. I have fun with them. I go on holiday with them. You know . . . and that's just it. What else would I do with my life?

Curiously, this obsessional involvement does not necessarily make them bad traders—people with this orientation do not automatically drop out of trading environments; those that stay with it are just more prone to highs and lows of emotion. However, the literature would suggest that a hazard for such people would be likely to be a risk of persisting overlong in their engagements with situations where early exit would be the best strategy (Sandelands, Brockner, and Glynn, 1988). Ego involvement is also likely to amplify reactions to sources of stress (Riess and Taylor, 1984), and since stress reactions tend to impair the ability to act or to think in a controlled manner, we can infer that it is a relevant factor in trader performance.

The assessment phase is also vulnerable to various problems of reasoning and calculus. Rational decision-making depends upon the accurate or effective allocation of decision-weights according to the expected value of outcomes and to the probabilities attached to the paths that connect outcomes with actions. These are more often subjective and implicit than objective and explicit. Traders need to bring this calculus into consciousness as much as possible, since they are close to the trigger for choice. Managers in our research talked about how they did not want traders to become too attached to particular stocks or sources because this represented a departure from objectivity of traders' analysis.

Trader Psychology

A factor that behavioural economists have recently begun to include in their treatments of decision-making is _regret-aversion_ (Kelsey and Schepanski, 1991), which we discussed in Chapter 3. This is the tendency for an agent to add hidden weights to the calculus by additional consideration of the psychological cost of missing out on non-chosen outcomes. There seems to be a curious but powerfully influential kind of computation going on that gives a discount value to any option that might entail consequent regret from not achieving other outcomes.

One of the more complex is insufficient _anchoring adjustment_. This is the tendency to fail to update one's targets as the environment changes (Rutledge, 1993). We saw earlier the perils of being too context dependent—allowing one's expectations to be overly influenced by local contextual factors. This extends the principle, but here the context is psychological—created by one's own initial reactions. Once a trader has dropped anchor, figuratively speaking, in some decision zone then this bias represents his reluctance to see that he might have done so in the wrong place. It is what happens when one has made a snap judgement and then disregards feedback that is inconsistent with this position. This is a bias that affects social as well as technical judgements. Making early decisions about someone—for example in a job interview—may put one in a more anchored position early in the process than one is aware of. Even if the interviewee says things that contradict the positive or negative image that was planted in the interviewer's mind at the start of the process, they come too late to shift the judge's opinion (Anderson, 1992).

Self-regulation theory accounts for how desire for consistency can overcome realism and rationality. These psychological processes only emerge as dysfunctional because of the unusual contextual demands of highly technical systemic environments. Confidence and self-esteem are qualities to be valued, but people with high levels of positive self imagery and affect are wont to interpret even bad events as opportunities, or more dangerously, to construe them as unrelated to any of their actions. Their self-regulatory process absolves themselves in order not to disturb the flow of their confident forward surge of agency (Whyte, Saks, and Hook, 1997). It is for this reason that self-confidence and self-esteem may be false friends in the trading environment. As one senior trader manager in firm A told us:

> I have seen about three people who thought they were top traders and they have made some fantastic money, but have all done the same thing . . . When they started losing money, instead of cutting or reducing the positions, they made the bets bigger and bigger and they expect to make more and more money. They ended up making serious errors of judgement, doing something contrary to the SFA rules and out of the job. They will not get another job. This has ended their career prospects.

To examine the extent to which traders are prone to overconfidence about the basis for judgements they make, we asked them to make estimates of five numbers they were unlikely to have good knowledge of[6] and then asked them to set an upper and lower bound within which they were at least 95 per cent confident the answer would lie. Given a 95 per cent probability of a correct answer for each of the five questions we can calculate the probability of each proportion of correct answers. If the confidence limits are accurate we would expect $0.95 \times 0.95 \times 0.95 \times 0.95 \times 0.95 = 77.4$ per cent of respondents to have all five correct answers within their confidence limits. A lower proportion is evidence of overconfidence in specifying the confidence limits. Both traders and students were much more likely to get wrong answers (i.e. the correct answer falls outside the limits they set) than they should be were their limits genuinely 95 per cent confidence limits. This exercise suggests both traders and students to be significantly overconfident in their estimates.[7]

The Challenge of Action

The implementation of decisions is often straightforward following the deliberations of diagnosis and assessment. However, there exist various forces that can impel the decision-maker towards irrationality, for what lies between deliberation and action is commitment. This is fundamentally a form of emotional engagement and various forces other than the coolly appraised merits of the case that can pull the decision-maker in a different direction, most of them social.

The phenomenon of *herding* is a case in point, where the actor retains their self-image as an independent minded and free agent, while being unconsciously swayed in judgement by awareness that some other respected person or group has followed a particular course of action (Prechter, 2002). The more the other is revered the more likely the influence and the more conscious the imitation. Traders are apt to rationalize herding on the basis of *ad hominem* attributions, disregarding the fact that their role models may themselves be constrained or misled in their actions. In species that herd the safest place to be is in the centre of the pack. This is the way herding operates psychologically. Even though fund manager performance has a low year-on-year correlation, at any time large numbers of investors are following last year's leader (Bagnoli and Watts, 2000). Flow traders, of course, see themselves as making rational judgements about market herding behaviour believing, sometimes with justification, that they may be in a better position than most investors to spot the end of the trend and make a timely exit.

Local *norms* are also influential. Between firms, or even between areas of the same firm, there may be quite different sets of standards and beliefs about the market and its opportunities. Within the social context there are other factors that may influence the trader. One is *impression management*. Another is *groupthink*. The former category includes actions that a trader undertakes in order to enhance his reputation among colleagues; excessive risk taking is a hazard in machismo trading cultures for this reason. Groupthink creates another profile, where people come into line with others, for fear of being exposed as deviant from the group norm, and make excessively risky or excessively conservative decisions (Janis, 1972). *Competitive pressures* similarly distort outcomes by, motivating one person to triumph over another more than to make a contribution.

A foreign exchange trader in bank C talked about the temptation to do this:

> When I trade a currency where it's say market making in a book, which I do less and less these days—I'm very emotional about it, because I'm not dealing with [X] bank, I'm dealing with the guy there, and it's not [X] bank, it's, if I know the blokes name, especially if I don't happen to like him very much or respect him, then it's actually very . . . it's a lot more emotion that comes into it, which . . . it sounds very childish, but in actual fact it is just whatever works to stir you up sometimes. . . . I want to take money off him and I want him to know. Maybe less now, maybe I'm more comfortable with myself than I used to be, but I used to want people to know I'd taken money off them.

I used to enjoy them talking about it, which is quite childish, but it's just the way it is. . . . once actually, with one counter-party in Switzerland, I just wanted this guy. I wanted his head on a stick. It meant that I was trading at levels that I really shouldn't have been. Not with any huge P&L implications, not to a level where it would endanger the overall result, but I was definitely leaving money on the table just because I was after this guy. I would say I was dealing on crappy prices just because I wanted to hit him, which is silly. . . . I wouldn't do it now anyway because I'm not in a position to do it. And if I see my traders caught—you know—after someone, I'm not impressed and I tell them not to do it.

The principal agent problem has a bearing on what influences traders during the action phase. This is the problem economists identify as arising from the distinctive and sometimes incongruent interests of owners (principals) and those whom they employ (agents). Specifically, it implicates the potential hazard of agents pursuing self-interest at the expense of their employers (Jensen and Meckling, 1976). The outcomes that matter to the trader may not be aligned in value with those that are important to the firm. However, the problem is broader than just economic value. What is at stake for the bank is money. However, what is at stake for the trader is also reputation and other psychological outcomes, which may have greater pull than mere avarice. This makes traders inherently vulnerable to the likelihood of economic rationality being overridden by social and contextual influences. As we shall be discussing in Chapter 8 it is alignment of these interests that an incentive system is designed to achieve. In the world of trading this often does not succeed.

Post-Decisional Processes

Many of the problems with decision-making arise in the aftermath. Outcomes are the subject of analysis by many parties in a trading environment, and what cause-effect linkages are attributed retrospectively has a major bearing on the effectiveness of the decision-maker and the decisional process more generally. Reactions to outcomes may defeat rationality—storing up a legacy of unhelpful orientations to be carried forward into the next decision (Brehm, 1956; Elster, 1983). We will discuss several of these before focusing on one in particular: *illusion of control*.

The drivers for these post-decisional processes are factors we have already discussed as playing an important part in self-regulation—the need for internal consistency, to maintain positive motivation, to make sense of the world, and to have a positive connection with one's social group. Throughout this chapter, an underlying rationale has been the human desire for order and control over a world full of randomness and happenstance. One way of expressing this is to claw back some control by acting on the world and then making a favourable interpretation of the outcome and one's influence over it. Most of the post-decisional biases have this character, for example *the hindsight bias* (Fischoff, 1982). This is being wise after the event—turning 'I might have known' into 'I suspected all along this might happen'.

> It's pretty rare that something is screamingly obvious. It happens once in a while but you don't know in advance whether you were right or whether you were lucky. But you know what happened.

Hindsight bias is part of the price we pay for the benefit of reconstructive memory—and the ability to forget what we do not need (Hoffrage, Hertwig, and Gigerenzer, 2000). As self-regulation would lead one to expect, the bias tunes itself to the type of feedback being received (Louie, 1999). But from here it is a short step to *rationalization* —the tendency to re-evaluate negative outcomes in a positive light. This may be done for a mix of psychological and social reasons; to feel good about oneself and to look good to others. When the outcomes are favourable you hear this expressed as by the trader who claims 'You make your own luck'.

Louis Pasteur is credited with having said more memorably, 'Chance favours the prepared mind'. This is the essence of effective trading under uncertainty, and of conduct in many other kinds of enterprise and activity. More often as we noted in Chapter 4, being right, and being seen to have been right after the event have important reputational effects and may even attract rewards.

In logic the fallacy that dignifies this error is called 'affirming the consequent' (Rude, 2000). This is where the true assertion, if p then q, is converted into the erroneous reverse formulation: q, therefore p. For example, true assertion: if I am a good trader I will make money. False reversal: I am making money, therefore, I am a good trader. This is actually a pervasive logical error that is very commonly and unwittingly evoked. Unscrupulous sales people, politicians, and other professional influencers all recognize and play upon our susceptibility to this error. It emerges in trader comments such as from the individual, quoted earlier, who thought that 'by definition' his decisions were correct if he was making money.

More easily spotted are a range of _attributional errors_, in which we ascribe outcomes falsely to specific causes (Martinko, 1995). We have already mentioned the tendency to overattribute to human agents— we are much more reluctant to find no one to praise and blame. It is unappealing to say that good fortune was serendipity or that a negative event was no one's fault but was a system failure.

As we have already discussed, in trading environments the most dangerous attribution is to assume that random events are non-random. Trends, such as _regression to the mean_ are fuel to this fire. A classic example cited by Kahneman and Tversky (1973) is the case of the Israeli pilots whose performance improved after punishment, and deteriorated after reward—attributed to the reinforcement regime but actually randomly varying around a fixed mean. Regression to the mean consists of these kinds of ceiling effects and floor effects. In a randomly varying population, something that is at the upper end of a normal distribution is more likely to move to a lower than a higher position over time, and something that is low will be more likely to move up. A study of US futures and bond traders found traders' performance following a random walk with this kind of regression to the mean (Hartzmark, 1991). An equities trader in firm B described the problem of identifying when there is a genuine underlying trend:

> Trades in general are in 2 categories either range trading or there's some sort of trend, either up or down. The worst experiences are always those when you think there's a trend and your stock is trading in a range so every time when it's at the top you start to buy because you think it's going up further and it goes down and then it goes down you sell it and then it goes up again. These situations are the worst.

Negative events are especially prone to dysfunctional attributions. We shall be discussing in Chapter 7 the problem of why we do not learn better from failure, but the core cause is that when something is strongly aversive, that is when the agent feels tarred with the brush of failure, then the natural human motivation is to seek to avoid its recurrence at all costs. The emotional heat of this desire scorches out the possibility for dispassionate and reasoned analysis of causes. So it is that when people are recollecting failures they become prey to kinds of magical thinking that will feed and satisfy their elevated emotions (Cannon, 1995; Cannon and Nicholson, 1996). The most common faulty attributions post-failure can be characterized as:

(1) *Vigilance*: the belief that one can be, by act of will, more alert to the unexpected;
(2) *Efficacy*: the conviction that one can enhance one's coping skills and ability to deal with challenges of this and other kinds;
(3) *Identity*: the idea one can more effectively be oneself or reform derided aspects of self-identity to 'be better' in the future.

All of these remedies might, theoretically, be possible, but the reality of human adjustment to failure is that these general aspirations have more the character of wish-fulfilment than problem solving. They come more from the self-regulatory drive to claw back control by force of will. They do not come from reasoned analysis, which argues first for dispassionate analysis of causes before seeking remedies. These are magical beliefs that spring from the pre-eminent need to avoid the future aversive experience of failure, and the need to reassert self-control. A related phenomenon that has been the subject of huge volumes of research is *escalating commitment*. This takes two main forms, both of which have the same effect. The first is the sunk costs effect (Arkes and Blumer, 1985): the tendency to continuing investing time or energy because of the mental calculus that says that efforts expended so far would be wasted if one withdrew, like the aversion people have to quitting a long queue once they've been in it a while. The second effect is the escalation effect, which involves not just maintaining but redoubling (Staw *et al.*, 1981). The consequence in a trading environment is severely negative: to persist in certain trades because one has expended resources in them already.

The escalation effect is what derails rogue traders—loss aversion combines with it to elicit not just loss chasing but the redoubling of bets to claw back to neutrality. Dostoyevsky describes it memorably in his short story *The Gambler* (ironically, written to pay off his own gambling debts), though in recent times the cases of Leeson at Barings, Hamanaka at Sumitomo, and Rusnak at Allied Irish Bank all illustrate the same tendency in the finance context. The key element in many everyday cases is more of a psychological than a material claw-back (Staw, Sandelands, and Dutton, 1981). The underlying motive is self-justification: the drive to prove oneself right in one's original course of action.

The common theme in all these cases is how one decision and its outcomes can be a trap for the next. The unwary can be blind to the degree to which a residue of emotion and reasoning is being carried forward to bias the next decision. The guard against this in trading environments is the manager's injunction to trade as if one had a flat book; that is *de novo*, without any prior history of gains or losses. Of course, this is very hard to do, not just because one cannot put them out of one's mind, but because they colour self-perceptions and motives more deeply. The person who is inflated with self-confidence or deflated by pessimism as a result of a good or a bad run cannot be brought to a point of neutrality by managerial exhortation.

So what can managers do? Well, one immediate recommendation might be training in the psychology of biases for all traders and their managers. We will elaborate on the further implications for management later in this book. But first let us bring our attention to one of the biases we found to be especially pervasive, combining many of the features we have reviewed here, and one which we found to have a strong direct bearing on trader performance. It is the illusion of control.

5.3   Illusion of Control[8]

The illusion of control is the tendency to act as if chance events are accessible to personal control (Langer, 1975). The illusion is exemplified in a quote from an equities trader. 'Every year I have improved my information filtering process so now I can beat the market.'

As we have argued, cognitive biases exist for sound adaptive reasons, to help us get to acceptable and operable conclusions with speed and efficacy rather than logical nicety and computational efficiency.

Control is a central consideration in all of them—of self and of the outer world. We are powerfully motivated to restore control when we feel it is threatened (Fiske and Depret, 1998). In order to do so effectively we need to be supported by a framework of self-belief, that is, self-efficacy (Bandura, 1989), and to sustain belief we need evidence. In a world where much that happens is uncontrolled our self-regulatory systems encourage us to make favourable attributions about what we have and have not influenced (Bandura and Wood, 1989). Mood and self-efficacy are maintained by taking credit for positive outcomes and attributing the failures to third parties or to a capricious world.

There is an important distinction to be drawn between realistic and unrealistic control beliefs (Zuckerman *et al.*, 1996). Realistic control beliefs concern circumstances where control is objectively possible. Unrealistic control beliefs concern illusory perceptions of control in circumstances where control is not objectively possible. Several studies have demonstrated these two dimensions of perceived control to reflect different mental states (Wannon, 1990; Zuckerman *et al.*, 1996; Knee, Zuckerman, and Kieffer, 1999). While a case can be made for the psychological benefits of high realistic control beliefs for their positive effects on motivation and persistence (Taylor and Brown, 1988), high unrealistic control beliefs are less likely to be beneficial. As one trader warned:

It's very easy when you're making lots of money to double up and double up and take unnecessary risk. This is just human nature. You think you've become slightly God-like and you can actually see a lot more than the market can.

While illusory beliefs about control may promote goal striving, they are not conducive to sound decision-making. They may cause insensitivity to feedback, impede learning, and predispose toward greater objective risk taking, since subjective risk will be reduced by illusion of control (Gollwitzer and Kinney, 1989).

Langer (1975) coined the term illusion of control to denote the pervasiveness of false and unrealistic control beliefs. People differ in their susceptibility to the illusion, sometimes as a function of personality and sometimes because of the context and external influences. In Chapter 6 we shall consider what might be some of the former factors—the deeper underlying individual traits. At the same time there is a substantial research record that shows how illusions can be induced by the surrounding milieu (Taylor and Armor, 1996). Research on the outcomes of the illusion of control underlines its importance—it has been found empirically to link with a tendency to perceive situations as less risky than they actually are (Houghton *et al.*, 2000), and in consequence to take greater risks. This has obvious relevance for a trading environment where people are supposed to perceive risk accurately and to take greater risks on the basis of higher order mental calculus rather than deluded judgement.

The questions that are posed by this research tradition for the trading environment are (*a*) does trading have a tendency to attract people who are prone to the illusion or might it attract those who are immune to it; (*b*) is the trading environment especially conducive to the formation of the illusion or is it one where the illusion is difficult to sustain; and (*c*) is the illusion of control detrimental to trading performance?

We shall address the first question in more depth in the next chapter; though a preview of our answer to this question is that we find no evidence that trading environments have a selective bias in favour of hiring people with control illusions. In fact, we expect the reverse; that people with persistent tendencies toward delusional attribution are sooner or later screened out. However, as we shall see, there are special issues associated with the profile of people who are attracted to trading floors.

We sought to study illusions of control more closely through a computer-based experiment, designed specially for the purpose. Before we look at what this revealed, it is well to consider what features of the trading environment might be relevant to fostering this illusion. A review of research suggests the trading environment may be especially conducive to development of the illusion of control because of five features:

Stress: It has been shown that stress induces the illusion (Friedland, Keinan, and Regev, 1992). Trading is a highly stressful occupation in terms of workload, time pressure, visibility, and uncertainty coupled with limited control opportunities. We have already noted that traders are more vulnerable to what psychologists call 'free-floating anxiety' than the general population (Kahn and Cooper, 1993). In line with our earlier discussion, which defined stress as the product of high load plus low control, the illusion of control can be construed as an attempt by the self-regulatory system to mitigate the stress by increasing the sense of control.

Competition. Langer (1975) found competition to be an antecedent of illusion of control. We tend to take competition as a cue that control is possible. The process of trading is intrinsically competitive. The other players are usually invisible in today's screen-based trading environments (though not so long ago traders were face to face in the pit), but traders often know who are their specific market adversaries around the globe in specialized markets. The market itself is often conceived as a disembodied competitor, in exactly the sense that traders talk about 'beating the market'. Other traders on the same trading floor or desk are also visible competitors for reputation. Bonuses heighten this competitive ethos. As Kahn and Cooper found in their study, competition is a major associate of the stressfulness of the environment.

Implemental Mindset. This term was coined by Gollwitzer and Kinney (1989) as the alternative to the notion of a 'deliberative' mindset. We all move between the two as we navigate through events and decisions. The implemental mindset occurs when we are focused on goals. A deliberative mindset occurs when we cease acting in order to reflect on the causal links between actions and outcomes. The distinction is akin to focusing on ends versus means. These researchers found that illusions of control were heightened when their subjects were induced to adopt an implemental mindset. Although good trader–managers encourage deliberative practices, for example by encouraging analysis of the rationale underlying trading decisions, there are several factors pulling in the direction of an implemental mindset. First, there is the focus on profit and loss, an ever-present and highly visible end result of actions, and second there is the bonus system, which acts as a multiplier pulling in the same direction, amplifying the focus on outcomes. Third, the short-term nature of information advantages also means that traders are unlikely to forgo the opportunity to trade in order to learn more about the value of information or a strategy, by observing the market.

Choice, Involvement, and Familiarity. Langer (1975) focused on the key role of what she called 'skill cues' in inducing the illusion—factors in an informational array that would support the attribution that one is in control. Choice, involvement, and familiarity all can act as skill cues. Trading involves continually making choices but more importantly often requires close focus on a particular type of instrument or market. Traders are often highly identified with the instruments or markets in their area of expertise. So all these conditions could be held to apply.

Our programme of interviews suggested, as did the quote at the start of this section, that traders routinely make favourable assumptions about their control over outcomes—after all, it is what they are paid so much for! In a situation where the locus of control might be ambiguous, traders, like the rest of us, orient towards a view of themselves as people who are having a meaningful influence over surrounding events.

We wanted a more objective test of susceptibility to this illusion and so devised a novel test, in the form of computer game, written in visual basic and programmed on to a laptop computer, which we asked all the traders in our study to play. First, we asked them to complete a short questionnaire estimating their own trading performance on four dimensions:

- Contribution to trading desk profits
- Skill in managing risk
- Analytical ability
- People skills.

They were asked to mark their position on a linear scale from 0 to 100 as if they were percentiles (e.g. to mark 60 would imply they are better than 60 per cent of traders doing similar work). At the same time we got ratings of them on the same dimensions from a senior manager with a close knowledge of their performance. As an additional performance measure we got each trader to tell us his or her total annual earnings including bonus. We then asked them to play the game, telling them that this was a test designed to improve our understanding of the way in which they take decisions. We used the game for three main reasons. First, a computer-based exercise would be novel and more likely to capture their attention than a paper-and-pencil questionnaire measure. Second, we wanted to create a test that mimicked trading in two important aspects: noisy feedback and decision-making under conditions of limited information. Third, we wanted to test illusions of control by means of some measurable active behaviour.

Once the trader started the computer program, this is what happened: A welcome screen introduces the program and collects some personal details. The program then informs the subject the following:

When the game starts you will see a chart, similar to the picture shown below. The vertical axis represents an index with values between −2000 and 2000. The horizontal axis shows time. The index starts at zero and every half second for 50 seconds the index is increased or decreased by some amount. Changes in the index are partly random, but three keys on the keyboard may have some effect on the index. The possible effects are to raise or lower the index by some amount to increase the size of the random movements or no effect. There is some time lag to the effects. The keys are 'Z', X', and 'C'. There is no advantage to pressing keys more than once in any half second. Your task is to raise the index as high as possible by the end of 50 seconds. At the end of the game the final value of the index will be added to your pool of points.

The display subjects viewed is shown in Fig. 5.1.

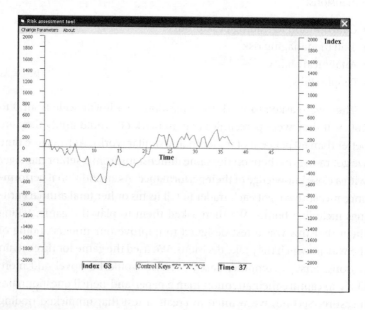

Fig. 5.1   RAT Screenshot

The game then runs, with the trader pressing the keys and watching the line rising and falling over the period of 50 s. At this time the trader is told their score, and asked to rate their success in increasing their overall score by setting a slider bar from 1 'not at all successful' to 100 'very successful'. The game then runs as described, a total of four times, and after each round traders are asked to rate their success in raising the value of the index.

The experience proved to be highly engaging, with traders earnestly pressing keys and rating their performance. The trick to the whole exercise was, however, that *the keys had absolutely no effect on the rise or fall of the moving line at all*. The index movement was pre-programmed— in rounds 1 and 2 it yielded a guaranteed increase in points, in round 3 it delivered a loss and in round 4 maintained the same level. The traders' estimates of their success in raising the value of the index at each round were thus a pure measure of their illusion of control in the game. This was pretested on a pilot sample of 130 MBA students, to verify the statistical reliability of the measure. The validity of the measure—that is, whether it was measuring what it was purported to measure—was cross-checked on a separate sample of 117 management students correlating scores with a published and validated measure of realistic versus unrealistic control beliefs.

The results of the test for traders showed first that there was variation in the extent of illusory beliefs, but that most participants felt they had some success in increasing the index. Note—at no time did we say that the keys affected the index, only that it might or might not. As we can see from the histogram of trader results (Fig. 5.2), scores on the test were normally distributed and spanned the full range from 0 to 100. Often, the interviews with traders reflected their illusion of control scores. The following quotes are from traders with high scores on our control illusions measure. Note how they stress strategies for maintaining a positive self image.

You need a positive view of yourself, self questioning makes this too difficult and you tend not to perform well under pressure. Stories about traders being arrogant and nasty—that sort of person does perform rather better. You need to have a lot of common sense, be down to earth. You can question yourself, but you have to have decided that you are good. Most traders would rate themselves on your scale as in the top

Trader Psychology

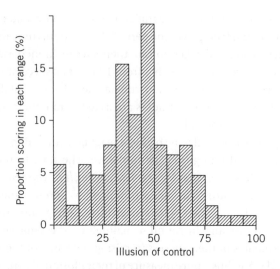

Fig. 5.2 Distribution of traders' illusion of control scores

section for the analytical ability and if they put themselves at the bottom, I would question that. You need to believe in your own ability because when things go wrong, how will you cope? You have to think you are better than average in the market.

If you make a decision, based on either running risk or increasing risk, you always want to feel that you have made the right decision and then it's not whether you get beaten up if you lose some money, it's more whether or not you can justify the decision. If you lose half a million dollars, you go home and think it's not very good, but if you can justify to a manager and have discussed it with people, then that is fine. You logically go through it and say I made this decision, it went wrong because of this and we lost money, that's fine. If you don't discuss it and don't try to justify the risk, then you'd probably get more stressed about the position.

The following quotes are from traders who have low illusions of control scores. Again the quotes concern reactions to things going wrong, but the emphasis is less on protective self-justification than on honest appraisal of own mistakes and reactions.

Traders by default always make mistakes. A good trader will look back at all the trades in the last quarter and not say weren't we clever, but look at where we went wrong. It is important to learn where you went wrong and the opportunity cost of not doing more than you did, even though money was not lost.

Emotion and rationality are not at opposite ends, they co-exist the entire time. You buy in at 50, they go to 48, you refuse to believe it. Your rational side says you've got it wrong, your emotional side says the market is wrong so you buy some more. They go to 46, you're really pissed off now, you're not going to sell them, you're not going to take a loss. They go to 42; your rational side kicks in and says I got this wrong and I am out and it doesn't necessarily. . I am not suggesting it happens in that sequence every time but the two always co-exist. The two always co-exist.

The next step was to see if illusion of control was related to performance—both self-rated and manager rated. This was conducted by means of regression analysis, which measures strength of association, holding other factors constant statistically. Other factors entered and controlled in our analysis were educational level, job level, and trading experience.

In relation to the trader self-ratings, the results produced a statistically significant negative association between illusion of control and both total remuneration and contribution to desk profits, but not risk management, analytical ability, or people skills. Among the control factors more highly educated traders had higher total earnings and scored higher on analytical ability. Job level and trading experience were also positively associated with total earnings.

The associations are not just due to self-perception, but hold up for the manager ratings also. Traders with higher propensity to illusion of control are rated by their managers as less effective (compared to peers) at risk management, market analysis, and as contributing less to desk profit. As we predicted there was no association with people skills. This skill criterion was included to test that our performance measures really were discriminating aspects of real performance. Finally, traders with higher illusion of control had significantly lower total earnings.

So there is a clear case for saying that illusion of control is associated with poorer performance and lower earnings. The next question to be addressed is what can be done about this, since it has major implications for all trading environments—indeed for any area of business where people are being required to make frequent decisions under conditions of uncertainty and risk.

One implication is that managers should assess to what extent the contextual factors we discussed as contributing to the illusion can be removed or attenuated. In particular it may be possible to reduce excessive stress, guard against unhelpful extremes of personal competitiveness, and encourage the regular adoption of a deliberative mindset.

The reward system in many trading environments is unhelpful in this regard. However, changing it is difficult for any individual bank, because of the first-mover disadvantage of doing so, in relation to competitor institutions that persist with high bonus payments. In terms of deliberation, the best managers encourage traders to analyse the underlying processes for making and losing money on any given trade—especially major losses—though much more general encouragement could be given to deliberative practices. Stress is harder to reduce—it is endemic to the trading environment, though individuals can be selected for their ability to withstand pressures.

A second implication concerns the selection and placement of traders. At present, we know that there is a liability to illusion of control that is present in some individuals more than others, and its effects can be exacerbated by situational factors. We do not yet know the relative importance of the individual factor and environment issues. However, future research is likely to develop knowledge in this field and it will have important implications for the selection and management of traders and other professionals making decisions in uncertain environments.

In Chapter 2 we raised the question of whether professional traders are candidates to fill the role of the 'sufficient number' of rational investors required in any market to meet the assumptions of the efficient markets hypothesis. On the evidence we have presented here, it would seem not. Professional traders are, for the most part, just as prone to the biases and illusion that afflict us all. However, there is significant variability between the propensities of individual traders to suffer these deviations from normative rationality. Further, we have shown that, for at least one such illusion, this variability translates into differences in individual trader performance. We address the implications of these findings for trader management and the regulation of trading in

Chapter 9, but first we need to pin down more precisely what is the nature of these differences.

This we do in the next chapter, where we continue with our discussion of trader psychology, turning to the question of whether there is a 'trader psychological profile'. If such a phenomenon exists, where does it come from, and what might be its practical significance?

Notes

1. There is, of course, some variation in practice between individual firms.
2. The general framework within which we approach the field takes as given certain features of human psychology that govern how we make decisions. It is the idea that we do not acquire our cognitive capacities *de novo* over the early part of our lifetimes. For sure, we learn important principles and practices in the early formative years and beyond, but the basic parameters of thought and judgement are prepared pathways for normal environmental experience and exposure to build upon (Pinker, 1997). This is an area of vigorous debate, but there is now general acceptance that a tabula rasa account of human development is unsustainable (Pinker, 2002).
3. We use the term affect here in the psychological sense of emotional state or mood.
4. It is worth noting that this is a flow trading perspective as opposed to a fundamentals perspective.
5. We will focus principally on cognitive biases directly relevant to our data. For a more comprehensive account of human cognitive biases see Bazerman (2002).
6. These were the value of UK imports from the European Union in 1994, the value of UK imports from the United States in 1994, the number of people killed by cerebral malaria in India in 1992, total US health and medical expenditure in 1992, and the total land area of the Japanese mainland.
7. This result may reflect either overconfidence or failure to understand probability and sampling.
8. A more detailed account of this study has been published separately in the *Journal of Organisational and Occupational Psychology*, where full details of the hypotheses, procedures and statistical analyses can be found. See Fenton-O'Creevy *et al.* (2003).

Chapter 6

RISK TAKERS
Profiling Traders

The previous chapter raised a question that is major, controversial, and recurrent in all behavioural science; the extent to which any individual act is the product of the inner forces of the individual (agency) versus the surrounding circumstances (context). This becomes, at its most fundamental level, part of the debate about nature versus nurture. On the environmentalist side of the argument lies the persuasive possibility that contexts condition the drives of the individual. On the agency side is the idea that individuals shape environments to suit their enduring purposes and goals. Most social scientists now accept an interactionist position that does not set one of these views implacably against the other but tries to integrate them—nurture only works where nature allows it to and nature only emerges where the context permits. The complexities that this view allows are self-evident, but it is important for practical as well as theoretical reasons that we disentangle them. For example, it is important to identify causal cycles, such as where people create environments in order to satisfy their deep dispositions, but these contexts prove to be instruments of oppression for other individuals whose dispositions are significantly at odds with those of the more powerful members. Families sometimes have this character. So do organizations.

As we examine the work and behaviour of traders the nurture versus nature debate has several important aspects:

1. How much of trader performance is attributable to the enduring dispositions and characteristics of the trader: drives that have crystallized well before the individual took their current position?

2. To what extent are the behaviours that can be witnessed on trading floors attributable to specific shaping factors in the task environment—the kinds of markets people are working in, and the flow of challenges they are confronted with in terms of complexity, speed, loss, and gain?

3. What is the role of social forces and management systems—how traders are managed, rewarded, and trained?

4. Is cultural variation across firms attributable to different profiles of trader psychology, produced by the uniquely configured interaction between agency and context in each firm?

In preceding chapters we have implied support for all of these positions. We know that markets are not uniform and that the roles and performance of traders cover a wide spectrum of demands and constraints. We know that firms pursue profitable business by means of differing structures and cultures. We know that the micro-features of traders' roles induce a variety of curiosities and irrationalities, as we reviewed them in the last chapter, and later on we shall be discussing further the issue of the extent to which we can 'immunize' traders or any decision-makers against biases by training, insight, management, and incentive regimes.

What concerns us in the present chapter is the question of whether there is a 'trader psychological profile'. If such a phenomenon exists, where does it come from, and what might be its practical significance?

As a preface to these questions one needs to note and set on one side the common stereotypes that abound about the profession, heftily reinforced by media hype about rogue traders. It is often held that they have streetwise 'barrow-boy' mentality: young, male, sharp-witted, ruthless, self-interested, macho, materialistic, uncooperative, aggressive, and devious. This view puts them into a twilight zone of pretty unpleasant and unmanageable people. It also is a cause for alarm if these are the people on whom the security of your pension fund rests, for at the very least it suggests people who are addicted risk seekers. Such people do exist, and can be found on trading floors, but in this chapter we will be dispelling the myth that this is a general truth. First, though, we need to put a context around the identity of traders. That context is risk.

6.1   Risk: Types and Fallacies

We saw in the last chapter that a well-known fallacy under whose spell we frequently fall is 'affirming the consequent'. For example, moving from the reasonable proposition that people who are addicted to risk taking engage in risk-taking behaviours, to the fallacy that people who take a lot of risks are risk-addicted individuals. This fallacy has spawned a literature that accepts a presumption about people as being more or less 'risk seeking' versus 'risk averse'. But what evidence is there for the existence of such a trait or personality dimension? There is very little; though that little is important, especially in the present context. We wish to argue that most of the time:

(1) most people do not pause to think about the risks they are taking in everyday life;
(2) when people do, risk is conceived as a cost to be born for achieving what they want or need;
(3) there does exist a small group of people who are genuinely risk seeking for the sake of a particular kind of psychological stimulation, but they are a minority;
(4) people's conceptions of risk are often irrational and incoherent, and the scale of them perceptually distorted.

We shall illustrate and elaborate on these points throughout our interactionist reconstruction of risk behaviours.

Before we do this let us briefly consider why this is necessary through an analysis of the risk concept. Risk is generally defined as uncertainty about negative outcomes, and is quantified by the equation that multiplies the magnitude of loss or harm by the probability of its occurrence (Bernoulli, 1738). This is the negative expected utility of any risky decision. Of course, its positive counterpart, possible amounts to be won multiplied by likelihood of occurrence, could be equally considered a 'risk' of gain, though it tends not to be framed as such. However, considering the nature of the duality is vital, for this is where trading and gambling meet; value is put at risk for the sake of possible gain. Logically, one can identify four kinds of risk from the expected utility formulation, which have their parallels in finance, gambling, and life in general.

Type 1: The Pure Probability Calculus

This is the gamble where you know exactly the probability of outcomes (Brockner and Rubin, 1985). This is usually found only in highly artificial environments where the range of outcomes is strictly controlled and how they are arrived at approaches pure randomness. On a roulette wheel, probabilities are actuarially precise over a long run with a true ball and unbiased wheel, but on any trial what makes the ball fall in one slot rather than an adjacent one is caused by elements beyond observation or calculation, such as speed of the wheel and ball, ricochets, and air pressure. The purest forms of gambling rely on the unknowability or incalculability of causal influences. It is this combination of actuarial precision and unknowable influences that make gambling attractive to punter and investor alike—both can calculate risk–return ratios over the long run with precision. These people can apply their own control via knowledge of these probabilities and their own ability to determine the size of their stake (Klein and Kunda, 1994).

A precise mathematical calculation is possible about what kind of risk you want to take. It is rare in everyday life, outside the artifice of the gaming room, to have this kind of choice, but in the world of finance it is common. Some forms of trading with derivatives via partial hedging and spread betting can come to closely resemble this model. In these cases the trader can precisely calculate the value at risk, making a stake at a known probability that approximates to a precise level of desired risk–return ratio. The approximation comes from traders and their banks not knowing how much they are at risk from unaccounted for potential states of the world. For example the

Russian default on sovereign debt, behind the crash of Long Term Capital Markets (LTCM) or the Kobe earthquake in the Barings collapse.

Type 2: The Multi-Player Game

At one level, poker is a pure probability gambling game, since the probabilities of specific hands are finite and precisely calculable. Seasoned poker players match their stakes to their probability estimates of the superiority of their own hands, and the game at its highest level is played by both native and trained mathematicians (Alvarez, 1983). The added twist in this model is that winning and losing depends on the actions of others holding independent and unknown information about the same situation. One player's success or failure depends upon chance (getting good hands), risk–return strategy (size of stakes on hands of different quality), and social judgement (ability to read and influence the behaviours of other players).

Often, we are in situations where the last of these considerations apply, and in the realm of finance we see this model clearly in action. Market-makers may be able to figure out quite precisely the risks attached to different market movements, but they cannot always anticipate the actions of other players in the market, whose actions could affect the outcome and the current parameters of the deal. As in poker, there may be a lot of bluff and counter-bluff going on between the representatives of different banks competing for the same business.

Type 3: The Formbook Gamble

Once one moves away from the world of fixed probabilities in cards, dice, and roulette, people can be seen to be gambling on horses, dogs, baseball teams, political parties—just about anything unpredictable. The key to this kind of gambling is not that outcomes are random, but that they are the result of obscure, complex, and idiosyncratic forces. The punter can try to use his expertise and perspicacity to read the signs; for example, intimate knowledge of the runners, riders, and conditions on the track will lead him to place a bet that expresses a degree of confidence in the outcome. Generally speaking, the larger the bet the greater the confidence, yet in these cases there are real non-random forces underlying the outcome, so confidence can be either justifiable or misplaced.

Because of the complexity and obscurity of these forces—the mental state of rider or the condition of the horse, the mood of an electorate on polling day—often a hunch or a guess will yield as good a result as hours of study. But in the long run the knowledgeable punter should do better than the pure gambler. The type 1 pure odds gambler is best sticking with the gaming room where outcome determination is truly random. Fund managers trying to get better returns than the market average are in our type 3 category, but for most of the traders in leading investment banks, type 3 gambling is disliked as overly speculative. Often it is converted into type 1 'pure probability' risk taking by spreading the risk, hedging, and other devices that prevent one-way bets being made.

Type 4: The Incalculable Gamble

Much of our existence is in the third of these risk scenarios and a fourth—which is where neither probabilities nor value at risk are known. In the fourth condition we know neither what is at risk nor the probabilities, through ignorance, neglect and the transaction costs of finding out. Even when we traverse busy streets with the utmost care, our lives are still at risk from a driver's error, though such hazards typically do not break the surface of our consciousness. This category constitutes the everyday risks of loss to which we are continually subjected because of the ways we live and work. Most of the time we do not think about these risks, until they are promoted into the territory of type 3 gambles, that is, when we know something we value has been put at risk, or when the possible loss is quantified for us but we are uncertain of the odds. Near accidents, or witnessing some unexpected loss happening to an associate, can have this effect on our risk awareness.

In many of these situations we become vulnerable to a common fallacy about risk that is rarely mentioned in the vast literature on the subject, which we can call the 'actuarial fallacy'. We define this as the error of applying normative probability estimates to single future events. This finds respectable (but erroneous) expression by various professionals in many contexts. The person with a medical condition who is told by a surgeon that an operation would have a 50 per cent chance of success may be perplexed about what to do, but what actually has she been told? In effect, that in the history of similar cases half have succeeded, plus the additional assumption that with comparable sampling this result would be repeated for a future equivalent sample. The patient may feel reassured that the uncertainty of the risk has been at least quantified. Psychologically she might feel that the information turns the case into a type 1 pure probability gamble from an incalculable type 3 or 4 risk. But in fact it has not. The statistic does not mean the operation will be a 50 per cent success, for the outcome is binary: it succeeds or fails.

Unlike a type 1 gamble, where the outcome cannot be predicted, this could in principle be rendered significantly more predictable if one had sufficient relevant information. Knowledge about the condition of a patient's internal organs could in the medical case reduce the uncertainty considerably. Unlike the forces determining the roll of the roulette ball, the causes of the outcomes are not unknowable. Here, it is a case of the cost or difficulty of finding out the true risks being excessive. Actuaries alter the premiums for life policies according to predictive statistics and apply them to single cases in large numbers, because it is only over a series of cases that probabilities like this have predictive value. For the single case the answer cannot be derived from the actuarial statistic, but only from the specific knowledge about which factors apply that have the capacity to determine the outcome. This is of no interest to the insurance underwriter, but it should be to the surgeon or the trader.

The actuarial fallacy is pervasive. People routinely talk as if probability statistics were simply applicable to single cases, and traders are not immune from the fallacy. Traders are mostly making judgements across large numbers of cases, which is where risk statistics have genuine utility, but in any individual judgement call one is much better off looking for information about causes than for actuarial probabilities. Traders taking large long-term positions are often 'fundamentalists' for this reason. The only way to feel secure is to know as much as possible about causal factors.

6.2 Risk: Who Wants It?

Considering these types of risk, one may pause to consider who might be attracted to these risk situations and why. The answer is summarized in Fig. 6.1—our reconstruction of the notion of risk. The chief assumption of the model is that no one seeks risk per se, partly because people lack any coherent model of risk. What they really seek are gains that entail risks about which they have an imprecise and non-empirical imagery. The closest to being genuine risk seekers are those in a much smaller group who seek the stimulation that comes from uncertain gains and losses: what in the literature is called sensation seeking. Risk, as we have noted, is unreal to people for much of their daily lives. It is only when some event brings it into focus, such as a near accident or an unanticipated difficulty that one begins to think

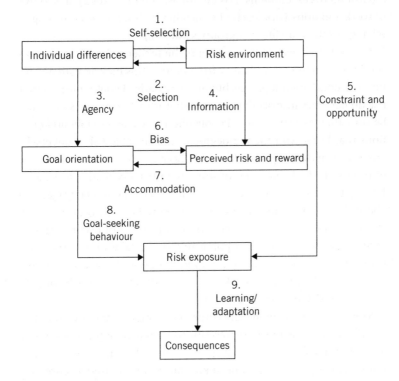

Fig. 6.1 A model of individual risk behaviour

about risk. In general people are not risk seeking in the true sense of the word; they are willing risk bearers or stimulation seekers. Both groups often only have a hazy sense of what real risks they are bearing. Risk cannot be 'sought' because it is not a meaningful goal for a person to seek. Let us use the model in Fig. 6.1 to explain.

At the top of Fig. 6.1 are two key sets of factors whose nexus is the substance of risk behaviour. On the one side are individual differences, which we shall be looking at in greater detail shortly, and which here is the repository of risk relevant person-specific drives, dispositions, tastes, abilities, styles, etc. (Sitkin and Pablo, 1992; Gasper and Clore, 1998). On the other side is the risk environment. This is the array of risks that exist at any point in time for an individual or group, which can be analysed as a set of opportunities, threats, with a profile of stability or change. In keeping with other scholars we think of environments as 'domains' (Weber, Blais, and Betz, 2002), in spheres of work and non-work, each of which has its risk profile according to what goals the individual or group is pursuing.

Arrow 1, 'self-selection', represents the tendency to orient towards certain environments and away from others. This may be with awareness of a domain's risk profile, but not necessarily. People enlist to enter risk domains because of other features that attract them, and sometimes because they have no choice. People often take jobs and join organizations that bring with them a degree of unavoidable risk. Conversely, environments select people (arrow 2) because they want to make use of their skills and character. In some high risk occupations—such as fire fighting, there is a conscious exchange at the point of engagement about the person's interest and willingness to bear the risks of the job (Guidotti, 1992). In other occupations this may not occur (Östberg, 1980), such as the job of a publican,[1] statistically one of the most unhealthy jobs in our society, but one about which one can infer that many incumbents did not take on the position with much thought about the risks they would be bearing.

Moving down the model are three key elements that flow from this nexus. Agency (arrow 3) represents how individual purposes, goals, and intentions arise from unique identity elements, for example, emotional sensitivities and personal capabilities. Arrow 4 represents the flow of information, imagery, and impressions about domains that capture attention. Our orientation to risk is entirely dependent upon this representation, which is filtered or amplified by media and other agencies. Arrow 5, *constraint and opportunity*, represents those features of the environment that, in the early stages of engagement with them, expose one to degrees of risk; often with quite inadequate information, as in our example of the publican who remains quite unaware of the health risks of his occupation throughout his tenure.

Arrow 8, *goal-seeking behaviour*, represents the heart of the argument: the idea that most people are exposed to risks not because of any liking they have for risk but because of the nature of their wants. An evolutionary biology construction of risk shows how this process can be quite devoid of any thought or risk conception. For example, the foraging behaviour of birds has been shown to become riskier the closer to the limits of survival their physical condition falls (Muller-Herrold, 2000). For humans also, loss avoidance is the greatest inducement to risky behaviour; as is known and feared in trading environments. With humans the capacity for self-consciousness affects this risk calculus, as shown in arrows 6 and 7, *bias* and *accommodation*, respectively. Arrow 6, *bias*, is the process identified within self-regulation theory through which people misperceive risks in order to remain aligned with their goals (Vancouver and Putka, 2000), as well as how they are framed (Fagley and Miller, 1987; Mittal and Ross, 1998). Wanting something very much focuses attention on the reward and blinds one to degree of risk exposure (McNamara and Bromiley, 1997). Interestingly, in the most extreme cases of want the connection is short-circuited, without even the need for judgement. Human behaviour has a non-calculative automaticity in some circumstances: for example, humans like other animals, will instinctively put their lives at risk to save offspring from danger. Accommodation (arrow 7) is the moderation of goal orientation in the light of risk information (i.e. from whatever processes are occurring under arrow 4) (Yates and Stone, 1992). The implication of arrows 6 and 7 is that ultimately it is in the control of the individual, how much they choose to be aware of and attend to risk information, except, perhaps, in life and death crises.

The last arrow, 9, *learning/adaptation*, represents learning from experience. This plus other feedback processes[2] represents the engine that drives a lot of risk behaviour, by reducing risk perception (Kogan and Wallach, 1964; Sitkin and Weingart, 1995; Slovic, 2000). It explains why people will run great risks on streets and highways, as drivers, passengers, and pedestrians, without even thinking about them. As has been pointed out, there is a kind of homeostasis in our everyday risk taking: our quiet and comfortable cars loaded with safety features can lull us into a dangerously passive stance in relation to risks (Adams 1995; Simonet and Wilde, 1997).

Finally, it is important to note that some of the most important risk-taking determinants come from biases that infect the aftermath of a risk episode. If people bear risks and suffer no harm then this may reduce attention to risk information and bias perceptual awareness. As we saw in the last chapter, one major input to this danger is people's unfounded beliefs that they are able to exercise personal powers to control or recover the consequences of uncalculated risks (Shapira, 1995). This may come as much from dispositions, such as high self-esteem, as from faulty learning.

So far we have not discussed people who have an appetite for danger: high stakes gamblers, mountaineers, bungee jumpers, and the like. These are not a homogeneous group, though many of them share one facet of personality: sensation seeking (Zuckerman, Ball, and Black, 1990). Within the model, sensation seeking is conceptualized as a psychological reward that arises in many risky situations. This has two constituents: the thrill of imminent great gain, married to the reward of feeling a sense of achievement in bearing the risk. It is the possibility of having these rewards while actually being safe that makes bungee jumping and big thrill rides in fairgrounds so popular with many sensation seekers. We shall shortly talk about the relevance of these motives to trading, but first let us summarize what the model implies for our understanding of risk management.

It indicates that risk behaviours are induced principally by four causes: (*a*) location: such as an imposed risk environment, (*b*) loss avoidance: the drive to avoid some known threat, (*c*) goal seeking: powerful orientations towards known gains, and (*d*) sensation seeking: the desire for stimulation through danger. The first of these, *location*, points directly to the processes of selection and self-selection into the trading context. As we discuss at greater length in Chapter 7 most trading floors have a simple policy of looking for 'quality' by hiring people with the best degrees from the best universities. More precise selection is deferred to the post-entry placement process, allocating hire's roles on the trading floor, or elsewhere, according to their presumed abilities. Those that attain and maintain positions as traders are those who are judged to have proven they can survive in this risk environment.

As we have discussed, management systems try to desensitize traders to excessive fear of loss, while establishing norms of vigilance and control over acceptable risk. Trading environments are as information-rich as any in the business world. Traders do not require an appetite for risk; they are constrained to take risks (arrow 5) by virtue of their roles and positions, albeit in many different forms according to the nature of markets and trading roles.

The challenge for management in this analysis is how to counter the three hazards of too much risk bearing, avoidance of risk, and errors of judgement about risk. The model suggests several paths to doing so, only some of which are currently practiced in investment banks and trading houses.

First, it suggests more attention could be given to selection, with a more intelligent modelling and matching of individuals to roles. Second, the information environment needs to be actively managed to ensure that traders are accurately apprised of actual risks, and avoid the clutches of the actuarial fallacy.

Third, their goal orientation needs to be monitored and managed. An important issue here is to avoid too close a coupling of risk with individual reward, such that risk bearing becomes unduly amplified.

Fourth, and this is probably the biggest gap, managers need to understand the psychology of decision-making, bias, and risk, to the degree that they can help train traders to avoid major pitfalls.

Fifth, the model stresses the importance of monitoring what traders are learning. Inaccurate inferences can easily be drawn from apparent consequences of actions.

6.3 Individual Differences: Trader Personality and Risk Profiles

As the model implies, individual differences play a critical role in who becomes a trader and how they discharge the role. The principal ways in which any individual may differ from another are physical attributes and constitution, temperament and personality, cognitive ability and style, attitudes and values, abilities and aptitudes, and background/experience. Not all of these are of interest or relevance in the present context, and not all are easily measured for research purposes.

One of the most immediately striking features in our study, and perhaps of any trading environment, is that there is not a lot of variation in some of these factors. In the case of *gender*, there is a predominance of young educated males. In our sample there were only two women. It is widely noted that trading environments are not perceived to be female-friendly environments, because of the macho culture they are seen to exhibit (Welch, 1999). More women are to be found in sales and middle and back-office functions than in market-making or proprietary trading. Ethnicity is irrelevant to trading, except insofar as it correlates with other biographical features on which traders select or self-select into this risk environment. Given that the chief pool in which trading houses fish for talent are the elite universities (or other trading houses) then one expects and finds ethnic profiles resembling those supply sources. This also brings to trading floors a social class bias, on the same principle.

Age is another compressed variable. Although traders do acquire skill with experience, it seems to reach a ceiling at middle age, for it is said that trading is a game for the under-35s and few remain beyond 40. The profile of our own sample is shown in the Appendix, but the age range was 24–48, with an average age of 32. Only 7 per cent were over 40. Why so few older traders? Is it that the pace and stress are more than a middle-aged person can handle? There is some folklore to that effect but it seems spurious, since there is no research evidence that suggests people's stress resistance declines post 35. There are two more parsimonious explanations. One is that younger people have a stronger goal orientation, to make money and succeed, which makes them willing to endure the personal costs of the activity. This declines as they get richer and more established. What starts out as exciting and challenging can become boring after several years.

This is why traders are apt to dream (unrealistically probably) of a life pursuing their favourite hobby or line of study on the back of their accumulated wealth (see Chapter 7). Others retain the desire to trade, but just do a lot less of it. This is often the thought in the minds of those who believe management is the next step for them. This too is often unrealistic, for it involves no reasoned analysis of what a managerial role would demand or what their capability would be to discharge it.

We had no measures of intellectual ability or cognitive skills, though these too could be expected to be subject to a high degree of range restriction, given the forces of selection and self-selection operating here. No doubt some people on trading floors are considerable brighter than others, but some trader–managers made the point to us that being too clever can be a disability, creating a susceptibility to analysis–paralysis. A senior manager in firm C told us his view of some of the hazards in recruiting the most highly intelligent applicants:

I want someone who feels comfortable making quick decisions with a limited amount of information. Not those people who feel that 'well if I just have that little bit of extra information, then I can make the decision'. You never have that, you never have the luxury of having that. That's why it's trading rather than portfolio management. . . . I want them to deliberate but I don't want them to over think it, and I don't want them to be brain locked, an inability to react to a situation. Obviously we recruit from the five or six best business schools in the States. I have interviewed a lot of people at Harvard Business School, some of whom have had 3 PhDs, from MIT, Harvard Stanford and wher-ever—Physics, Molecular, Biophysics and the like. They are probably capable of splitting the atom. But if I ask them a very simple question—Do you think the next 10% of the market is up or down. Not a right or wrong answer. Your opinion is as valid as mine. I just want to see a cou-ple of things. Number one—do you have an opinion? Given the infor-mation that you have right now, can you articulate that in a clear logical manner? That you can articulate to the sales force. That you could artic-ulate to a customer. Now a lot of times your come back from very very bright people is 'Well what's going to be the interest rate scenario?' Well the interest rate scenario is what it is right now—which means in order to come to a conclusion in terms of whether you think the market is going up or down by 10% you have to implicitly make a decision in terms of what you think the next policy decision will be or whether Russia does implode or the other million and one things that can impact the direction of the market.

Trading requires quite focused skills in its different parts—such as the capacity to engage in quick and concentrated analysis and the ability to influence a client. When we asked managers to sum up the qualities required, a certain degree of intellect was taken for granted, as a threshold value rather than something the more of which a trader possessed the better.

> You could be quite intelligent and be a money maker but not get along with people, so you're not going to fit in around here at least. We like people who feel comfortable buying and selling and have a commercial nose; math is less important than a commercial instinct and a sense of up and down. (senior trader manager)

> I'm looking for a lot of things in trader: solid, sound, understanding of the business and the bigger picture of the business. We want people who are smart, quick, people who can make quick decisions, market savvy, see opportunities, trading flair where they won't blow you up, intelligent thinkers, who can pounce on situations. (trader manager—equities)

> One trader I recently took on from another desk is not very quantitative, but he excels at getting information, getting customers interested and without him we would do less business. Another guy has a PhD, very intelligent, motivated and focused, very good. The 2 have totally different skills. They are treated differently and bring different things to the table. They make money in different ways. What more could you want than 2 people who make money in 2 totally uncorrelated ways? (trader manager—gilts)

As these quotes illustrate, the qualities that are most implicated are what might be called qualities of character and temperament—factors that enable individuals to withstand stress, hold their nerve, make dispassionate judgements, negotiate, and do deals (Bates and Wachs, 1994): in a word, personality. Risk orientation is also important, as a key behaviourally relevant outcome of personality and the risk environment. We collected data on both of these factors from most of the trader sample, which we were then able to compare with a large benchmarking database from executives and business students.

We will discuss each of these in turn and then their relationship to each other.

Personality

In the last two decades there has been a major resurgence of interest in dispositional approaches to organizational behaviour, led by emerging consensus around the 'Big Five' factorial model (FFM) of personality (Digman, 1997). The contents of the model are as follows:

N: Neuroticism/Emotionality

This is what separates people of a nervous, anxious, and moody disposition from the unflappable and emotionally invariant types. It can be conceived as a kind of smoke alarm. People at the high extreme are perpetually on the lookout for danger and hypersensitive to its presence and effects. Their alarm is calibrated to go off even when the house is not on fire. Low scorers tend to be more oblivious and have greater powers of recovery after setbacks. Their alarm threshold is so high that they tend to be devoid of empathy and awareness to the emotional climate around them. People who are high on N undoubtedly suffer more, though their suffering is often of their own making: their own imaginings, anxieties and fears. It is also due to their sensitivity to the world and its stresses; making them more empathic with the feelings of other people.

In finance, one may expect a normal range on the N dimension. There is no obvious selection bias on this dimension. Interestingly, in some structured environments high N scorers are more common, for it is in these more formalized environments that high N people may feel less exposed and more protected. High N scores can be seen as a liability in many risk environments, though they are useful in customer service oriented jobs.

E: Extroversion

Extroverts seek stimulation from people and action, whereas introverts are more content with the inner stimulus of their reflections and better able to endure slow-paced solitude. In the psychometric measurement of extroversion, two major themes tend to emerge. One is sociability, the desire for intimacy and closeness in warm relationships, plus a positive orientation to more casual social relations. The other theme is activity and dominance: the drive to be in charge of social situations, and to seek out the stimulation of highly dynamic action-packed environments.

Because the social aspects of financial firms are typically subordinated to their task focus and goal achievement; one can expect to find more introverts than extroverts in these organizations. This could be a problem on trading floors if social isolation combines with the competitiveness of trading role to produce a dysfunctional local climate in which customer relations and team working are neglected.

It is the activity, and dominance themes of E, rather than the sociability component, which is especially relevant to willingness to engage in managerial roles. However, one element of this theme may prove especially problematic in risk businesses like finance: the facet that measures sensation seeking. This facet is known to have a strong genetic underpinning and to be a key to the make-up of addicted gamblers and other thrill seekers (Zuckerman, 1994; Zuckerman and Kuhlman, 2000). High scorers are a very mixed blessing in finance. Their self-serving impulses could put others at risk as in some high profile rogue trader cases where whole firms were jeopardized. Yet, these may also be the people who could be most useful in the front line of fast-paced risky trading action, so long as they are very closely supervised.

O: Openness to Experience

This dimension measures radicalism versus conservatism. At one extreme are people with high tolerance for uncertainty and an appetite for change, and at the other are those with high needs for structure and certainty. The former are led by their curiosity into new situations. The latter avoid novelty and like to operate with routines and traditions. Creative people score highly on most facets of O.

In the finance professions the stereotype favours low O people, which would be consistent with the constraints that apply to many finance environments. Against this needs to be balanced the fact that high O scores tend to be associated with high general intelligence. High O people might not initially be attracted to finance, but those that do enter can find roles and situations where creativity and adaptability are needed and rewarded. In a previous study of Chief Finance Officers (CFOs), there was no particular bias in sample distribution, but those CFOs who were high on O had a predilection for strategic rather than operational roles (Nicholson and Cannon, 2000).

A: Agreeableness
This amounts to a tough versus tender-mindedness dimension, contrasting on the one extreme those who are nurturing, selfless, compassionate, and cooperative from those on the other extreme who are competitive, tough, and Machiavellian. It is said to be the most culturally conditionable of the Big Five (Buss, 1991). Business environments have a bias towards low A types, because the values that drive markets and competitive advantage also govern the way decision-making is practised, putting competitive individualism at a premium. There is actually a strong cultural bias here. Anglo-Saxon and North European management A scale values are generally lower than in the developing economies, Latin and Mediterranean cultures and the Far and Middle East.

Tough-mindedness on this scale might be acceptable as a necessary fact of life for much of business but there is one facet that can be a source of difficulty: trust. As measured by Big Five instruments this denotes the degree to which people believe others they deal with have good intentions and can be trusted. Much has been written on the topic of trust, for it is a key value in every kind of informal dealing and contract, and yet it is an obvious pitfall to be reliant upon people whose self-interests are incompatible with one's own. Too much trust is a hazard. Too little is a liability. The dangers for traders are on the one hand of laying oneself open to exploitation by others, and on the other of being the first mover in a spiral of negative tit-for-tat mistrust.

C: Conscientiousness
This is a control–achievement dimension. People high on this dimension are self-driven, disciplined, and orderly—at extreme highs they

are workaholics and control addicts. At extreme lows they are laid back, avoidant, and chaotic. Research has shown this to be the dimension most strongly predictive of work performance (Barrick and Mount, 1991), so scores tend to be elevated among high achieving populations. Within the world of finance an especially high value is placed upon order and control, those elements of the dimension that relate to the conscientious and scrupulous observance of regulatory authority. It is well established that personal discretion over decision-making domains increases as one ascends the hierarchy, especially in the highly layered order of big financial corporations. This creates a dilemma. People with high striving desires may not get through the hierarchy fast enough to satisfy them and thus quit, leaving the leadership to be selected from a survivor population of people whose biases are oriented more towards patient control than impatient ambition.

The NEO-PI-R

To incorporate the measurement of personality into our research, we opted for the NEO-PI-R as our preferred measure. This was because of its breadth and depth of coverage (thirty facets in five dimensions), and because of its impressive credentials for reliability, validity, and cross-cultural utility (Costa and McCrae, 1997; McCrae and Costa, 1997a). Also, at the time of the research at London Business School we held a database of around 3,500 executives and business students against whom occupational groups could be benchmarked, including a previous study of entrepreneurial leaders' personality profiles (Nicholson, 1998b).

The NEO-PI-R is a demanding instrument to complete: it takes a fluent respondent 45 min. It is thus hardly surprising that our traders, people in a hurry, were not the easiest to recruit to complete the inventory. Our sample size for the analysis was sixty-four, enough for some broad comparisons. We were aware also that the NEO-PI-R, although it would provide valuable insights into the questions raised at the beginning of this chapter, it would not tell us all that we wanted to know about trader dispositions to risk and decision-making. For these two reasons we developed our own new measure of risk orientation, based upon self-reported behaviours.

Risk Propensity

Our critique of the risk field earlier suggested that people are not truly risk seeking so much as risk bearing. Even in the case of sensation-seeking individuals, they are seeking a psychological payoff, and this may be delivered as readily by (subjectively risky) experiences that are objectively low risk as well as those where genuine risk is high. However, our model explicitly seeks to explain why, for various reasons, people will exhibit variations in their propensity to take or avoid risks. We sought to develop a short reliable measure, the Risk Taking Index (RTI), which would capture this propensity, not by asking people about their orientation to risk but about their actual risk behaviours past and present.

Previous research has looked at the intercorrelation of scores on a range of measures of risk taking in different decision domains, and typically found these connections to be weak, suggesting that people do not have generalized tendencies to take or avoid risk (Weinstein and Martin, 1969; Salminen and Heiskanen, 1997). However, research on managerial decision making by MacCrimmon and Wehrung (1986), showed that this pattern of results does not preclude the possibility of strong intra-individual convergence of different measures of risk taking. They found that a small number of people showed consistent responses on different measures of risk taking, and could be categorized as consistent risk seekers, or consistent risk averters. Weber and Milliman (1997) extended this analysis by finding that while the degree of risk perceived in a situation can vary according to the characteristics of the situation, attitude to perceived risk (the degree to which people find perceived risk attractive) remained stable across situations for a significant portion of their sample. This work is part of a growing stream of literature that combines situational and individual approaches to risk propensity by considering individual responses to different risk domains. The emerging picture suggests that it is possible to be risk taking in some areas of one's life and risk avoiding in others, while maintaining a relatively internally consistent attitudinal posture toward risk (e.g. Fagley and Miller, 1997; Weber and Milliman, 1997; Weber, Blais, and Betz, 2002).

Data from personality and perceived risk attitude studies suggests that both general (e.g. sensation seeking) and domain-specific (e.g. perceived risk) risk propensities are possible. Our premise in constructing the RTI as a measure of risk propensity was that it should encompass several risk domains, so as to capture the complexity of individual risk profiles, for example, by allowing us to identify people who are inconsistent in their approaches to risk in different risk domains. These individuals can be regarded as lacking a strong propensity to either take or avoid risks, but this could mask a propensity to take risks in some domains more than others, depending on the demands of situations. The inconsistency may be more apparent than real, such as the finance trader who takes risks routinely at work, but avoids risk when making family, leisure, and personal finance choices.

Our objectives for analysis were to put the RTI alongside the NEO-PI-R in order to check the degree to which trader risk appetite is underlain by personality dispositions, as has been found in previous research (Kowert and Hermann, 1997). Our particular interest was to test this both in the trader group, and with our much larger benchmark database, and specifically to see whether sensation seeking would emerge as a predictor of risk taking across any or all domains. We also expected the scale of Openness to experience to be a predictor of risk taking, since it embraces exploratory behaviours, tolerance of uncertainty, change, and innovation (McCrae and Costa, 1997b). These could be seen as factors that reduce the threshold to risk bearing to achieve personal goals. We had an opposite prediction for C conscientiousness: that high C would raise the aversion to risk bearing, by requiring achievement to be secured under conditions of conformity and control (Hogan and Ones, 1997).

The literature also suggests that consistent risk takers require resilience (Klein and Kunda, 1994), which would suggest that they should also score low in emotional sensitivity, the N dimension of personality. The same logic could be applied to A, the tough to tender-mindedness dimension. Robust pursuit of self-interest is coupled in the measure with a lack of interest in the consequences of one's risk taking upon others (West and Hall, 1997).

Thus, in relation to personality variation we hypothesized that traders with a high risk orientation would have high scores on O and E, and low scores on N, A, and C. The literature also indicates that there are age and sex differences in risk taking; young males being the most susceptible group (Powell and Ansic, 1997; Byrnes, Miller, and Schafer, 1999). Given the restricted age range and gender mix in our trader sample, this is a pattern we could only test for in the wider London Business School database, and use as a control when making comparisons.

The short RTI scale we developed to test these ideas is shown in Table 6.1. Statistical analyses[3] reveal that each two-item domain scale has high reliability and distinctive variance when compared with others. This supports the idea of domain-specific risk propensity: the likelihood, as predicted in our model, that people will be risk takers in one or more domains, but not in others. At the same time domain-specific risk scores were sufficiently intercorrelated to permit them also to be summed into a single index of risk propensity.

The data were used to create seven scales: one overall scale summing all elements, representing generalized risk propensity, plus six scales, one for each of the risk domains (recreational, health, career, financial, safety, social), the sum of the now and past scores in each domain.

Table 6.1   Risk taking index

We are interested in everyday risk-taking. Please could you tell us if any of the following have ever applied to you, *now* or in your adult *past*? Please use the scales as follows:
1 = never, 2 = rarely, 3 = quite often, 4 = often, 5 = very often

	Now	In the past
a) recreational risks (e.g. rock-climbing, scuba diving)	1 2 3 4 5	1 2 3 4 5
b) health risks (e.g. smoking, poor diet, high alcohol consumption)	1 2 3 4 5	1 2 3 4 5
c) career risks (e.g. quitting a job without another to go to)	1 2 3 4 5	1 2 3 4 5
d) financial risks (e.g. gambling, risky investments)	1 2 3 4 5	1 2 3 4 5
e) safety risks (e.g. fast driving, city cycling without a helmet)	1 2 3 4 5	1 2 3 4 5
f) social risks (e.g. standing for election, publicly challenging a rule or decision)	1 2 3 4 5	1 2 3 4 5

6.4 Data Analyses with Traders and the Benchmark Sample

We shall discuss the results in two main steps. First, we shall look at the pattern of average scores, to examine whether traders differ from other groups, in and out of finance, in their personality, and their risk propensities. Second, we shall look at relationships among these and other factors, to consider the implications for performance and other outcomes.

Personality

First, Fig. 6.2 shows our trader sample alongside other finance and non-finance samples on the NEO-PI-R.

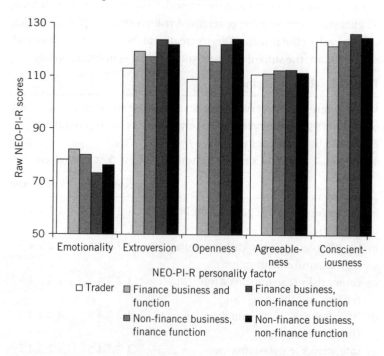

Fig. 6.2 Comparisons of personality scores by occupational group

Table 6.2 shows significant differences between occupational groups for each of the thirty personality facets.

Table 6.2 Personality facets—significant differences between occupational groups

Emotionality	B, C > D, E
N1 Anxiety	B, C > D, E
N2 Angry hostility	
N3 Depression	B, C, E > D
	B > E
N4 Self-consciousness	B, C > D
	B > E
N5 Impulsiveness	
N6 Vulnerability	B, C > D, E
Extroversion	D, E > A, C; D > B
E1 Warmth	D, E > A, C
E2 Gregariousness	B, D, E > A
E3 Assertiveness	D, E > A, B, C
E4 Activity	D, E > B, C
E5 Sensation seeking	
E6 Positive emotions	D > C
Openness	B, D, E > A, C
O1 Fantasy	E > D > A, C; B > A, C
O2 Aesthetics	E > D > C; B > C
O3 Feelings	B, D, E > A
O4 Actions	B, D, E > A
O5 Ideas	E > A, C; B, D > C
O6 Values	B, C, D, E > A
Agreeableness	
A1 Trust	
A2 Straightforwardness	
A3 Altruism	
A4 Compliance	
A5 Modesty	A, C > E
A6 Tender-mindedness	
Conscientiousness	D > B
C1 Competence	
C2 Order	
C3 Dutifulness	D > B
C4 Achievement striving	D > A, B, C; E > B, C
C5 Self-discipline	D, E > B
C6 Deliberation	

Notes: A: trader; B: finance business and function; C: non-finance business, finance function; D: finance business, non-finance function; E: non-finance business, non-finance function. Significance differences based on $p < 0.05$, for Bonferroni *post-hoc* tests.

The most striking feature is that what seems to make a difference is not the type of firm one is in, but the kind of job function held. Throughout Table 6.2 the main contrasts are to be found between finance and non-finance functions (A, B, C versus D, E). It is striking that there are few significant differences between non-finance function people in finance firms versus those who are in non-finance businesses (D and E). If there is a 'finance firm culture' these data suggest that it does not lead to a different kind of person being attracted to the industry than goes elsewhere. In contrast people in the finance function (finance professionals) are much more homogeneous regardless of whether they are in finance firms. The data show that people in finance functions really do differ from non-finance people. One may tentatively say that this suggests that selection and self-selection are at work more than socialization, which would be consistent with the evidence that personality dispositions are quite invariant for most people over long stretches of the adult lifespan (Caspi, 2000). Putting the traders into the picture shows them to be aligned with other finance professionals in most, but not all respects.

Looking at the results in more detail, first, there is some evidence that people in finance are more emotional, as measured by the N scale, than those elsewhere; the 'E' group, and with them non-finance people in financial services firms, are often low scoring. Finance is something of a refuge for some emotional people. It is notable that our trader sample, 'A', do not differ from the generality, that is, they are no more or less emotional or variable in their emotionality than other occupational groups. There are also major differences, on the next two dimensions, E and O, with finance people more introvert and conservative. The relationships are very strong, statistically, but also quite patterned. Traders are quite consistently in the low scoring group across most facets. Interestingly, the one on which they are undifferentiated is sensation seeking, the gamblers' scale. Although as we have shown this factor is a major predictor of risk taking, it is not one that divides traders from other finance or non-finance professionals. On the O facets finance people, particularly traders, are less experimental when it comes to action (O4), more concrete than abstract (O5), and less imaginative (O1). All these results add up to a consistent pattern. Careers in the finance profession have profiles that attract people who are disinclined to stand out from the crowd or to take chances.

As for leadership, we cannot say how many in our sample could turn out to be business leaders. It is commonplace for people from finance backgrounds to rise to lead companies, especially in the United Kingdom, yet our data do suggest that they emerge from a population where it is much more the norm to lack the drive that propels people into leading positions, especially dominance and achievement striving. For many professionals the route to leadership lies along the path through general management. Many engineers, marketers, human resource specialists, and finance people realize that they have to leave their profession behind to rise to leadership. An earlier study of CFOs in the United Kingdom's top corporations supported this position (Nicholson and Cannon, 2000). This work found that many who had risen to their position, at the head of a corporate finance function, had no ambitions to go further and become CEOs. The small proportion who did have this ambition had a predominantly strategic orientation, and personality profiles that would set them apart from the finance profile we have seen here. In other words, if finance professionals want to become leaders there is nothing stopping them except their own drives. For the majority however, their profession would seem to offer sufficient fulfilment without impelling them into management.

In terms of the *trader profile*, little separates it from other finance professionals, and of greatest note are those features that distinguish this group from non-finance professionals. These suggest that the personality predispositions traders bring into their occupation fall pretty much within the full range of varieties and types one would expect to find in the general population, apart from the marked tendencies toward introversion and conservatism we have discussed.

This pattern has a couple of implications. First, extreme types of one kind or another are as likely to crop up in trading environments as any other. There is nothing in the selection and self-selection of traders that is screening out the highly emotional; the extreme competitor; the workaholic; the addicted experimenter, etc. And it may be noted that each of these extremes represents their own distinctive source of risk in a trading room, as in any other occupational context. Second, the distinguishing features that do differentiate them reveal that consequences such as go-it-alone introversion, lack of initiative, and lack of interest in exercising authority are a constant hazard in trading environments. Perhaps it was in recognition of these hazards that two of the banks in our sample made strenuous attempts to incentivize cooperation and teamwork.

Risk Propensity

The RTI was designed around self-reported risk taking in six domains. One feature of the scale is the contrast between people's reports of past risk taking assess and current risk taking. The pattern was very clear as shown in Fig. 6.3: a highly significant decline from past to present in three domains (recreation, health, and safety[4]) and no perceptible change in three (career, financial, and social risk taking[5]). What are we to make of this?

The finding in itself is interesting but the explanation is not self-evident. Two explanations can be entertained. One is that risk taking declines over time; that is with age, especially in a population that is predominantly in its 30s and 40s, who perhaps are recalling their more reckless youth of wild recreation, unhealthy lifestyle, and dangerous habits. This would be consistent with the literature on

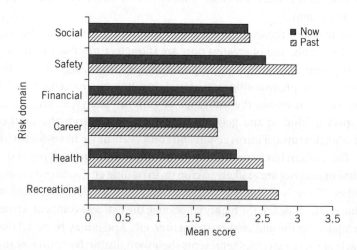

Fig. 6.3   Risk propensity, risks taken—now and past

youthful striving, especially among males (Geary, 1998; Byrnes, Miller, and Schafer, 1999). The pattern of the data shows that it holds for both sexes but differences are much greater for males than females on these three scales. And there is an intriguing additional factor: change over time in propensity for financial risk taking is clearly moderated by sex; among women it increases significantly from past to present while for males it decreases.[6] The second explanation is that respondents are engaging in systematic retrospective perceptual bias; immunizing themselves to their present levels of risk taking by believing they have reduced their exposure over the last years. We have no way of choosing between these explanations, though the consistency of the data with theory and the clear discrimination between domains favours the former explanation, that these are genuine shifts with time and age.

Looking at occupational groups (Fig. 6.4) we also get a clear result. Overall, traders are more risk averse than other groups. In particular they are notably less inclined to take social or career risks. This demonstrates that, contrary to popular belief, people with risk-taking personalities are not attracted to the world of trading, but the world of trading does teach them how to be risk takers in their work.

Relationships and Outcomes

Several relationships here are instructive: the link between the two sets of measures, personality and risk taking; the relationship of biographical and demographic factors to both of them; and other indicators.

Let us start with how the NEO-PI-R personality dimensions and facets relate to the RTI and subscales, using our large benchmark sample. Table 6.3 summarizes the results of a regression analysis across our total sample (traders and non-traders, $N = 1638$), where personality factors are used to predict risk taking.[7]

Results strongly and clearly supported our expectations for overall risk taking. The common pattern is that people with a high risk propensity across all domains, that is people with a general willingness to bear risks in all areas of their lives, are high on extroversion and openness and low in neuroticism, agreeableness, and conscientiousness. The relationships are very strong and highly consistent. Statistical procedures that separate out and cross check findings for

Risk Takers

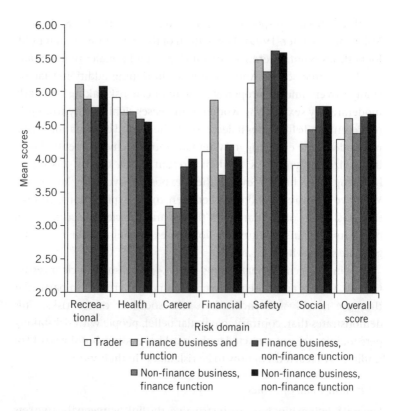

Fig. 6.4 Comparisons of risk propensity scores by occupational group

Table 6.3 Relationships between RTI and Big Five personality factors

	Types of Risk						
	Recreational	Health	Career	Finance	Safety	Social	Overall
Neuroticism	−0.16***	0.11***	−0.11***	−0.14**	−0.09***	−0.12***	−0.18***
Extroversion	0.17***	0.17***	0.01	0.09**	0.22***	0.22**	0.26***
Openness	0.20***	0.06*	0.34***	0.10**	0.05	0.32***	0.36***
Agreeableness	−0.12***	−0.17***	−0.18***	−0.21***	−0.19***	−0.16***	−0.31***
Conscientiousness	−0.09**	−0.13**	−0.08**	−0.17***	−0.16***	−0.07*	−0.20***
Variance explained (R^2)	0.35	0.18	0.42	0.34	0.31	0.37	0.41

*$p < 0.05$.
**$p < 0.01$.
***$p < 0.001$.

subgroups show that this finding holds with the high consistency across groups.

What does this mean? The high E and O (extroversion and openness) imply an appetite for stimulation and change. The low N and A (emotionality/neuroticism and agreeableness/tender-mindedness) denote the toughness necessary to bear the attendant risks. However, the clincher in the pattern when it comes to risk taking is the low C (conscientiousness), what one could call the get-rich-quick factor in risk taking. In terms of our model this is the factor that impels the actor to bear the risks in order to reap the possible rewards. Low C denotes spontaneity, lack of discipline, and willingness to take shortcuts to save effort. People with high C might take controlled risks, but their nature makes them more ready to take the pains to lay the groundwork that delivers outcomes. Low C people will prefer the short and risky route.

Traders are subject to the same general pattern. Those with the high risk-taker profile we have identified will be generalized risk takers outside their work domain as much as within it. Of course the converse is true, people with the opposite pattern of high N, A and C, and low E and O (should they survive in this environment) will be conservative in their approach to risk. But our earlier result suggests that the socialization of traders to take financial risks is a persistent overlay, so compelling is it. In other words there are many traders who take big market risks who in doing so are swimming against the tide of their risk-avoidant natures.

A more detailed analysis of the relationship between the individual personality facets and the RTI subscales shows there to be quite differentiated patterns for each scale but some common themes (for simplicity we simply show here whether there is a significant relationship and in which direction) (Table 6.4).

Among these is the finding that sensation seeking (one of the extroversion facets) is the primary predictor of the RTI in four of the six domains (Recreation, Health, Finance, and Safety) as well as for the overall risk-taking scale.

The O4 (actions) facet, which taps individuals' openness to trying new experiences, is also linked with risk taking in four domains. It is the facet that most strongly predicts career risk taking, and the second strongest for the recreation and overall risk-taking scales.

Table 6.4 Relationships between RTI and Big Five personality subscales

	Recreation	Health	Career	Finance	Safety	Social	Overall risk
Emotionality							
N1 Anxiety	−		−		−		−
N2 Angry hostility							
N3 Depression		+	−				
N4 Self-consciousness							
N5 Impulsiveness		+	−				
N6 Vulnerability							−
Extroversion							
E1 Warmth							+
E2 Gregariousness	−						
E3 Assertiveness						+	+
E4 Activity	+				+	+	+
E5 Sensation-seeking	+	+		+		+	+
E6 Positive emotions							
Openness							
O1 Fantasy				+		+	
O2 Aesthetics				−		+	
O3 Feelings							
O4 Actions	+		+		+	+	+
O5 Ideas			+	+		+	+
O6 Values	+	+	+			+	+
Agreeableness							
A1 Trust							
A2 Straightforwardness	−		−	−			−
A3 Altruism				−			
A4 Compliance	−		−				
A5 Modesty	+						
A6 Tender-mindedness	−		−				
Conscientiousness							
C1 Competence			+				
C2 Order			−	−	−		−
C3 Dutifulness			−	−			
C4 Achievement striving	−					+	
C5 Self-discipline				−	−	−	−
C6 Deliberation			−		−	−	−

Notes: + indicates a positive relationship; − indicates a negative relationship (at significance level of $p < 0.05$).

The openness to values facet (O6), which could be interpreted as tolerance for multiple perspectives, is a predictor of the RTI in four risk domains plus the overall risk scale.

Competitiveness (A4), a preference for a fast-paced life (E4), low levels of anxiety (N1), lack of straightforwardness (A2), lack of self-discipline (C5), and spontaneous decision-making (C6) are all also significant predictors of risk taking across several domains.

The repeated emergence of this subset can be interpreted as strong evidence of the existence of a common set of dispositional factors that consistently influences risk taking across different situations. Among other findings, the most notable finding is that the health scale of the RTI has a different set of predictors to the others. People who take risks with their health are high on neuroticism, unlike other high risk takers, whose N scores are low. This is consistent with the idea that people resort to health risk behaviours to alleviate anxiety and other negative emotions (Vollrath and Torgersen, 2002).

Looking at demographics, analysis with the benchmark sample confirmed the 'young male' effect (Finucane *et al.*, 2000), especially in the recreational, health, and safety risk domains. These are risk domains that we saw earlier had most reduction from past to present risk taking, confirming the idea that this is a genuine shift with time.

6.5   Illusion of Control

In Chapter 5 we reported that traders with high illusion of control perform less effectively and we suggested that the trading environment is rich in elements that might encourage this illusion. If this is the case, what can we say about individual factors that might predispose traders to the bias?

First, there is some evidence that traders may have somewhat lower susceptibility to illusion of control than other groups: mean scores on our illusion of control measure for traders were some 10 per cent lower than for our MBA students. Nonetheless as we saw in Chapter 5, the traders in our sample had scores covering the full range of levels of illusion of control. One explanation for the lower average illusion of control among traders might be that they become less prone to it with training and experience. We tested for experience, looking at their backgrounds, but found no link to experience. This inclines us toward the more plausible explanation that selection processes operate to select out traders with high control illusions.

We also looked at the relationship between personality and the illusion of control. We found that illusion of control was significantly related to extroversion ($r = 0.21$, $p < 0.05$). There was no correlation with the other four personality factors. Looking more closely at the sub-facets of extroversion on the NEO revealed significant correlations with two of them: E4 activity ($r = 0.21$, $p < 0.05$) and E5 sensation seeking ($r = 0.32$, $p < 0.01$). These two associations (activity and sensation seeking) may reflect a bias to action and a greater tendency to adopt an implemental rather than deliberative mindset that researchers have found to be associated with illusion of control (Gollwitzer and Kinney, 1989). On other measures, traders who were high on illusion of control were also more likely to enjoy recreational gambling, more likely to take risks with their personal finances and reported themselves to be less likely to think through all costs and payoffs when making personal financial decisions.

6.6   Trader Profiles and Performance

We saw in Chapter 5, that a propensity to illusion of control was associated with poorer trader performance. What of other aspects of the trader's profile? We carried out regression analysis on the traders in the sample for whom we had NEO personality data, examining the association between personality and total remuneration. As before, we controlled for experience, job level, and education. We also controlled for the effect of illusion of control. Table 6.5 summarizes the results.

As in our earlier analysis we can see that illusion of control is significantly associated with lower remuneration. In addition, personality also accounts for significant variation in earnings. If we accept total earnings as a proxy for trader performance, the results suggest that the higher performing traders in our sample are emotionally stable introverts who are open to experience. Given the small size of our sample

Table 6.5 Regression on total remuneration

	Standardized regression coefficients
Experience	0.44**
Job level	0.36**
Education	0.23
Illusion of control	−0.28*
N	−0.42**
E	−0.28*
O	0.41**
A	−0.23
C	−0.05

$*p < 0.05.$
$**p < 0.01.$
$***p < 0.001.$

of traders with personality data ($N = 64$) we have to be cautious about generalizing from this result. However, the pattern makes sense.

The story would go as follows. Emotional stability immunizes individuals against the stresses and strains of a job that places a premium on maintaining detachment in the face of large gains and losses. Introversion insulates traders against social distractions including the need to be liked and accepted: useful especially where there is a need to seek or tolerate contrarian positions. Finally, openness is associated with intelligence and ability to adapt to fast changing environments.

We also examined whether there were links between our risk measures and performance. We found none. This is consistent with our earlier argument that underlying risk propensity is only one factor in trader risk behaviour, which as we shall see in the next chapter is highly conditioned by training, socialization, and context.

In this chapter we have considered whether there is an 'ideal' trader profile and what might be the important dimensions of individual difference on which traders vary. While we have some evidence that emotionally stable introverts who are open to experience will perform well, it would be unwise to suggest that this represents the ideal trader profile. Rather, we would suggest that the principle value in profiling personality and risk propensity is to enrich the dialogue between traders and their managers in achieving the best person–job fit, especially at early stages of the trader's career, and to enable the most effective management of each individual trader.[8] In the next chapter we focus more directly on the process of trader development and learning.

Notes

1. Proprietor of a pub/bar.
2. Feedback arrows between levels of the model have been omitted, in order to keep the model simple and focused on the areas of causality of greatest interest here.
3. For a full description of the development and performance of the Risk Taking Scale see Nicholson *et al.* (2004).
4. Two-tailed *t*-test significant at $p < 0.001$.
5. Two-tailed *t* -test non-significant at $p < 0.05$.
6. Two-tailed *t* -test significant at $p < 0.05$.
7. We used structural equation modelling to estimate regression coefficients simultaneously for all the risk subscales. Adjusted goodness of fit was 0.93. We also looked at direct paths to the overall measure of risk propensity (modelled as a second-order factor). Adjusted goodness of fit was 0.92. For a more detailed account of this aspect of our study see Nicholson *et al.* (2004).
8. We return to this theme in Chapter 9 as we discuss the implications of these results for trader management.

Chapter 7

BECOMING A TRADER

We have already seen at several points in our analysis that traders undergo a range of formative experiences during their first years on the job. Some of these are programmed; some are not. Becoming a trader involves more than skill acquisition; it involves tacit knowledge, learning a new language, knowledge of procedures, analytical tools and shortcuts, and a broad understanding of the industry. More deeply, it is a process of acquiring a web of relationships through which acculturation takes place: the internalization of the boundaries of acceptable behaviour, underlying assumptions, and ways of seeing the world. The learning process involves acquiring an identity as a trader and entering into a community of practice.

Traders are subject to a range of intensive experiences, some of them emotionally powerful, and some of the most important and emotionally charged learning occurs through immediate experience of loss and gain. Managers and reward systems punctuate the process to amplify or dampen the beliefs, knowledge, and motives that are being acquired. Much of the learning is informal, mediated by the trader's individual actions and reflections, and a web of informal influences and relationships. Mentors and peers take on an especially important role as trusted informants about 'the way things really happen round here'.

To complicate matters, it is a moving picture. Markets, information, and demands all change. Becoming a trader is not just about learning a static body of knowledge; rather it is about learning ways of doing things, how to adapt to new situations and modify decision rules, and how to use history and experience to make decisions rapidly and with confidence. Experienced traders need to constantly draw on and modify tacit knowledge. Managers need to ensure that traders develop the correct attributions: traders need a critical approach to the relationship between a decision and its outcome, and not simply to commit the fallacy we examined in Chapter 5, that a good outcome implies a correct strategy.

The process of formal and informal socialization will take some, but not all, new recruits through the transition from novice to full members of the trading community. The learning process is long, complex, and some are unable to make the metamorphosis; as described well by one of the managers that we interviewed.

I have thought very hard and often about what makes a good trader, and there is something unidentifiable in it. You always know when it's there and you definitely know when it is not there. The only word that really sums it up, in cash traders, is one of these all-encompassing words like savvy or 'nous'—street-smart. You can never be specific with these words. You can never say, this person has got this, or hasn't. It tends to be a quality which, over time, you can see when it's there and when it's not. You have to give people quite a long time for it to come forward because people initially are nervous; they are trying too hard, they are not trying hard enough, they haven't got to grips with working in a big organisation, they come from all sorts of different backgrounds. I've often found there can be up to a year and a half lead-time, but sometimes it can come out in 3 weeks. They have produced something, tapped into something and you think that's great. They've got into the market psychology and pulled it out and their development starts there. Sometimes people need a kick-start and you need to nurse them and prod them along a little bit. It's more of an intuitive feeling you get from somebody than a case study where you can tick boxes. When it's not there, it's usually because someone has evaluated the situation incorrectly. They find the market perplexing. Some people don't seem to understand or comprehend how a free market works and how the mechanisms in that market occur and they never quite get it. They're almost like a step behind it all the time rather than a step ahead.

In this chapter we consider some of the experiential and psychological factors that shape traders' development and can, for some traders, develop and foster illusions of skill.

7.1   A Transitions Model

The idea of transitions having distinct interlocking phases, the transition cycle (Nicholson, 1987), can be invoked to help describe how traders develop, and to discuss the influences on learning at each stage. The transition cycle comprises four stages:

- preparation and anticipation
- encounter
- adjustment
- stabilization.

The transition model has three essential characteristics. First, it assumes that all of us are at any one time at some stage of one or more cycles, and that movement to subsequent stages and to the next cycle is normal, though the time taken to do so will vary. Hence, all traders are at some stage of adjustment to change or awaiting some upcoming development, such as vertical progression through the trading hierarchy or a move to a new role. Second, each stage involves distinctive psychological processes. The appropriate strategy for one stage is different for subsequent stages. The challenges, problems, and solutions alter. There can be adaptive and maladaptive learning at each stage, and each can produce both positive and negative outcomes. Third, the stages are interdependent; strategies, events, and activities at one stage have consequences for the nature of the challenge presented by subsequent stages. In other words, development through transition is a process that requires multiple levels of awareness, planning, and engagement.

7.2   Preparation and Anticipation

Socialization into any complex professional role begins even before the person has taken the job, and trading is no exception. The professions rely on prior educational systems to have delivered to them well-socialized individuals who are in a state of readiness to accept the imprint of the profession's acculturation and training. In highly stratified societies, such as the United Kingdom and most other Western countries, selecting from top universities does this, and indirectly and implicitly introduces a degree of social class bias by doing so. Such anticipatory socialization, as this is called in the careers literature, means that the mores of the environment they are about to enter do not have to be learned afresh. It is a two-way process of matching expectations about the kind of world they are entering and the kinds of behaviours that would be considered normal or acceptable.

The process is one of selection and self-selection, as we saw in the risk-taking model presented in the previous chapter. Interestingly, though traders may enter with quite aligned general perceptions of the kind of environment they are entering, they are likely to be very poorly prepared and informed about exactly what they will do. This is a common feature of the bridge between college education and the business world; the former teach almost nothing of direct application in the latter, except in the technical domains of such areas such as law and medicine. Further selective biases are introduced by selecting from specific disciplines.

This raises a question we have already considered: what kind of person is attracted to financial services and, more specifically, a trading environment? In the area of investment banking potential traders come with initially inaccurate perceptions of the kinds of demands that will be made on them; full of wild exaggeration, thanks to the portrayals in popular culture of the kind to be found in 'Liar's Poker' (Lewis, 1989) or 'Rogue Trader' (Leeson, 1996).

The selection model adopted by organizations, implicitly rather than deliberately, has a critical effect on the recruitment process and subsequent trader development. Every seat on a trading floor is worth a lot of money and every wrong choice can lead to opportunity costs, losing trades, and reputational damage to the company. Some of the managers that we talked to discussed how some of their young hopefuls had started out as traders, but found the demands too great and were moved to a sales position or, worst case, fired, as illustrated by the following quote from a senior manager.

We have two people on the desk at the moment, both of whom started at the same time, from relatively similar backgrounds and one of them has just hit the ground running and he's gone right up the curve, well on his way to being a pretty good risk taker and price maker and a pretty useful trader. The other trader has actually failed miserably and is miserable in himself. He is really struggling with the whole issue of what the market means to him. Yet academically they are very similar. It has been interesting to watch, but I'm disappointed that we've actually had a failure.

The upcoming socialization process is being rehearsed during the process of the interview and induction stage. Research has shown that interviewees tend to assume that their interrogator, foibles and all, is representative of the company, and the decision whether to join is often based upon this single impression (Feldman, 1988). Ideally, the recruitment interview provides an opportunity for the prospective trader to learn about the organization and job demands, and the interviewer to get an accurate idea of what to expect from the new recruit and a reliable idea of where to place them post-entry. In investment banking this is quite important, since the various job functions have quite distinctly different features. A rigorous selection process should also be able to screen out most of the people who will not thrive in a trading environment and identify the potential rogue traders.

Our data indicate that these hopes would be misplaced. The selection systems that we witnessed in operation tended to emphasize an intuitive rather than a systematic appraisal of individual differences. The policy of choosing talented people and trying them out to see where they will fit is a respectable strategy. It is, though, a little expensive with human resources, by virtue of concatenating selection and placement, as discussed by one of the senior managers that we talked to.

People accumulate experience and become integrated in a team. Even though someone might not be perfect for a job, replacing him is difficult.

First of all there's the human equation and you try your best to counsel and advise people so they get better and maybe they will, so it's the first restraint on letting them go. Second is, how to replace them? If you're testing football players, maybe you can see how well he kicks, how fast he runs. You can't do that with trading, it takes a long time so there's a risk in hiring anybody new. After all, the person you are about to replace, you thought he was really good and you were wrong. Even if you saw a person you want to bring in, it would only be after you've done hours and hours of searching and interviewing and making sure that they will integrate on the interpersonal level with the team, even if he's a good trader in the economic sense. Then there is the opportunity cost of when the first guy leaves and the second is operational, which could be 6 months, a year, or even longer. So once you've made an investment in one person, there is a price to pay if you say OK you have made a mistake, we need a change.

By relying on prior selection processes, embedded mainly in education systems, employers are vulnerable to whatever else may follow from the sampling bias this represents. The judgements of interviewers cannot be taken seriously as a forensic defence against the hiring of maladaptive or rogue traders. Research suggests that only highly skilled and trained interviewers, operating with a validated semi-structured schedule might be able to achieve this; that is interviewers need to use interview questions consistently and base them upon a thorough analysis of job requirements, in conjunction with a well-designed application form and relevant biographical data (e.g. experience of decision-making, business knowledge, and exposure). The combination of these elements was not present in our sample.

Some organizations used a range of psychometric techniques and trading simulations. However, the final selection decision often consisted of a line manager making idiosyncratic judgements. As reported in the previous chapter, our data suggest that the detection of likely misfits could have been enhanced by the use of psychometric testing.

An unintended consequence of this process is to reduce diversity. Relying on the somewhat formulaic approach of narrowing down via disciplines and universities carries the risk of reducing the variance in people's work orientations, and the possible negative impact this might have on creativity. Having a relatively shared background from which to commence learning is advantageous in some respects, efficiency for example, but it also means that one can create an environment in which there is an absence of challenge or questioning of basic assumptions. The point was illustrated by the comment of one trader in our sample.

The intellectual diversity is not as much as it should be. I didn't go to university. I'm quite a senior person and I'm quite good at what I do and yet I would not be able to join the business now. It's rather like the British aristocracy, it can be inbred. We hire 90% from Oxbridge, Harvard and Wharton, so it's intellectually focused on the small group of people. This affects everything. The firm is made up of individuals and people not of codes and numbers and if you have individuals all the same then you get flabby and die out. So it is a concern.

One of the authors had the experience of conducting a seminar on the subject of diversity with an assembly of managing directors from the trading floor of a major European investment bank. On pointing out to them the irony of addressing around 50 white males in blue shirts and ties on the subject of diversity, after the amusement had abated one attendee gave voice to the unspoken sentiment in most investment banks: 'We're making plenty of money as we are—why change?'

The absence of women from trading floors in the United Kingdom can be considered a major limitation; especially when there is some evidence that women can be better traders than men, by virtue of a less strong tendency to overtrade (Barber and Odean, 2001). Many investment banks increasingly recognize the need for greater diversity. A senior manager in firm B, interviewed in 2002, reported on changes to the selection process that reveal the nature of the impetus towards greater diversity:

A few years ago the typical employer would be a rowing blue from Cambridge. Now we are trying to broaden the selection process, for example by hiring from a wider range of universities. One example was when we were doing a presentation at university X [a new, technology-based university rather than a traditional academic college]. We were approached by someone who had long hair, an earring and was overweight. He was persistent and one of the savviest people that was interviewed. He was hired. He has turned out to be one of the best cash traders. This hire would not have taken place five years ago.

However, the nature of the anticipatory process does vary as a function of organizational cultures and structures, for norms and practices differ. We observed large inter-firm differences in culture. Firms B and D had the strongest orientations towards cultural fit. Learning how to behave within those cultures was a critical part of a trader's development. In these cases, there was a markedly greater emphasis on whether prospective traders' existing attributes fitted into the culture, and their willingness to adapt to the culture. Once established, they were likely to remain in the organization for the long term. As one senior manager in firm B pointed out, 'We try to create a culture where someone would be embarrassed if they had to walk in one day and say to the guy next to him "I'm leaving" '.

Firms A and C were less uniform in their cultures. We observed quite marked differences between desks. One can infer that in these cases trader success is less a matter of ability to absorb the acculturation of the powerful firm-level ethos, so much as being appropriately placed within the firm in an area where one's abilities can be realized.

The transitions literature shows three important strategies for successful negotiation of the preparation/anticipation stage of the cycle. First, a realistic preview of the organization is needed. Job candidates need to look beyond the marketing and typically hard sell of the interview process to assess what the daily demands and environment are actually likely to be. Second, organizations can bring forward the challenge of adjustment by a programmatic introduction to the firm; making advance contacts available. In investment banks this is mostly *ad hoc*; applicants who know people in the industry have prior network intelligence. Where these networks do not exist, employers can assist the process by helping to broker such contacts. The objective is interaction with organizational representatives to help individuals make accurate self-assessments and informed choices about the suitability of the job for them personally.

Perhaps the most important asset in preparation is self-knowledge. Having a clear idea of one's own biases and development needs is a powerful aid to path-finding in a new environment. Our research did not capture what kinds of insights newly recruited traders had about themselves prior to joining, but we do know that it is typical for smart well-trained graduates newly on the labour market to have given very little time or thought to who they are (Arnold and Mackenzie Davey, 1992). They are too busy striving and living. One would like to think that the selection–recruitment process might help them towards personal insights, but it contains few elements that might, apart from the natural process of self-discovery that comes through subjecting oneself to choice and deliberation. At this point some conclude that this world is not for them, but for many it comes much later than the point of recruitment. A few world-weary traders we spoke to clearly felt they were stuck in a role that did not really fit them as people. The rewards of the trader's world make it compelling and hard to quit, even for misfits.

My ambitions are to make a huge amount of money. It would be naïve not to consider looking at moving to other firms and management would expect people to. I will continue to work here while it is in my interests to do so. Most people would say they are trying to work towards financial independence—pay for house and school fees, save some money which gives you the option not to work. If you have houses and families this is a worthwhile goal, why shouldn't people be working towards that? So if you know you are being underpaid at one firm and you can get another job elsewhere, it doesn't really matter where you are looking at a computer screen. There are also loyalty factors, but if you add them up and someone is going to pay you $750,000 instead of $400,000 you say hey, extra $350,000, I can probably change my computer, I can change my seat, I can get to know a new set of people. Everybody has a different price, but everybody has a price.

7.3 Encounter

It is in the Encounter phase that first impressions and early actions coalesce; what might be called the initial 'learning the ropes' stage of acculturation. This has several layers. At the surface lies the need to acquire knowledge and skills. This is the zone where most pressure is felt and which most preoccupies new entrants. Some of this is a kind of mental mapping: figuring out who does what, and how day-to-day events unfold. At a slightly deeper level it is also a critical period of forming working and personal relationships; a process that can prefigure much future development and satisfaction. Relationships with managers, known to be one of the most common cause of quitting through dissatisfaction in most organizations (Mobley, 1982), are especially important at this time.

During the encounter phase, traders are beginning to construct their identities as traders and to enter into the trading community. This stage can be characterized by four main processes and events: working with mentors, managing emotions, the experience of making mistakes, and the first tangible losses and gains in trading.

The most critical relationships in this phase are essentially mentoring in character. A typical programme involves traders attending formal classroom sessions, followed by sitting by their more experienced colleagues, talking through decisions, and being challenged to make hypothetical decisions. This apprenticeship process, also referred to in Chapter 4, has been described by Lave and Wenger (1991) as legitimate peripheral participation, which they assert is central to joining any community of practice. Participation in practice is a vital component of learning since, as Wenger (1998: 102) describes:

> Practice is a shared history of learning that requires some catching up for joining. It is not an object to be handed down from one generation to the next. Practice is an ongoing, social, interactional process, and the introduction of newcomers is merely a version of what practice already is. That members interact, do things together, negotiate new meanings is already inherent in practice: that is how practices evolve. In other words, communities of practice reproduce their membership in the same way that they come about in the first place. They share their competence with new generations through a version of the same process by which they develop.

For traders important elements of this participation are the opportunities to gain a shared language and to engage with what we described in Chapter 4 as 'theories of how to work the world'. This is not simply the acquisition of a body of knowledge. Rather it is the beginning of engagement in the construction of practice and the opportunity to build an identity as a trader, which includes a personal style of trading and a repertoire of approaches. To be effective, peripheral participation must provide access to engagement with other members of the community; engagement with their actions and with their repertoire in use.

The managers we interviewed talked about the importance of mentoring, how they would try to match traders with a mentor that seemed to fit their style, and how they would switch traders to different desks to expose them to a range of experiences. One senior equities manager told us:

We move new recruits between mentors who all have different styles. Some of them are more technically orientated, some people are between technical and fundamental, some people have more the gut feel for the market, some people are better short players and these people hate playing things from the long side. Some people are momentum players. This way we can find a trader's individual style.

This participation is, though, necessarily peripheral. Novices do not have the expertise to put money at risk and require a period of observation and learning. This stage of learning is a process of moving from the periphery to the centre of the trader community. In order to make this transition, newcomers need to be granted sufficient legitimacy to be treated as potential members. Granting them a status that allows for peripheral engagement is important since at first they are likely to fall short of what is regarded in the trading community as competent practice. One trader described this process:

First, you watch what other people are doing, follow and react. You don't buy unless somebody else buys. If a customer buys from you, you buy it back straight away because you don't know whether you want to stay short in it and so on. Secondly, you understand what is going on, you can predict the price action, you begin to realise that you predict it right more than you predict it wrong but you haven't yet discovered the appetite of putting money at risk and it is at that stage that some people never progress. And if you don't get me on that point there are a lot of people in our industry that will stay in jobs but frankly, will never make or lose a great deal of money for anybody. It is only the transition into the third phase where you put money at risk that really determines in my mind whether that [learning] curve develops. This can take three months, three years or never happen for some people.

To some extent the new trader can 'borrow' legitimacy from a mentor. Legitimate peripheral participation allows a period in which inevitable mistakes and violations of community standards are opportunities for learning rather than cause for censure, neglect, exclusion, or dismissal (Wenger, 1998: 100). Thus, in this period new traders are engaged in a continual negotiation of their status as they seek to both learn and build trust with the other traders around them. One equities trader described his experience:

> The first time I ever looked after a trading book on my own was after I'd been here about six months and I was sitting very close to someone else who watched pretty much every trade that I did. I think it was another six or eight months after that, when I'd been around for about a year, that the guy that I worked with, who then traded the utilities and oils, went away on holiday for a week.
>
> I think getting complete responsibility for every trade in a stock is a formative experience in your career because it's at that point you realise that you're not peripheral to risk making decisions you are the decision maker. It can come as a shock because when you're sitting with someone you provide information to them and you do small trades and small size but you don't have overall control over the picture and I sometimes think that it might be good for us to get people to make that transition by giving them a small number of stocks, 2 or 3 stocks in a sector to take complete decision making control over but most traders are pretty proprietorial about their sectors and don't want to give away stocks to someone who they don't fully trust. But the whole point is that at some stage someone has to make that leap of faith and it's good that someone goes on holiday and leaves you with it and you then only refer on large positions. I remember in that week I did a trade in one of the stocks that we traded, far bigger than any trade we'd done in the previous 12 months. It involved a considerable amount of risk and although I was liaising with someone else on the desk he was pretty confident that I had it under control and was happy to leave me to make the call. It could have gone horribly wrong. I could have lost a reasonably significant amount of money but as it was it was fine and it forms your decision making process and makes you more confident.

The mentoring model brings three notable challenges. First, mentors themselves might be regarded as 'good' traders. Yet, it is a certainty that mentors, like anyone, are going to have a number of habitual biases and illusions that have become built into their decision-making, which can be unwittingly reinforced among new recruits, unless they have taken steps to be aware of and counteract their biases. As we saw in Chapter 5, the more crude errors and biases are countered by various means such as, technology, self-exhortation, and introspection, but many of the more subtle ones are not. Equally, while the shared norms, models of the world and modes of behaviour of this community of traders reproduce and continue successful practice; they can also reproduce practice that no longer suits the conditions traders face. For example, practice relevant to a long-term bull market may persist at a time of market collapse.

Second, much of an experienced trader's knowledge is tacit, codified at a subconscious level, abstract in nature (Reber, 1989) and varying in its retrievability. Tacit knowledge is, by definition, information that is difficult to codify and communicate. Nor, as we saw in Chapter 4, are traders always willing to transfer such knowledge. This makes information transfer patchy at best.

Third, mentors have no control over the market events that a new recruit will be exposed to. The natural variability of market movements, losses and gains, has significant and enduring effects on trader development. Their reactions to these experiences require careful management, not least through an awareness of the emotional content of these events.

Coping with emotions is an aspect of encounter that is a considerable challenge for many new traders. The range and depth of feelings at this time can seem overwhelming.

My reaction to losing money has changed over time. It is not fun for traders to lose money, but my loss tolerance has got bigger. I remember the first time I lost $10 million about 7 years ago. I was shattered. I couldn't sleep and I felt sick. Now I think it's important to be supportive of a trader when he is losing money.

As we have seen in our discussion of personality, we know that people vary in the extent to which they experience anxiety, tension, and positive emotions, and these variations are as common on the trading floor as most other working environments. The relationship between personality and emotions in trading is best thought of as a set of thresholds. Potentially stressful events or negative experiences will evoke quite different reactions, according to the traders' susceptibilities. A successful strategy for managers is to adapt their supervisory style to the personality of trader. One expressed it to us that some of his traders 'need a kick to get them going' whereas others need constant encouragement or 'to have an arm round their shoulder'.

Once individuals start trading on their own account, without the direct involvement of a mentor, their early experiences of loss and gain are the principal source of strong emotions. For most new traders this is a roller coaster ride for their first few months. The quality of this emotional journey can have a long-lasting effect on their development. For example, one manager talked to us about how he deals with traders who have big successes early on in their career.

> If we do see it [early experiences of success], understanding the trader's personality is important. How they interact with peers. What their life style is. We do watch out for it, but it's rare. The nice thing about this firm is that we have a wonderful way of keeping arrogance in check. We are a very big team, and personalities keep that in check. Managers hear about it from peers if people are too cocky, and they talk to them directly. People come to us, not in a competitive back-stabbing way, but because they care. Most people have been trained from within. Even external hires get mentored in the same way, so when someone goes astray we get to hear about it.

He also talked about his own experiences of negative emotions early in his career.

> I would cite myself as a great example of someone who started trading when I was 18 and got terribly emotional about everything, every loss. I'd lie awake at night and think everything through and try and replay the tape. I wish it had happened a different way. I'd get irascible with sales people and shout. Over time you realise that nothing matters and you not only realise that nothing matters in here, it doesn't matter outside here either. At the end of the day as long as you have your sanity and your health, there is not an awful lot that can touch you and so you get a sense of security from the company that you work for and in life as well. It took me a long time to get that, but my job is to make sure that my younger people get to that point pretty quickly.

Some traders we spoke to talked about jumping with joy and the overwhelming good feeling of a successful trade. Even more graphic were descriptions of despair, black holes, anger, and anxiety.

One study of the physiological emotional responses of traders to losses and gains found that both novice and experienced traders had emotional reactions to financial information that significantly influenced their decision-making, but these reactions were weaker for more experienced traders (Lo and Repin, 2002).

One way in which emotions affect trading and the development of traders is through their influence on memory functioning and decision-making. Memories are often ordered in terms of emotions (Bower, 1981) and emotions provide 'markers' for memories (Damasio, 2000). So positive mood states make the recall of information associated with positive emotions more likely, and negative moods facilitate the recall of negative memories (Fiske and Taylor, 1991). Such is normal human susceptibility to loss that in general the negative experiences tend to be more easily recalled, unless they have passed into the cultivated oblivion of repression.

The effects of recollection are often self-reinforcing, as self-regulation theory maintains (see Chapter 5). Traders making gains may be induced into states of overconfidence, aided by recall of other positive experiences. The opposite negative spiral is less common, since it is effectively disabling, though sometimes this happens, as noted by a trader we interviewed.

You definitely get on a roll, things happen. You make them happen probably, but they seem to happen when you are on that roll. By the reverse, when things are going badly it doesn't matter what you do, things always seem to go wrong.

Managers reported occasionally having to pull traders off the floor to give them a break to rebuild shattered self-esteem. As we suggested in our model of risk taking in the last chapter, experienced emotions can also have an effect on the use of decision rules (Forgas, 1989) and degree of risk that one is willing to take. Negative emotions can lead to risk taking (via loss aversion, as postulated by prospect theory), and positive emotions can lead to risk aversion (Isen, Nygren, and Ashby, 1988).

In addition to emotional reactions to early losses and gains, trading experience at this stage has an important influence on the development of decision-making rules, values, and acceptable behaviour.

We asked traders to rate the perceived importance of major early events. About 25 per cent felt their learning was relatively continuous. About 25 per cent described their learning as punctuated by a small number of highly significant events that had shaped their trading style, and the remainder described a combination of both types of learning: a stop–start pattern of experience. An important theme in the early phase of trader learning is developing understanding of the causal relationships between decision inputs, executing a position, and the subsequent loss or gain.

The mentor's role is to help traders to develop this understanding, via analysis of critical incidents. Although the actual size of a loss or gain is limited by the value that a novice trader is allowed to put at risk, emotional reactions are often stronger than a more experienced trader's response to a loss or gain that is larger in value. Moreover, managers and mentors need to rebuild the confidence of traders who suffer a major loss to preclude inhibition from future decision-making, and to ensure the reasonable risk taking that will develop a trader's resilience. Mostly managers are alert to the dangers of traders being incapacitated by loss and a major emphasis of trader socialization is making traders battle-hardened enough to cope with the experience. This is not true in the opposite case. Little attention is paid to the dangers that may flow from gain-making trades. As one of the bond traders that we spoke to reported 'It is the hardest thing in the world to critically analyse someone when they are making money'. Yet, this is exactly what must occur if illusion of control, overconfidence and an inflated sense of ability are to be kept in check.

The concept of learning from mistakes is firmly established in managerial rhetoric. As we mentioned in Chapter 5, reality often departs from this rhetoric because the emotion associated with errors makes individuals more disposed to find quick and comforting magical beliefs about ways of avoiding their recurrence rather than achieving a more analytical understanding.

During this development phase, traders can make mistakes for several reasons. They might have a poor strategy or apply a good strategy inappropriately to the current situation, or through inexperience not yet have a mental model to guide their actions. If traders can achieve a sufficient level of emotion management, making errors of judgement[1] can have a positive effect on learning. The trader who can exercise some freedom to experiment and make mistakes during learning is more likely to avoid becoming fixated on particular models and heuristics. A trader told us the following story.

> I took an enormous position because I was convinced that something was going to happen as a result of a client trade. I thought that the client was wrong and I decided to keep the trade. I made one of those fundamental errors that traders make from time to time. The position had a big percentage movement very quickly. I thought it was too late to cut the position so I doubled the position, and then it went wrong. It was a short position and I cut it right at the top. It cost a lot of money. Luckily it was at the beginning of the trading year. I felt I was immature and stupid and I should have known better than that.

If the position had made money, the trader might not have given his decision-making a second thought, but in this case the decision was in error. Making mistakes is not just useful but essential, because errors present a challenge to decision-making assumptions and reduce the likelihood of routines becoming automatic (Frese, 1995). Training should provide opportunities to explore both decision processes and the decision context, so that traders can transfer their learning from one situation to another and become more able to deal with novel situations (Heimbeck *et al.*, 2002).

The approach to error management differed within the four organizations that we worked with. There were no clear inter-firm differences, but there was variation between desks in what has been called 'error management style'. This has a significant impact upon people's reaction to errors in the way that errors are dealt with, and errors are reported, if they are reported at all. Successful error management comprises several facets (Grefe, 1994): rapid detection, analysis of causes, and fast resolution. A supportive organizational culture is critical to successful error management. This type of error reporting was exemplified by one senior manager:

> We have firm policy of filling out error memos—saying what they did, who was involved, why it happened, and what are the best ways of improving it. That provides a nice structure for any error at any level of seniority. You make the person repeat and say to you what happened.

Sometimes when you listen the details will not be fine-tuned or incomplete, and then you can explain to them that's why errors happen. You have to treat it not like it's the end of the world but you do have to take it very seriously. The other thing we do, which I initiated about a month ago, is every Monday morning we send an e-mail to the entire department saying how many errors we made the previous week and how much that cost us. Last week we made three errors, two minor. We detect most of them. Managers always have to assume there is always a possibility that someone would want to conceal an error, but our firm has always been very good at being willing to ask people to admit wrongdoing and get it out in the open.

Fostering a positive error climate has been found to be associated with acceptance, communication, and prompt action and recovery after error incidents. Less successful companies tended to focus on checking, control, and blame. Research suggests that the virtuous cycle does not commence with the culture, but with performance. High performing organizations develop a climate in which errors can be discussed and dealt with constructively (Dormann and Frese, 1994).

Probably the greatest challenge is the development of a culture where errors are not seen as a punishable offence, unless they have an ethical dimension. Ethical breaches are unacceptable in trading communities because they have the capacity to threaten the organization economically and reputationally. Edmondson (1996) compared different approaches to error management to explain the differences between effective and unsuccessful teams. She found that the managers of effective and successful teams were accepting and lenient, recognizing that individuals punished themselves to a degree that obviated the need for further discouragement by management. Research shows that nurturing an individual sense of responsibility for errors, combined with a team spirit and acceptance will lead to higher error reporting and learning.

On the trading floor we saw the potential for effective error management, illustrated below.

New traders need a clear understanding [of their role]. So they sit on the desk, learn and repeat what they are hearing. We ask a lot of challenging questions. Most will have come through training with a broad understanding of trading. We challenge them to understand what they are looking at while they still have formal lectures etc. Finally, we let them make mistakes and give them a certain amount of freedom. Traders are wrong a lot and they need to learn that being wrong is OK and the key is to be right more than you are wrong, and to accept that there are variables that you can't always see.

Error management processes that are less likely to lead to openness and learning were also in evidence, as seen from the following two quotes from managers in two different organizations.

Accountability is an important issue. This has been a problem at [this organisation] and people tend to back off until no-one is accountable. There can be undiscovered losses.

I am very strict with the guys that work for me. When they make a mistake I am very hard. They know that 10 minutes later I will be laughing with them, but I can't stand stupid mistakes. If you're wrong, you're wrong. If you're right, you're right. But if you forget something and you lose a small amount then I can't stand it.

7.4 Adjustment

In this third phase of the transition cycle traders have begun to participate in trading as a full member of the community of practice. They have begun to develop their own style and repertoire. The most common aspect of this transition is attenuation of the emotions that had characterized the trader's first months, though the Encounter stage of emotional adjustment can take up to the first 2 years in a job. An equity trader in firm A provided an illustration:

The depth of emotion between making money and losing it, between feeling good and feeling bad is a tenth of what it was 3 or 4 years ago. I never get particularly overwrought because I consider it a longer term situation and think that the blips in between all pretty much even out over the horizon of a career. My main goal is, when we are losing money, not to get emotionally brought down by it. I don't hold myself back from getting excited when I am making money, but even when I am making money, I do not think it changes my whole outlook because then you are fairly comfortable and can carry on working and it is better. I feel emotion the most when I am losing money and I tend to feel it especially on the market-making side.

The process of feeling emotions, yet buffering their impact on daily decision-making can have an additional benefit of understanding and predicting the emotions of others (Humphrey, 2002). This can be a source of comparative advantage in the world of trading. Some traders attribute their skill to market feel: an ability to intuit what others will do and then pre-empt them. A gilts market trader told us:

> The world to me is event driven, so those events are important. But the markets are emotionally driven so there is emotional reaction to those events . . . I am a mathematician and I have always loved maths and done maths, but if I was a mathematics geek I don't think I could trade. I think it's the blending of the quantitative skills with an understanding of how people react. Let's face it: what is the market? It's you and me and a hundred other people sitting around and playing poker through screens. You can't see each other, but that is emotion.

At the adjustment phase there are three important components to the trader's role that require skilful behaviour. First, interpersonal skills are central to the development and maintenance of client relationships. Traders work in a competitive, consolidated industry where customer service is a priority. Second, team working is a key feature of most trading floors and central to skill development, decision-making, and risk management. It is for this reason that, in all our firms, evidence of collaboration and team mindedness had become an explicit component of performance appraisal. Interpersonal skills and teamwork require the development of sophisticated insight into the reactions of others.

This is what is commonly called empathy, the successful attempt to understand others by taking their perspective (Davis, 1996), a fundamental aspect of interpersonal relationships. Empathy is part of what cognitive psychologists call everyday 'mind-reading' (Whiten, 1991), and is considered to be a key part of 'emotional intelligence', a factor which has been suggested to be central to many aspects of work, including leaders' ability to deliver financial performance (Golman, Boyatzis, and McKee, 2001), and a significant influence on individual cognitive-based performance (Lam and Kirby, 2002).

A number of the traders that we spoke to in our research talked about how they use empathy to help them make judgements and to reach decisions. Can one generalize empathic understanding to the reading of market sentiment? The following quote from an equities trader illustrates how he uses his understanding of the market to inform his decision-making:

> My competitive advantage is being able to ascertain what is the reaction of the market. What are they going to do? What is the market going to think about this particular thing, or this particular fact? If you are able to anticipate this and get it right, you are able to make money. The emotional element is a big part of what I do. These are Latin countries so there is a lot of emotional reaction and you have to integrate this. This is why being a Spaniard helps because I can understand how Spanish people think and feel about things and how they will react. It's a combination of rational and emotional reactions. I am a Latin person and more hot-blooded. I get more crazy about things and more depressed about things. I have seen quite a lot, though, and gut feelings are about having seen things. Experience gives you the ability to guess what is going to happen.

The development of market empathy is a goal for some managers, both for themselves and for their traders. Managers talked about how they instructed their traders to think about, and take advantage of, the emotions of others: for example, exploiting the panic behaviour of other players, judging the emotional conditions of the market, and the sentiment surrounding particular stocks.

> What I ask the trader to do is look at each one of those stocks and try to judge the emotional conditions, the sentiment regarding each of those stocks individually, thinking what is the momentum, has it gone too far, is it just starting to turn?

If one assumes that empathy confers an advantage, can it be trained? Researchers agree that it has a strong stable individual differences component to it, and indeed a number of managers talked about the difficulty of developing interpersonal skills and empathy among their traders. Referring to the personality data, although the trading sample tends towards introversion one facet of the Openness dimension of personality tells us that many traders have at least some degree of interest in their own and others' feelings, which may be a good basis for enhancing empathic skills. Experience and maturity also clearly matter here, since our interviews suggest that for many inexperienced traders the emotional 'noise' of their own reactions to markets can crowd out the space required to judge others reactions.

A second important process at the Adjustment stage of traders' development is feedback on the trader's autonomous decision-making. As we have seen, the relationship between decisions and outcomes is noisy and traders need assistance to understand the causal chain. Feedback from managers and mentors is an aid to this kind of analytical insight and, to be effective, it needs to be delivered immediately and directly (Brehmer and Allard, 1991).

7.5 Stabilization

In the stabilization phase the performance curve has flattened. Adjustments at this time are more continuous and organic. The goal here is to reach a dynamic equilibrium whereby continuous adjustments can be made to trading models and practices as new information and feedback become available, as voiced by one bonds trader:

> I think my strategy is a mix of being consistent versus flexible. I think it is just something you develop over a period of time. You have to have an overall strategy for your business. The way we tend to do it, say 50% of our business will be client driven so therefore really we are acting on clients' feedback on whatever they're doing, and 50% of our business is going to be our view. Some of that will be a strategy which is longer term, some of that will be obviously moving on short-term news or whatever but I think you have got to have both strategies. You've got to mix and match them. Clearly if you've got a long-term view and some news comes out you're going to have to change it pretty sharpish so you've got to be aware of everything.

Advanced skill development involves the acquisition of tacit knowledge: a subconscious library of memories, events, patterns, product histories, and people that can be drawn upon rapidly and adapted to be fitted into new situations. Moreover, traders are not simply responding to the demands of their situation. As we have seen in Chapter 4, they are engaged in the development of the practice of trading and theories of how to work the world. In doing so, they are actively shaping their environment, by developing new approaches to decision-making and building relationships with new customers and markets.

Traders learn about the boundaries of the trading community, including a culture that extends beyond the firm. They develop a shared awareness of events in the trading world, via intelligence that traverses companies by means of social and friendship networks. The propensity for inter-firm migration is also an individual difference; some individuals are genetically disposed to be more career mobile than others (McCall *et al.*, 1997). In our sample, 45 per cent had worked for three or more employers in their career. The causes have deep roots in character. There are also major contextual differences. Some firms are much more comprehensive, consistent, and effective in their acculturation of individuals, so that the individual's professional identity becomes thoroughly intertwined with corporate identity. This was true of one of our four firms, where it was reported that individuals rarely if ever 'walked' to take up attractive competing offers, so entrenched did they become in the culture and such were the efforts to place people into suitable roles.

Managing Stabilization—Three Challenges

Although newcomers absorb a disproportionate amount of attention, most management activity is focused upon traders in the Stabilization stage, since these are the most populous. Stabilization is characterized by a flattening performance curve, a platform of knowledge about the social and operational environment, and understanding of local norms, achievement of which, most managers agree, takes around 2 years. In the next chapter we look more closely at the manager's role as a communicator, incentivizer, and controller, but it is worth drawing attention here to three key issues of concern: the trader's management of emotional dissonance, the state of traders' knowledge and practice, and future developments.

Emotions and the Management of Dissonance

In all jobs that involve customer service, a degree of emotional labour is demanded; that is, employees need to conform to particular organizational rules about the emotions that they display, and how they are displayed (Hoschchild, 1979, 1983). It is paradigmatically associated with the work of people such as airline stewards, IT customer services representatives, receptionists and other occupations where there is economic advantage to be secured from making the customer or client feel good.

Trading would not normally be put in the same category. However, many firms do recognize that a client focus is a key to competitiveness, because the way that service is delivered can differentiate between firms who offer equally suitable products. As we started our research it was clear that one of the firms had a much stronger customer focus. However, by the time of our follow up interviews, in 2002, there was much greater convergence with all the firms emphasizing customer service at a time of intense competition for a shrinking pool of client business. An equities trader described the effort involved in emotional self-management.

> Staying emotionally calm all the time is the hardest. It's not so much the making or losing money because that's more clinical. It's the constant staying calm and emotionally neutral when people are shouting, yelling, screaming and asking stupid questions.

The emphasis on a cool head has important implications. Traders face a challenge of emotional management; how is one to control emotional dissonance: the mismatch between what is felt and what must be expressed? Authenticity, being oneself, is highly valued by most people and a source of motivation in terms of a drive to affirm and express our real selves (Erickson and Wharton, 1997). A number of the traders in our study talked about the importance of feeling that they were in the right job and working in a role that they felt gave them some sense of self-worth. For these people, although a large bonus was valued as compensation for the toil and effort that being a trader demands, they also needed to feel that they were doing something of intrinsic worth.

> I would like to make a little bit of money. I would like to stay as a trader and I'm happy at this firm. But I think it's shallow if someone wants to stay on Wall Street all their life. You are not a great contributor to society. I would not like to follow a career path, which I have seen a lot of other people do, which is to be fired, quit in disgust or die. I have seen all three happen in a firm like this. Very rarely have I seen people say I have enjoyed it, thanks, I'm moving on. It's sad that you don't see this.

Inevitably, some situations are more conducive to authentic responses than others. Polite and positive customers are more likely to be met with a genuine positive response from traders than angry, anxious clients (Ashforth and Tomiuk, 2000). The days of throwing phones and smashing screens are past history on most trading floors, and more the stuff of legend than reality. The contemporary trading organization is well aware of the need to engineer conditions that will evoke the 'right' response in the trader (e.g. Leidner, 1993; 1999; Fineman, 1996). To achieve this requires a culture of customer service combined with rewards for teamwork and maintaining relationships. Financial bonuses and reinforcement from managers are structured, in theory, to provide incentives for learning how to behave appropriately. In practice, as we shall see in the next chapter, what managers do and how traders react is not always in accordance with this model.

The people who find it easier to adapt their emotional responses are those who enjoy their role as a trader, are intrinsically motivated, have the ability to see issues from multiple perspectives, and have internalised the culture and values of the organization. The traders who have reached the point of authenticity, who really believe in what they are doing, have an increased sense of personal effectiveness resulting from their skilful self-management and a genuine belief in their actions (Brotheridge and Grandey, 2002), as illustrated by this trader.

I have tried to get a happier balance in my life between work and non-work. This has made me happier as a person. If there is such a thing as trader burnout it's because people work 20 hours a day and they have gone bust. Whereas hopefully, having organised my life so there is a happier balance, I can just keep on doing it. I think if you come into work and you are refreshed, feeling vibrant and looking forward to it, then I think you do a better job overall.

This contrasts with the trader who told us about his concern at feeling he was 'not a great contributor to society'. Authenticity, as we have characterized it, matters more to some traders than others. Many do not pause to consider the degree to which their lives may be out of balance, and for some of these the danger of strain and burnout may come upon them unexpectedly. The stress literature has consistently found people who suppress symptoms to be at greater risk than those who verbalize their distress (Ganster, Fusilier, and Mayes, 1986).

In sum, the chief implication for managers is that they need to create a climate that truly fosters core values, such as customer service, and rewards traders for appropriate learning. It is important for managers to help traders achieve authenticity by seeking roles and strategies that match their skills and aptitudes.

Assessment of Current Practice
Earlier in this chapter we raised the question of whether traders really learn how to be effective traders, or whether they developed biases and strategies that enable them to survive in the trading environment. Management has an important role to play, throughout progress towards stabilized performance, by identifying and taking corrective measures with traders who have become entrenched in their maladaptive patterns of thinking and behaviour. By the time they have reached this stage, traders' ability to smoothly control their conduct makes it more difficult for deeper differences between them in terms of underlying awareness, habits of thought and assumptions to be detected. Managers need to pay close attention to their assessment model if they are to round off a learning curve. In particular, managers' need to de-bias their own ideas, via strategies such as taking multiple perspectives, accepting that their way is not the only way (Bazerman, 2001), and developing insight into the cognitions and emotions of their traders. Some of the managers we spoke to had great insight into these issues and were skilled at assessing the needs of individual traders. For example, the following manager in an equities division talked about how he managed people in situations of loss:

> It's quite easy to get traders' block and with the wrong type of management, that's exactly the effect you produce. If you make someone scared, or nervous or insecure and any element of insecurity creeps into that person, they won't do the right job for you. The markets are fluid and you can generally unwind most things, unless they have gone bust and companies tend not to go bust, especially in the FTSE. People tend to report in pretty quickly. We know where the problems are and sometimes you can see if someone is having a problem, they are sitting there and fretting about it. You go and say, listen, maybe you should think

about this in a different way, let's pull some charts up, or switch off the box, forget about it and talk about football; a diversion of some sort, which tends to happen spontaneously. I start from minute one. If someone has come in and lost £5k in the first 5 minutes, you would have that conversation and say this is not a problem, talk to them straight away, I can help them out. Once they have got over the suspicion, which is there and they might think oh he'll get me to do that 5 times and then he'll fire me, once they realise, they never have problems. I have never come across a position where someone is hiding a loss.

However, managers have vulnerability to cognitive biases themselves, making for clouded assessments of traders' learning. For example, a highly respected, experienced and very well-paid manager of a team of traders, each of whom had large budgets and considerable latitude in their decision-making, talked about his own biases.

I have assimilated a lot of knowledge and I can short cut decision making. I know previous situations, know what can happen and that makes me more confident. The times I have lost money are when I am up [in P&L] a lot. I feel very relaxed and put on trades that I shouldn't. I'm not disciplined in that respect and in retrospect, I tell myself I have to be disciplined even when I am up several thousand. Sometimes because I need some excitement I do something sub-optimal. When I lose money, I have full concentration, I go home and think about that issue, or when I think of a trade idea, I completely focus on it. But only when I think it is an exciting idea. When I am doing well I am too relaxed. When I am doing badly, I focus. I try to be aware of this and if it happens to me, it probably happens to others as well. I want to make sure others are focused.

Despite this manager's worrying confession one can be reassured to a degree by his insight. Perhaps this enables him to have a greater awareness of the likelihood that the same habits might be forming in new traders, but the risk remains that his own biases could also make the detection of biases in other traders difficult. This manager reported how important he felt it was for traders to be able to explain their positions, yet the traders in his team did not bear this out. Several declared that his style of management was very non-interventionist and that there were only a few occasions when a managerial point of view had been imposed upon them, for example, when facing a significant risk or loss, or where a decision could contravene the regulators' rules.

This analysis defines two challenges for managers. The first is to identify, and to work to correct the biases we reviewed in Chapters 5 and 6. The second challenge is to take a broader perspective on the direction of a trader's future development.

Future Development
Once traders have reached the phase of stabilization some are beginning to think about how to take their careers a step forward, while others are settling in to their routines and rituals without much thought for the future, for as we have found, motivations for development vary widely. We asked traders about their career path, and found responses that could be categorized into four themes.

First are the traders who have become deeply involved in their role and their organizational culture. This group is particularly prevalent in organizations with strong cultures that direct much conscious effort towards the enculturation of new recruits. Traders working within this group reported that they would not thrive in a different culture. Some of these traders expressed satisfaction with their current role, but gave little thought to their career development. This implies that conscious assessment and intervention by management would be needed to help move this group on further in their career development. A second group, like the first group, were satisfied with their role, but gave more thought to the future development of their role performance and responsibilities. Typically, this group is thinking about how to attain increased scope and authority, through skill development or by taking on an expert role, with specialist responsibility within or for a section. A subset of this group was interested in conventional career-ladder progression with ambitions to reach the top positions within their firms, like the trader who reported that he 'would not stop until he got to the top'. This group of traders can be thought of as implicitly at the preparation/anticipation stage of a new transition cycle—one that involves an intra-organizational shift to a new role, e.g. the transition to a managerial role. It is in the nature of managerial and professional job change, and human psychology, that people are generally poor at predicting upcoming change opportunities, which makes it difficult to prepare for specific change (Nicholson,

West, and Cawsey, 1985). Moreover, the trading environment is problematic for many other reasons when it comes to identifying and developing traders who might become managers, as we shall see in Chapter 8. For this group, the focus needs to be upon developing and supporting managerial skills.

A third group comprises those traders who want to leave their jobs when they have made enough money, with the aim of pursuing some personally rewarding activity that they would find less stressful than trading. One can interpret this as a kind of reverie, induced by the ambient pressure of their existence, though some do have specific ambitions grounded in reality. Examples included an equities trader who had already taken the first steps to fulfilling his dream by setting up a special effects company, to which he intended to move full time. But in the main this group of traders were much vaguer in their aspirations: unspecified dreams of a quiet life in which they could enjoy their accumulated wealth.

A fourth group was those traders who had started out enjoying their job, and then become dissatisfied with the demands of the role, yet found the job had locked them in with golden handcuffs. They were unable to leave the trading environment because they found themselves committed to a lifestyle that would be unsupportable through any other line of work.

The implications of these variations are that career ambitions have an impact on work orientation during the stabilization phase. The long-term ambitions of traders may colour their decision-making and risk taking. For example, a trader with short-term money-making ambitions might be more willing to take risks than one with ambitions to climb the managerial ladder, and the unambitious lack the drive to seek opportunities or develop new approaches to decision-making.

The data about the career management of traders raise several implications. Our four firms, highly effective in day-to-day job control and market management, did not incorporate consistent clear processes of career development review. This is surprising for such world-leading organizations and suggests that this deficiency might be commonplace in trading firms. One can recommend that management takes an active role in helping ensure that traders' expectations about their progression within the organization are realistic. Second, the goals of individual traders have an impact on their decision-making. The committed trader who seeks vertical progression through the hierarchy is likely to attend more to trading protocol, to develop long-term relationships within and outside of the organization, and to place greater emphasis on learning and development than their less path-directed colleague.

In addition to the qualitative data, we measured the number of each individual's past employers and their expectation of future career changes (Figs 7.1 and 7.2). We found no significant relationships with age or personality factors, but there were differences between the organizations.

Firms B and D stand out as having the most stable trader population, with significantly fewer past employers than firm C and traders in firm D significantly less likely to anticipate a career change in the next 5 years than traders in B and C. Given the difference in emphasis between organizations, it seems possible that strong organizational cultures, particularly those that emphasize individual learning and development

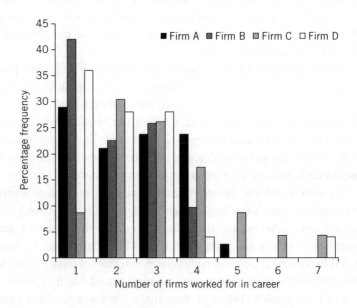

Fig. 7.1 Career mobility to date

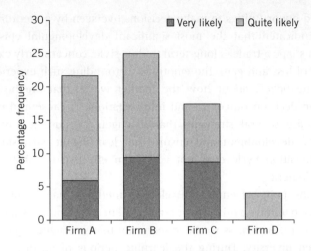

Fig. 7.2 Likelihood of a career change in the next 5 years

and appropriate person–job fit, are successful in reducing the movement of traders between firms.

7.6 Achieving the Metamorphosis from Novice to Expert

To become an experienced, skilful trader requires a sophisticated understanding of a complex, uncertain world. New traders need to combine focused, explicit skill acquisition with the development of numerous, often subconscious, heuristics concerning decision-making, self-management, and how to match behaviour and values with organizational culture.

In this chapter we have discussed five significant stages of a trader's development: the initial selection process, and the four stages of the transition cycle (anticipation, encounter, adjustment, and stabilization). Each stage of the transition cycle requires traders to face different challenges that engage distinctive psychological processes, and each holds a range of implications for managers.

Typically, traders start in the classroom and then work within an apprenticeship framework; learning to trade is via observation and limited opportunities to make decisions overseen by a mentor. Our data indicated that the most significant developmental episodes, which shape a trader's long-term trading style, concern early experiences of loss and gain, the emotions surrounding such experiences and the beliefs about how the market works that are built up around decision outcomes and interpretations of cause and effect. There are several strategies that managers can use to optimize traders' development and ensure that learning at each stage of the transition cycle does not veer from effective to maladaptive development.

At the point of entry, the selection methods that we observed tended to involve a mix of formal assessment and informal, subjective judgement, which, as we have seen, can be the unwitting cause of reduced diversity. During the learning periods of encounter and adjustment, we observed some good practice in de-biasing decision-making by means of asking traders to explain their decisions, but this can only be as effective as the people who are judging the explanation. It follows that it would be beneficial to involve people with varied experiences and perspectives through this learning period. Managers admit the importance of diversity, though there is some way to go in achieving it at both the levels of psychological as well as social profiles. A wider selection pool, thorough analysis of job requirements and a more standardized selection procedure are strategies that could be employed.

Maximizing trader performance was also an underdeveloped managerial activity. The traders and managers that we spoke to were almost all clear that superior performers had 'special' qualities, and yet no one was able to articulate clearly the precise set of skills and attributes implicated. There seem to be few resources directed towards identifying what makes a top trader, despite intense speculation on the subject, the large costs of recruiting a new trader and giving them several years to see how potential develops into skill. We discuss this issue in more detail in the next chapter.

The main implication for managers is the need to understand where individuals are in terms of their development, and to ensure that interventions are not simply based on a trader's level of experience. The interaction between the nature of experience and individual skills, personality, motivations, and reactions to experiences should be significant considerations in managerial strategy.

Note

1. 'Error' is often used on the trading floor to mean a factual error such as hearing '15' for '50', or incorrectly recording a trade. We are using the term in a broader sense to include errors of strategy and decision-making.

Chapter 8

MANAGING TRADERS

Two particular aspects of the behaviour of traders in financial markets have often attracted attention. First, regulatory authorities are concerned that reliance on high bonus payments is depressing profits in the investment-banking sector and may expose firms employing traders to high levels of operational risk. This has, in the past, supported a proposal to raise the capital adequacy requirements of those firms that rely primarily on contingent pay. Second, periodic publicity surrounding the concealment of losses by traders, which has led to the failure of at least one major bank, has resulted in regulatory intervention as well as public concern about malfeasance. The picture of trading implied by this publicity is one of incentive driven gambling; risk seeking motivated primarily by pursuit of personal gain within the context of fairly loose managerial controls.

In some ways, this is surprising. As we have shown, while individuals vary in their risk appetites, traders are not especially risk seeking and the trading context is closely monitored. Moreover, supervisory controls are strict. In the United Kingdom, the Financial Services Authority (FSA) is moving towards a rigorous risk-based approach to supervision which, in addition to assessing capital, liabilities, earnings, and market risk, seeks to evaluate controls and management structures within firms (FSA, 2003; Bank of England, 1997*a*, *b*[1]). Theory, policy, and public image are not aligned.

In this chapter, we seek to further understand this apparent paradox by looking directly at how traders are managed. There is a regulatory concern, specifically to 'consider management's appetite for risk and its attitudes towards controls' as part of a wider risk-based approach to the assessment of firm behaviour (Bank of England, 1997*a*,*b*: 36). The FSA has made clear its intention to incorporate requirements on the measurement and management of operational risk into its supervisory framework (FSA, 2003). Management failures of various forms were identified as significant factors in several well-publicized cases of malfeasance at Barings, Morgan Grenfell, Daiwa, and Sumitomo. In the case of Barings, the failure of managers to analyse 'large (reported) profits from activities perceived to be essentially risk free . . . was a serious failure' according to the supervisory body (Bank of England, 1997*b*). However, to date there has been little empirical research on how traders are managed and the extent to which managerial behaviour either fits academic models or complies with regulatory concerns.

This chapter examines the management of traders; it focuses on the risk implications of the manager–trader relationship. Section 8.1 looks at relevant theory. Section 8.2 presents the data. Section 8.3 assesses implications; our central argument is that the main concern of managers of traders in investment banks is with mitigating the effects of loss aversion rather than the pursuit of profits. We seek to outline the circumstances that drive this concern and assess broader implications.

8.1 Relevant Theory: Economic and Psychological Approaches

Expected utility theory predicts risk aversion. However, the argument applies most directly to individual decision-makers in the market. By contrast, in most cases, traders are employees of firms and act as agents for principals. They may trade the assets of the firm (proprietary trading) or of the firm's customers, but in both cases, agency theory may be applied. Agency theory also assumes consistent risk aversion on the part of agents acting for principals who manifest risk neutrality. The basis for this assumption lies in the sunk costs agents carry with respect to employment in the firm. Risk aversion is manifest in decisions made by agents primarily concerned with protecting personal wealth. Principals, who are assumed to be risk neutral since they can diversify their share holding across firms, must either incur opportunity costs in monitoring agents or set up incentives which align agents' risk orientations with their own (Jensen and Meckling, 1976; Tosi and Gomez-Meija, 1989; Beatty and Zajac, 1994; for a general review, Eisenhardt, 1989). Risk aversion by traders is thus predicted by both expected utility and agency theories.

Agency and psychological approaches to risk differ in that the former sees risk preferences as emerging from incentive and monitoring effects, whereas the latter sees preferences as emerging from a combination of decision context, as in prospect theory, and the individual propensities we have discussed in Chapters 5 and 6. In the former approach, risk aversion results from the absence of effective monitoring (Jensen and Meckling, 1976). In the latter approach, the crucial issue is the avoidance of loss rather than monitoring effects or outcome uncertainty. Whereas conventional finance theory has used principal agent theory, behavioural finance draws on the study of decision biases, particularly framing effects, to examine aggregate irrationality in the market.

We argue here that the empirical application of a model to trading which integrates both approaches may advance the debate over the management of irrationality in financial markets. Such an integration has been attempted by Wiseman and Gomez-Meija (1998: see also Wiseman and Catanach, 1997). Their contingency model allows for differential governance and framing effects. Agents may exhibit both risk-seeking and risk-averse behaviour in different contexts and their preferences are influenced by both monitoring intensity and incentive structures.

Wiseman and Gomez-Meija (1998) argue that agency theory is too restrictive in making the assumption of consistent agent risk aversion. Prospect theory posits framing effects; agents are prone to risk aversion in the domain of gains and risk-seeking loss-aversion in the domain of losses. Wiseman and Gomez-Meija argue that the framing of problems by agents is influenced by the nature of the surrounding monitoring and incentive regimes, together with performance history, which sets the reference point for the framing effect.

Three elements of their model are important here. The first is the idea of risk bearing, defined in terms of the agent's perception of risk to his or her own wealth, particularly that resulting from employment loss (1998: 136). Risk bearing is the extent to which the agent, not the principal, carries the risk of the agent's actions (1998: 138). It mediates the link between problem framing and risk taking. Positively framed problems increase perceived risk bearing (because there is something to lose) and this in turn encourages risk aversion. Negatively framed problems decrease perceived risk bearing and encourage risk seeking; 'there is nothing to lose but loss itself' (Wiseman and Gomez-Meija, 1998: 134; see also Sitkin and Pablo, 1992). For example, a trader expecting a good performance (and thus bonus) outcome will be reluctant to put those anticipated gains at risk whereas a trader anticipating a poor outcome will be more willing to take risks to avoid that negative outcome.

Second, as we have noted, the reference point defining framing effects may not be zero. This may arise because performance history affects trader aspirations. A history of strong performance may raise aspirations reducing the probability of performance outcomes being framed as gain. A trader who has achieved high levels of bonus and perhaps committed to expenditure such as a large mortgage on that basis may experience a modest bonus as in the domain of loss. On the other hand, performance targets can also affect aspirations. If targets exceed performance predictions, again this can cause anticipated outcomes to be framed as a loss. Both effects are predicted to induce risk taking by agents (Wiseman and Gomez-Meija, 1998: 137, 142).

The third element concerns the balance between monitoring and incentives. Wiseman and Gomez-Meija propose that strong supervision will lead to higher performance targets and that supervision will focus on agent behaviour rather than performance outcomes, which are contractually more efficiently specified in advance. They also propose that the use of behavioural evaluation criteria, particularly retrospectively, will increase risk bearing and thus induce risk aversion (1998: 144–145) since behavioural criteria are often idiosyncratic to the monitor and not specified in advance. Use of accounting performance criteria (P&L), by contrast, decreases risk bearing and may thus increase the probability of risk seeking.

The approach implies that risk aversion in the domain of gains will be caused by relatively weak supervision, low performance targets, high risk bearing, and behaviourally based, rather than performance-based, evaluation. Risk seeking in the domain of losses will result from weak supervision, performance targets exceeding predictions (particularly where past performance has been high), low risk bearing, and evaluation by accounting performance. This is consistent with the brief picture of the industry painted at the outset of this chapter: high bonuses eating away at profits combined with occasional malfeasance based on the concealment of high risk behaviour in loss situations. However, it remains unclear whether it is an accurate picture of trading conditions; we turn to this in the following sections.

We are concerned here with the role of managers. The managerial role may be examined in terms of the monitoring of inputs, processes, and outcomes (Mintzberg, 1983); it is a mix of the agency functions of monitoring and providing incentives. Managers may not recruit to the firm but, typically, they induct and socialize new recruits to their group or desk. For existing staff, input monitoring may consist of discussing traders' positions and examining the logic that sustains their trading behaviour. In at least one case covered by the data, managers had dismissed traders not because they made losses but because they could not explain their positions adequately. Monitoring the process itself, that is directly supervising trades, is difficult for three reasons: first, because of the sheer complexity of trades; second, because of the existence of wide spans of control; third, managers spend time trading as well as managing. Measuring performance outcomes may be formulaic; dependent purely on the individual trader's profit and loss account, perhaps modified by some more general form of retrospective and subjective behavioural evaluation.

8.2   Managers and Traders

In this section, we first present data from managers in our sample and assess the implications. Second, we examine management controls, management style, and their consequences. Third, we look at the experience of gains and losses. Fourth, we examine the influence of bonus targets and the nature of bonus calculation. Throughout, we are concerned with the impact of managers on risk taking in gain and loss domains. Our argument is, first, that managers focus attention primarily on the domain of losses (monitoring prevails) and that bonus attainment is a crucial influence on risk propensity in the domain of gains (incentives prevail). Managers attempt to eliminate loss aversion but tolerate risk aversion.

Managers

Managers of traders within the sample are generally ex-traders. This was explained by respondents in terms of the need to comprehend the markets technically and the need to empathize with the stress and complexity of the traders' role. This presents a familiar dilemma; highly expert traders are needed in managerial roles but there are at least two sets of issues involved. The first concerns the opportunity costs involved in the promotion of good traders into managers. The following quotes illustrate.

> Sometimes the worst thing that you can do is take someone who is a brilliant producer and because he is a brilliant producer assume that he can mentor, communicate and develop other people to have a similar skill set and the answer to that is that a lot of people can't make that adjustment . . . We have people who are great producers—great producers who would not be great managers, and who we can pay higher than managers. (manager)

> Traders are often terrible managers of people and businesses. You just cannot take your top producers and make them managers. (manager)

> We are very poor at managing in this company . . . we generally take the best traders and the best salespeople and we make them managers. We don't give them any training . . . non-production managers are looked upon as being a cost to the organisation which is poor because we need more people who understand business than know just how to trade. (trader)

> Ninety-five percent of the time, managers are traders who have been in the business a long time and they had no real management skills. Some make good managers, some make bad managers . . . I think the majority

of them are very bad managers because they've never been in the situation before. (trader)

Demographic data are relevant here. There was wide earnings variation within the sample, from under £100,000 per annum to well over £500,000.[2] Over half of the sample earned over £300,000 per annum. Educational levels, tenure, and trading experience are all positively associated with total earnings. Based on unstandardized regression coefficients, an increase of one educational level (e.g. from bachelors' to masters' degree) was associated with an increase in pay of £88,000 p.a. An increase in tenure of one year is associated with a pay increase of £29,000 p.a. An increase in experience of one year is associated with an increase of £19,000 p.a. However, there is no significant relationship between pay and job level; managers did not earn more than traders and, in some individual cases, they earned substantially less (cf. Abolafia, 1996: 33). This may indicate that a move into a managerial position is associated with a loss of earning power, perhaps related to lower levels of trading activity by managers. Alternately, it may be that those who became managers were not previously among the higher earning traders.

In practice, most managers sought to continue trading both for credibility and by preference, but some noted the severe problems in doing so. Here are two examples:

I cannot run a book; management is becoming more and more a full time job . . . I don't think it is very good that I am seen as competing with my own traders because either I would do better than them because of what I know, or I would do worse and this would undermine my authority. (manager)

Running a position as a manager is difficult because you have to be totally dedicated to it if you want it to work. (manager)

This tension was noted by both traders and managers; both in terms of the difficulty of being a good manager while trading and in terms of the opportunity costs of management activity. Many comments from traders relate to the role of managers as trader–mentors. For example

I think when it's busy and there's a lot of management issues for them to cover it can be a conflict with them being away from the market but I think they're both very interested in trading and make the effort to do as much trading as possible and keep management issues to out of hours. (trader)

In practice, there was variance in the volume of managerial trading. In one firm, the Head of Arbitrage thought that around 75 per cent of his time was spent trading. The Head of Bonds did not trade at all. He reasoned as follows;

> I chose not to so I could manage the department. I don't think I would be a very good trader because I would be distracted by other responsibilities. Managing traders is very different from trading . . . when you are a trader your job is quite well defined, you try to make money over a period of time . . . as a trader manager you tell people what risks you want them to have or not to have but you just do not know enough about the markets to intervene. (manager)

This is the source of the second set of opportunity costs. If there are fee-earning opportunity costs involved in promoting traders to manager, there are additional agency and monitoring costs in allowing managers to continue trading. Role conflict may reduce managers' ability to assess and control what other traders are doing. In practice, the granting of autonomy to traders is both inevitable and considerable.

Trader Autonomy

In the firms we studied, we found there to be a strong ethos of autonomy and responsibility, shared by managers and traders alike. Traders wanted autonomy and managers wanted them to exercise it responsibly. In general, the balance was felt by both sides to be about right, with strong emphasis put on the quality of communication. One trader noted;

> Each product is run by product leaders and they're responsible for that business and beyond that there's no micro management that goes on by anyone other than the heads of desks and that's a good thing as far as I'm concerned. There's a healthy involvement with issues that go on day to day and the business as it is being developed but no micro-management. (trader)

Managers tended to hold similar views:

> I consider I have a veto on any positions my traders take, even when they are within their limits . . . but, to give you an idea, I think last year I used it once, the year before twice and this year, not at all. (manager)

Managing Traders

Phrases used by traders about managers included 'laid back', 'non-interventionist', 'individualistic', 'loose'. Managers were often seen as 'very good, very relaxed, they have some pretty talented people and they let them get on with it'; 'managers provide an environment in which I am able to perform'. However, on occasion, management support was seen as important 'you need the confidence that management has bought into an idea'. The organizations were perceived, by many, as flat and non-hierarchical in the main 'it is collegiate, people don't pull rank'. One respondent thought he worked in a 'think tank atmosphere'. In general, there appeared to be a feeling that reporting relationships were often beneficially submerged within more collaborative, problem-solving team relationships. One senior manager described himself as having the 'casting vote' on his team. One trader noted; 'my manager works for me'. In a similar vein

> The managers give you complete freedom to do what you want as long as you do it in the [company] way. If you don't fit into the equation they'll be down on you like a ton of bricks. (trader)

> I have a direct boss who is theoretically my boss, but he does not get involved in anything at all.

> (Interviewer; 'Do you think that is a good thing?') 'Personally, I don't care, as long as he leaves me alone . . . ' (trader)

Several managers indicated the importance of trust. Specifically, it was generally not possible to have close knowledge of the positions all traders were taking, but only to communicate well with them and have faith in their competence. Managers might test out understanding or openness by asking questions about positions and their rationale within risk limits, but:

> There are accidents when things go wrong . . . Honesty and integrity are vital—if I do not have confidence in any of them, they would not be doing what they are doing, it's as simple as that . . . I would be sitting next to them, I would be watching what they do. And in fact out of one ear I listen to what they are doing the whole time and I make it my business to make them talk to me. I do not expect any one to come to me at the end of the day and say 'I've lost $100,000 today'—I expect them to come to me in the middle of the day and say 'I've got this position'. (manager)

As one manager put it 'non-intervention is the most productive style'. However, some traders described this style as 'a free market for individuals', and as 'Darwinian'. The amount of latitude given caused anxiety for some traders;

> Well I'm pretty pleased but I would say that to some extent we're not very managed in the sense that, at least in the day to day work, you're more pooling information than being managed in the traditional sense. You have a series of problems that you have to solve and you would go to a number of places for resources and the manager or somebody who has been here for a longer period and has a longer list of contacts may be able to help with that, but we're basically given a lot of latitude. (trader)

> There is sufficient autonomy and responsibility given to you and again it depends on the sort of person you are. I suppose your manager is there, very accessible and very approachable. (trader)

The implicit model of effective trader management is of a mentoring or coaching relationship within broadly specified and agreed risk limits.

> Management . . . is the setting of broad goals, such as risk limits, broad philosophy of the trade you want to do, setting up a mandate . . . the role of the desk manager is to set an agenda. (trader)

> You are left to your own devices . . . the overall desk has a limit and if that is exceeded the positions have to be hedged, so it is managed. (trader)

In practice, this autonomy is conditional on avoiding significant losses: management style, hands-off in general, tends to become interventionist in the domain of losses.

Controlling Loss Aversion

If upside risk is lightly managed, downside risk is actively controlled. Consider the following:

> I have two rules for people, don't lose more money than you want to and don't lose more money than your boss wants to and keep those two and you will sort of be fine. So I don't think we do lose more money than we want to and I don't think we take too much risk because it is my job to make sure that we don't. The flip side of the coin is this . . . I don't

think we take enough risk . . . invariably they find good ideas and you say it is a very good idea but the position could be ten times larger. (manager)

There is intervention when something is going very, very wrong or once a year at your review. (trader)

My veto works only one way—to reduce risk. (manager)

As long as I am making money, he [the manager] won't put controls on me. (trader)

Both managers and the managed felt that active management of downside risk was at the expense of managing the upside, and that this was rooted in the belief in the importance of trader autonomy.

The biggest thing [that we try to manage] is an ability, willingness and discipline to cut your losses. (manager)

My role as a manager is to cover the downside rather than the upside. I try to enforce the discipline of cutting losses rather than pushing them to add to positions. (manager)

We are not very good at getting traders to bring the best out of themselves. We should walk around and help them to gear up their abilities, for example telling them to look at a scenario and come back with an answer. Managers should be trying to maximise returns continuously. I don't think we do that at all well. (manager)

Most people have a tendency to cut their profits and let their losses run. (manager)

Traders knew their risk limits and, provided they made money within them, they had freedom. One expression was that you 'only get managed if you get out of line'. Management processes are only there to deal with exceptions and difficulties

Hands on when there is a complicated problem, hands off when it is not—if it is not broken, why fix it? (trader)

Some recognized asymmetries here;

If you make money you think 'oh well I just got it right'. If you make losses then you do actually sit there and analyse that and think—'how did I go wrong here?' When it comes down to it I reckon that 67% of this job where you make money is pure luck not skill. It's playing the numbers. (trader)

When losses were incurred, there tended to be a rapid shift in management style. As one manager put it:

As a trading manager, and this is the toughest thing, as a trading manager, when things are going well, they are used to being just left alone to run their business, especially if you have OK traders that you want to have on the desk, you just let them get on with the job as long as they don't blow up. So to switch from this mode to being very dictatorial and say—this is emergency time, we are losing money, I should make the decisions—this is a difficult switch and I think I have failed on this. (manager)

However, both traders and their managers acknowledge the importance of managerial interventions when losses were mounting.

Management do influence how people are feeling when they are doing badly. The way my boss treated me when I was losing money is the reason why I am happy taking risks now. (trader)

You can always tell if you are looking at a good or bad trader when the position is losing money . . . it's a question of vision, discipline, courage and understanding the environment . . . When the position is making money, it's much more difficult to see. (manager)

As we noted in Chapter 7, many described a learning process in which the first experience of incurring losses had been traumatic and the intervention of a manager who had seen similar circumstances was vital in re-establishing confidence.

Unless you've been in a black hole yourself, you can't explain it to anyone; you see someone just staring at the screen and they can't get out. When you have a position like that, you just look at it. You need someone to come along and say 'OUT'. So traders have to be approachable; there's a lot of repetition in this market. (manager)

There was a role for managers, accepted by both managers and traders to facilitate trader learning to improve risk performance in the longer term. However, consistent with our discussion of monitoring, where this coaching role was apparent, it was activated around experiences of loss not gain.

Managing Traders

Bonuses

Details of incentives differed between the four firms, but the following features were common. First, contingent pay was a very high proportion of total pay. Second, although there were acknowledged 'desk (i.e. market) effects', contingent pay was based on individual performance. Third, the precise performance bases used by managers for evaluation were kept deliberately unclear to preserve managerial discretion; market and internal behavioural criteria were mixed. Fourth, managers retained discretion over contingent pay, and bonuses were not known until announcement at year end.

The compensation year seemed to have an effect on risk behaviour in all firms, but the direction of the effect differed between individuals. For example

> I have two or three big plays a year and if these make money, I just shut up shop. (trader)[3]

> November is a notoriously bad month for the firm. It is a less profitable month, particularly from a trading point of view because who is going to go out there guns blazing when you think you have made a safe profit for the year. (manager)

> During the last month [of the compensation year] because everything has been set—and you can screw up—you become risk averse. (trader)

These are statements about risk aversion for the protection of personal wealth. However, there were other traders who would *seek* risk under these circumstances:

> Risk tolerance becomes infinite at the end of the year because we don't have any personal exposure to our result in the last couple of months, we can almost become less discriminating in the trades we put on. (trader)

> I think there is a certain comfort factor from having made money—your willingness to lose it is probably slightly higher. (trader)

In all four firms, according to their own accounts, managers did not monitor such individual differences closely. Risk aversion to protect gains and risk seeking on the basis of gains are implicitly treated as individual responses to meeting performance targets, not standardized by managerial intervention.

In summary then, the role managers play in active monitoring and intervention is reduced by role conflict in their joint roles as traders and managers. Traders achieve and welcome substantial autonomy within broad limits. Managers become interventionist in the domain of losses; in the domain of gains, autonomy prevails and there is no active management of the upside risk. There is limited awareness of the implications of this and little action to counter it. We explore the implications of these tendencies in the next section.

8.4 Modelling Utility?

We have described the nature and potential impact of one form of agent monitoring in financial markets; the role of trader management. We have done so both for policy-based reasons, managerial failures have been identified as contributing to serious examples of malfeasance, and for theoretical reasons, models of influences on decision-making under risk in this context theorize managerial influence in a very restrictive way. Our focus solely on trader management gives this argument two limitations which are sufficiently serious to bear restating. First, managers are only one source of agent control in this context. Other forms of control within the firms or the markets, for example, computer-based restrictions or those enforced by compliance functions, may mitigate some of the effects we have discussed. Second, the seriousness of the effects we have identified depends on the underlying pattern of trader behaviour. If traders are perfectly rational then the role of managerial behaviour may be marginal.

We have not examined trading behaviour directly.[4] However, we are relatively confident, given the analysis in earlier chapters, that there is non-trivial incidence of irrationality[5] in trader behaviour. The industry spends a considerable amount of money trying to control it and occasional public lapses reveal that it has not been eradicated.

How generalizable are the findings? We interviewed in London, and there was considerable folklore among respondents about different trading and managerial styles in other markets.[6] There is also other evidence that trading styles and behaviour vary between markets as a function of their institutional structure (Abolafia, 1996). There may also be differences over time. Data were collected principally in 1998 after a long bull market run. The advent of a bear market may subsequently have changed trader behaviour and management styles.

191

Managing Traders

Follow up interviews we conducted in 2002 suggest that one way in which London based investment banks have reacted to the fall in business brought about by stock market collapse has been to place greater emphasis on client relationships. There may be cohort differences: several managers in 1998 expressed concern that very few traders working with them had experienced a major market crash, such as that of 1987. There is evidence from traders in Abolafia's work (1996: 138) and more concretely in option prices in some markets (Mackenzie and Millo, 2001) to show that 1987 had a long-term impact on those who experienced it; specifically, both imply that those who went through it subsequently tended to overestimate the probability of extreme events. Finally, we excluded certain types of trading and markets from our sample. We have not covered sole traders, or commodity or foreign exchange markets,[7] or open outcry markets. In all these respects, the ability to generalize from these results may be compromised. We proceed with these reservations in mind.

Prospect theory suggests that traders would be risk averse in the domain of gains and loss averse in the domain of losses. The 'ideal' trader bias, enshrined in the trading maxim, 'run your profits and cut your losses' implies risk neutrality in the domain of gains and risk aversion in the domain of losses. These are almost opposites. If traders are to maximize profits and control losses, they must behave counter to the predictions of prospect theory. Incidentally, they must also act in the domain of gains counter to the predictions of both expected utility theory and of agency theory.

We found little to encourage the 'ideal' trader bias. Managers become most closely involved with traders when they are losing money. This monitoring effect does not seem to enhance risk bearing; it is perceived by both traders and managers to involve help, enhancing learning, rather than discipline. However, trader managers have only limited time available for monitoring. If loss-averse traders can evade such monitoring, there is the potential for a debacle, such as Barings, resulting in the failure of a bank and revisions to the regulatory framework.

When traders are making money the incentive effect may dominate.[8] However, both risk seeking and risk aversion may exist and individual differences in risk propensity become important. Traders' reference points dividing perceived gains from losses may be highly idiosyncratic, depending on past performance, the difficulty of the performance target, beliefs about the bonus system, and peer pressure. Managers in the four sample firms were not excluded from influence over bonuses, which included judgements after the event about trader behaviour in addition to the individual profit and loss account. However, across the course of the trading year, there is considerable trader autonomy.

We have not tested behavioural agency theory here, but it is useful to summarize our empirical findings in terms of it. Table 8.1 lists the controls which mediate or influence the predictions of prospect theory. It is drawn from Wiseman and Gomez-Meija (1998). When traders are making money (domain of gains) they are given considerable autonomy, judged mainly on how they describe their positions, they carry the risk of not making bonus, which is a substantial amount of total pay, and, in the market environments we studied, have a very good chance of hitting performance targets. This combination is likely to generate risk-averse behaviour. On the other hand, when they are losing money (domain of losses), the combination of factors is likely to generate loss aversion. Again, they are in practice loosely supervised; managers are concerned with loss but their spans of control are wide. Monitoring activity focuses on P&L. Since losses accrue to the bank

Table 8.1 Controls and incentives associated with framing effects—empirical findings

Control/Incentive	Effect Domain	
	Risk aversion (gains)	Loss aversion (losses)
Supervision	weak/loose	weak/loose
Evaluation	Behaviourally based	Accounting based
Risk bearing	High	Low
Performance target	Low	High

Source: Wiseman and Gomez-Meija (1998).
Adapted from Table 1 in Willman, P., Fenton-O'Creevy, M. P., Soane, E. and Nicholson, N. (2002) 'Traders, managers and loss aversion in investment banking: a field study', *Accounting, Organizations and Society*, 27(1/2): 85–98.

not the trader, risk bearing is low, but as the bonus target recedes, riskier bets may seem more attractive.

Recall that framing effects in prospect theory are the reverse of the 'ideal' trader bias. Two of the contingencies, risk bearing and performance targets, are highly influenced by individual differences, as described below. The former may depend on career history and wealth accumulation, the latter on the trader's own reference points. Loose supervision and a mixture of behavioural and accounting-based evaluation are present in all four firms. In short, framing, risk bearing and situational factors all militate against developing the 'ideal' trader bias.

Figure 8.1 introduces the reported effects of monitoring and incentives into the framing picture of prospect theory discussed in Chapter 2. Again, it does not consider the complicating effects of individual differences. First, consider the domain of gains. Between O and A, reference point and the bonus target—risk neutrality prevails on the part of the trader. Incentive effects align the interests of principal and agent. In the domain of losses, OB, the figure depicts a managerial

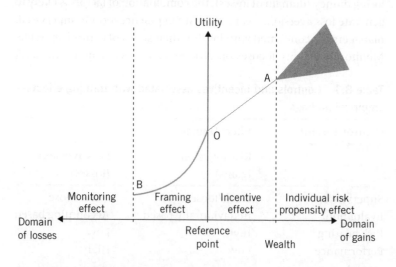

Fig. 8.1 Introducing incentive and monitoring effects to prospect theory description of risk behaviour

Source: Adapted from Figure 2 in Willman, P., Fenton-O'Creevy, M. P., Soane, E. and Nicholson, N. (2002) 'Traders, managers and loss aversion in investment banking: a field study', *Accounting, Organizations and Society*, 27(1/2): 85–98.

intervention point intercepting a loss aversion curve; the intervention reasserts risk neutrality, cutting the position.

Above A and, if intervention does not occur or fails, below B, families of curves may exist, reflecting the range of individual differences in the risk preferences of unmonitored agents. We argue that this is a micro-level contributor to the macro-level phenomena, falling profits, increasing bonus share and periodic malfeasance, noted at the outset. Figure 8.1 is not only a summary of our findings, it is also a behavioural agency model and, we would argue, a managerial 'theory in use'. Specifically, we argue that the objectives of managers in our sample may be summarized as

(1) minimize OB by effective monitoring of loss positions;
(2) extend OA by retaining discretion over bonus allocation.

Complexity is introduced by the individual differences between traders discussed in Chapter 5. In Figure 8.1 these differences tend to assert themselves outside AB, that is, where monitoring and incentives fail. However, in practice, the trader's reference point may not be zero and the target may not be the bonus target. In fact, some traders described the bonus target as the reference point, implying that they would engage in risk seeking behaviours if they fell short towards year end (i.e. in OA). Others described their objectives in bad market circumstances as minimizing losses (i.e. risk averse in OB). Individual differences in attitudes to risk are not dealt with by prospect or agency theory, but managers can only be effective if they know individual differences in risk propensity.[9]

8.5 Implications

We close with some practical issues. Assuming managers wish to act more consistently for risk-neutral principals what could they do? From the principal's perspective, the distance OB is a measure of the effectiveness of managers' loss-control function and loss avoidance remains a central managerial function. In the domain of gains, two suggestions arise. First, managers could reduce the volume of their own trading and monitor or coach more intensively in the domain of gains. The risk here is one of credibility loss, but this might be mitigated by credit for direct involvement in enhancing the returns to individual traders. It would generate important managerial information about traders' own reference points. The second suggestion involves reconsidering the bonus system. Cumulative performance to a bonus target also subject to retrospective behavioural evaluation may tend traders towards risk or loss aversion. Trading 'theory' suggests that all trades should be considered on their own merits, and that previous experience of profit or loss should not affect traders' decisions. Yet, the consequences of history tend to become embedded in the compensation structure. This could be more fully accommodated by moving away from single year accounting towards rolling bonus targets.

We argue that such changes are important. The approach adopted here has allowed us to highlight important links between micro- and macro-level phenomena. Specifically, agency and framing effects at the individual level can be seen to generate the conditions for occasional malfeasance and suboptimal profits at the industry level. While we have not analysed all relevant features of the agency relationship here, we conclude that changes to managerial practice in trader management could have substantial industry level effects.

Notes

1. The FSA has taken over the supervisory role of the Bank of England.
2. These data exclude stock options.
3. This trader was proprietary, that is, he traded using the bank's own capital rather than acting for a bank client.
4. For example through examining records of trades.
5. In the financial economic sense.
6. Several traders had worked in other financial centres, particularly New York. New York was regarded by those with experience as a more intense and client-focused work environment; managerial styles as discussed here were not reported as substantially different.
7. Some of the traders we interviewed operated in foreign currency derivatives markets but not principally in plain currency trading.
8. It is important to bear in mind, as we noted in Chapter 5, that trader incentives may include non-monetary factors such as reputation.
9. We dealt with these in greater detail in Chapter 6.

Chapter 9

CONCLUSIONS

In this concluding chapter we review our key findings and their implications for management, trader development, regulation, and future research. Throughout this book we have tried to describe the behaviour of traders in financial markets and to identify some of its determinants. We differ in approach from financial economists, who might try to describe a perfect market and from behavioural finance academics, who might be concerned to describe deviations from it. Rather we have sought to deploy a multidisciplinary perspective to convey some of the complexities in understanding how such markets operate. We have collected in-depth data on traders and their environment by means of multiple methods: qualitative interviews and observations, psychometric tests, survey material, a computer-based experiment and archival exploration. The markets we looked at in equities, bonds, and derivatives are highly structured and closely regulated. At the same time, they are socially constructed by those who operate within them. Traders enact theories of 'how the world works' (often in ways which make them come true), but they also develop theories of 'how to work the world' oriented towards success and survival, which they articulate and pass on to others.

The individuals who trade are agents, but their behaviour is also influenced by the fact that they can generate substantial personal rewards by successful trading. They do not bear the full risks of their trading activity. They operate under uncertainty in an electronic environment where successes and failures can unfold very quickly.

Conclusions

The people who become traders are not on our evidence super-rational individuals. They vary considerably in background, personality, and propensity to take risks. All are susceptible to a range of cognitive biases. They get lucky and they make mistakes. They become emotionally involved in the work they do. They trade on beliefs and hunches. Some have contrarian tendencies. They become traders through a fairly opaque and intuitive selection process and they do not endure long in their careers as traders.

Traders are tightly monitored but loosely managed. Valuing autonomy and being managed by ex-traders who feel similarly, they enjoy a freedom to experiment as long as they do not lose money. The drive towards maximizing profits is significantly underpinned by the pursuit of large bonus payments, which in practice are the main management device. Where the bonus does not work, there is very little else to ensure traders operate as economic maximizers. In practice, there is a lot of performance variance. The hierarchy of authority and control is flat, and management is by exception, mainly by means of intermittent operational intervention.

What do these findings tell us about the traders and about the operation of financial markets? In this conclusion, we first summarize our main findings then we pursue three questions. First, how should traders be selected, developed, and managed to improve performance and avoid costly errors? Second, what are the implications of our findings for the regulation of investment banks and trading? Third, what do our findings suggest as useful directions for future research?

9.1 Understanding Markets and the Traders World

In our introduction to this volume, we characterized the trader's world as a 'noisy borderland'. A world in which the assumptions of the efficient markets paradigm both breakdown and are brought about through the arbitrage activities of traders.

The Limits of the Efficient Markets Paradigm

As we have argued in Chapters 2 and 3, the efficient markets paradigm has been highly successful, within limits, in explaining aggregate market behaviour. However, those limits are significant.

First, much that is of interest about the behaviour of markets concerns the processes though which markets move towards never-quite-achieved equilibria. As we noted in our discussion of LTCM, arbitrage is not riskless and apparently irrational prices may persist for some time. Professional traders not only act to reduce such discrepancies through arbitrage, but may also amplify them through flow trading strategies. Further, professional traders are not immune to the many illusions and biases that drive the behaviour of more naïve investors. Indeed we have argued that professional traders are major contributors to 'noise trading' for a range of reasons which include susceptibility to biases, illusions, and learning processes.

Second, the efficient markets approach has little to say about many market phenomena such as bubbles, mania, and crises; beyond appealing to external shocks. A more nuanced understanding of the social and psychological processes enacted within financial markets offers the prospect of addressing these phenomena in terms of the internal dynamics of markets.

Reflexivity

As we discussed in Chapter 4, reflexivity in markets has two important implications for trading. First, the reflexive nature of markets means that as particular theories become more widely adopted, market behaviour changes in consequence: theories of how to work the world are often both dynamic and provisional. It is for this reason that we have argued effective trading to be less about the adoption of particular theories than developing the capacity to create and modify theories in response to changing conditions. Second, traders need the ability to draw conclusions about other market actors' motivations and models of the world. An important aspect of this skill is the capacity to make sense of emotions in markets.

The Pervasive Role of Emotion

A significant finding of our study has been the importance of the emotional life of traders, in two senses. First, we have noted that a crucial theme in trader development is reducing vulnerability to emotional swings brought about by losses and gains. Importantly though, this is not simply a matter of suppressing emotions; since this removes the opportunity to benefit from the second sense in which emotion is important. For a significant number of more experienced traders, emotion was an important and perceptible thread connecting market movements. Traders reported using their own capacity for emotional empathy to understand market trends and to predict turning points. This was particularly important for traders concerned with short-term market flows.

9.2   Traders as a Community of Practice

While formal financial economic theory provides an important framework for traders' work, it cannot provide a guide for action or a basis for comparative advantage. Rather action is guided by the development of practice within a trading community, or within multiple, overlapping trading communities. Traders' success depends not simply on their own skills and knowledge, but also on their social capital: their membership of networks and the nature of the trust and reciprocity within those networks.

Flair and Intuition: The Role of Tacit Knowledge

Through their working experience and their membership of networks, within and across firms, traders constantly develop their working practice. They depend on theories of how to work the world, which, as we have described, are shifting, provisional, and to some extent privately held. These theories are tacit in two senses. What we have characterized as Type 1 inappropriable tacit knowledge concerns heuristics and trading styles, which are learned and grounded in experience but difficult to articulate. It is this form of knowledge which is often experienced as intuition and described as 'flair' or 'getting it'. Type 2 inappropriable tacit knowledge is contingently tacit, kept so for profit by the originating trader or traders. This knowledge is in principle easily articulated, but is protected by individuals or groups of traders as an exclusive basis for their continued trading success.

This tacit and provisional nature of work the world theories poses problems both for trader management and development. One way in which the firms we studied met the challenge this posed to trader development was through an apprenticeship process.

The Role of Apprenticeship

What we have described as 'legitimate peripheral participation' in the trading process directly addresses the problems posed by both forms of tacit knowledge. Type 1 knowledge, not being clearly articulated requires immersion in practice to acquire. Novice traders sit by a series of more experienced colleagues trying out trading approaches both through thought experiments and in small stakes market plays.

Through these processes they are engaging in sense-making as they observe and discuss trades conducted by their mentors. By these means they begin to acquire both explicit and tacit knowledge about trading practice. At the same time, through exposure to working with a range of different colleagues, they can begin to develop their own distinctive styles and approaches.

The apprenticeship process also addresses the problem of Type 2 knowledge. Since such knowledge is protected and a basis of advantage, knowledge acquisition requires that traders develop their social capital. They must earn membership of the right networks and develop reciprocal relationships. Again, it is through the apprenticeship process that traders begin to engage in such relationships and earn a legitimate role in the trader community.

9.3 The Nature of Trader Rationality

Economic Rationality, Heuristics, and Self-Defensive Attributions

We have set our discussions of traders' decision-making within a framework of self-regulation. This framework draws our attention to the role of internal goal states in driving decision-making, not least the need for a consistent positive self-image and a sense of control over the world. In pursuit of these goals, traders, like the rest of us, are prone to the full range of biases and defensive illusions. Traders do, of course, rely heavily on economically rational tools and decision processes. The models and tools that they employ can be a powerful defence against bias and illusion. However, as we have repeatedly stressed, traders also work in a context where feedback on the success of actions is highly noisy, where information is often of uncertain value and where advantage may be fleeting and hard to grasp.

Conclusions

This context produces a necessary reliance on tacit, difficult to articulate knowledge, heuristics, and private information. Thus, it will always be hard for traders to distinguish between knowledge which is a source of genuine advantage and beliefs arising out of bias or illusion. However, as we have shown, there is great variability in the extent to which traders are subject to biases and illusions; and for at least one of these, the illusion of control, this variability translates into significant performance differences.

Risk, Personality, and Decision-Making

There is also significant variability between traders in their personalities and approach to risk. As we have shown, this is only to some extent a matter of deeply rooted dispositions. While a small subset of traders may have an appetite for risk founded in sensation seeking, as a group traders are, if anything, risk averse, introverted and conservative compared with other groups. Most traders take risks, not because they are innately risk seeking, but because the role demands it and they are rewarded for doing so. The nature of traders' early trading experience, the way they are monitored and managed and the bonus system are important influences on their risk behaviour. The issues raised by our analysis of trader personalities and risk behaviour do not primarily concern the 'right' trader profile. Rather they emphasize the need to deploy an effective framework for understanding individual differences when managing traders and assigning them to roles.

Emotional Competence

As we have already noted, the emotional life of traders is highly relevant to their functioning and effectiveness. On the one hand traders need to achieve sufficient separation from the outcomes of their trades to ensure that they are not disabled by their emotional reactions. On the other hand, they need to draw on their capacity for empathy to understand and predict the behaviour of other market actors. For many traders the increasing emphasis on customer service also brings a need to engage in the emotional labour of displaying an appropriate emotional front to customers and counterparties, often in fraught circumstances.

202

All of this represents a major challenge for the people who would manage traders. Let us look at what this picture of trader psychology implies for their effective supervision.

9.4 Implications for Trader Management

We shall start with the difficult question of getting the right people into the right seats.

Selection, Placement, and Individual Differences

As we have observed in Chapter 6, there are some prevalent stereotypes of traders. The reality is that the universe of types in trading is much more mundane, as elsewhere. However much trading organizations may seek to induce them to look alike by their socialization methods, traders remain a very varied mix of individuals. On trading floors, many managers entertain their own theories of individual differences, which they will share with little prompting. Some of these are perceptive and constructive, but they are almost invariably untested and not rooted in any empirical discipline. For the most part, our observation is that in environments where traders are employed, even among those where highly sophisticated attention is given to individuals at all career stages, little trader selection and placement is based upon more than a hazy and impressionist understanding of the factors that might have most bearing on risk taking and other relevant behaviours.

There are some firms that have set up mock trading environments, and a few that use psychometric tests, but even the latter tend not to use the best available instruments or to have a viable model of what they are looking for in relation to the various roles they are seeking to fill. Train them and hope for the best, is the principle operating strategy for dealing with psychological dispositions, aptitudes, and foibles.

Our findings on risk taking show that it can be socialized and controlled, but the prior question is what does one want? In selection would one wish to select on the basis of high or low risk propensity? There is no simple answer to this, but this is not a reason for avoiding

Conclusions

sophisticated assessment. Measurement and monitoring can be desirable and useful for ends other than selection. Placement is often much more important. In every investment bank and asset management business there are roles and locations suited to the risk-robust and others for the risk-shy individuals. The important issue is to know how to put people into roles that will grow their talents rather than destroy their spirit. The supplementary management considerations are to do with individualized treatment: how best to support the learning and performance of an individual through how one communicates with them and administers incentives and controls.

The purpose of profiling should not be to homogenize working communities. In fact, it can be most valuable as an aid to securing the benefits of synergy from a diverse talent pool. Building collaborations between people who have different values, styles, and skills can sharpen performance, increase innovation, and make life more interesting for everyone.

Even without access to the kind of instrumentation we have described in Chapter 6, managers in financial services, as in other organization types, can derive great benefits from acquiring a more precise lexicon of ways to think and talk about the people they deal with, through a better understanding of what underlies motivation, performance, or work satisfaction. The Big Five personality framework is a useful starting point for this. There are also powerful analytical frameworks for understanding the other dimensions we have considered, such as abilities and skills.

So, our recommendation is that people who employ traders begin to make better use of the sophisticated measurement models and methods that now exist, to see just whom they are hiring and to appreciate what they are doing to them. With this intelligence one can raise the level of conversation that it is possible to have about the challenges around their roles and strategies for dealing with them. We are not advocating the extension of the use of selection tools. One might want to screen out certain people who would have trouble maintaining effective performance in any job, but one does not need a lot of psychometric technology for that. Work experience is the best guide to person–job fit, but better assessment tools will make the dialogue and search for improved fit much easier.

Managing Apprenticeship

One of the constant themes that emerged throughout our interviews was the importance for many traders of formative early experiences: encountering large early losses or gains often proved to be a formative and lasting emotive experience that influenced their approaches to trading. The extent to which this apprenticeship stage was actively managed varied considerably. Some reported sensitive handling of these experiences by their managers, leading to useful learning. Others had clearly been less effectively managed. Given the importance to traders of reducing their vulnerability to the emotional impact of gains and losses and consequent biases in decision-making, effective management of their early experiences is vital. Similarly, we found wide variation in the extent to which managers carefully planned the mentoring of novice traders.

Errors

As we noted in Chapter 7, there is considerable variation in managers' approaches to errors. The most productive approach to error management can be summarized as a combination of high standards with forgiveness. Punitive approaches to error management are counterproductive: they reduce error disclosure, impede learning, and fail to reduce the incidence of error. By contrast, an open approach where errors are freely discussed enables learning and reduces the motivation to conceal errors.

Managing Illusion and Bias

Our theoretical position suggests there is no point in trying to alter human nature by eliminating all sources of bias. People can be trained to high degrees of computational sophistication, to be very clever reasoning machines, but biases are never completely removed, and motives can only be hijacked or derailed, not created and destroyed. Self-regulation theory suggests that the best strategies, therefore, are methods that raise self-awareness. If people are more aware of influences on their perceptions and decision-making they can partially self-correct, if they are motivated to do so.

Technical aids have a major role here. The discipline of statistics was invented to overcome our inabilities to make correct judgements in numerical environments. Logic and decision protocols exist to ensure that we do not draw false conclusions from evidence or miss some option in an array. In many situations traders do rely on machines to help them with such calculus, from the pocket calculator to the market simulation or option-pricing model. But at the end of every mechanical computation there is still a human agent who has to decide to accept or reject what the process delivers. The infinite patience and extreme accuracy of mechanical computations can be easily defeated by human opinions and beliefs, as it has been in a string of finance catastrophes and errors.

Some investment banks are increasingly alert to the limits of rationality, as are theoretical economists. The awarding of the Nobel Prize for Economics in 2003 to a psychologist and a behavioural economist (Daniel Kahneman and Vernon Smith) shows the increasing importance of these ideas. The next practical step for the investment banking community is to look more systematically at the decision-making hazards facing traders and start thinking about how traders and their managers can protect themselves against them. Some of this starts in the training environment, where the use of simulations and other instructional aids could illustrate and bring home the reality of many of the sources of bias, along with opportunities to practice one's defences against them.

This is more easily said than done, for many biases tug hard at emotional and motivational orientations. Just exhorting oneself to cut losses and let profits run is not always enough. The remedy is for traders not to be left in positions of isolation as decision-makers. On the best trading floors, desks have a climate of experience sharing, support, and exchange that enable people to correct each other without loss of face or rancour. In trader teamwork there is always the danger of groupthink, collusive relationships that yield support without critical analysis. The defence against this lies in ensuring that desks include (a) diversity of experience, knowledge, and approach, and (b) norms of open dialogue and legitimate inquisitiveness about each other's business.

Establishing this culture is a key element in the role of management. So, of course, is the dialogue between managers and traders. It is one of the most important raison d'êtres for management. Indeed, one (self-serving) recommendation we might make is that every manager undergoes a crash course in the psychology of risk and decision-making.

How might these ideas extend to illusions of control? The dilemma here is that strong realistic control beliefs are quite helpful to us when we are struggling to overcome difficulties. There is an apocryphal story of the survivors of a plane that crash-landed in the northern Arctic wastes who navigated to safety over several arduous days with the aid of a map they found in the plane, only to discover on reaching their destination that it was a map for a completely different area! Self-belief, even when based upon false assumptions, can promote persistence in the face of adversity. Fortunately, the alternative to illusions of control is not a depressive surrender into helplessness, nor is it reckless abandonment to the will of the gods. It is a reasonable attribution of causes and effects, a balanced mental accounting of responsibility to self and circumstance based upon realistic appraisals. Humility in the face of markets does not entail a lack of self-belief. This is an area where people differ, and the support that each individual needs or will welcome also differs.

Managing Risk Appetite

In Chapter 8 we looked at how trader risk taking is managed on a day-to-day basis. Observing how managers operate, we became concerned that both risk aversion and loss aversion were not well managed. The combination of trader autonomy, reliance on bonus and management spans of control generates an environment where managers see themselves as a safety net rather than as creators of value or profit. Put another way, trading environments rely too much on managing outputs.

Of course, we found variance. Some managers used their intuitive understanding of traders' risk preferences and bonus positions to describe a form of portfolio management in which they hedged the behaviours of risk seekers with risk avoiders to try to generate an aggregate behavioural risk exposure for a desk or department. They were not, though, always working with the best data either on underlying risk preferences or on positions. Overall, there remained in all four institutions considerable scope for trader risk preferences to influence trading behaviour.

Conclusions

9.5   Implications for Regulation

We have described a picture of an institutionally structured risk environment of enormous cognitive complexity in which decisions and innovations occur locally and competitively under circumstances of high stress and high rewards. Survival strategies consist in exploiting information advantages quickly, probably before their true nature is established, and then protecting that advantage as long as possible. This is what we described in Chapter 4 as the pursuit of Type 1 and Type 2 inappropriability.

Regulators want markets to operate efficiently in the Fama sense that prices reflect all available information. They may not want such markets to be perfect since there need to be a number of players in pursuit of profit at any one time. However, one could say that they often regulate against the creation of long-term imperfections and information asymmetries that might generate rents for certain players. In this sense, the interests of traders and regulators do not coincide. In the larger sense that both traders and regulators wish to attract investors to a market on a large scale, all have an interest in that market (or set of markets) having a reputation for transparency and open competition. To resurrect Lee's analogy from earlier in the book of markets as an ocean: regulators may wish to have a calm pond and traders may wish to surf but neither would welcome a maelstrom. However, regulators have an interest in making rules which traders have an interest in breaking.

In financial markets, regulators primarily regulate market activity but to do so they must regulate firms; often large ones such as those employing the traders in our sample that have huge resources and global reach. Although there are many regulatory differences across exchanges, most financial markets rely on a large amount of self-regulation in which settlements, compliance, and other departments within firms monitor and report on the market activities of the firm.

Regulators may make rules about how prices are set, for example, in rules about market-making, or they may make rules about how deals are closed but they do not regulate price. One may contrast this with the situation in utilities regulation where regulators fix prices but rely less on the firms' self-regulatory activities. So, the balance of regulation in financial services often focuses on agreeing or imposing rules on firms which the firms would not adopt for their own competitive advantage. These rules aim to safeguard investors' interests at the same time as allowing traders and their institutions to pursue profits. Traders as we have seen pursue their profits under conditions of considerable autonomy and trading rules need to accommodate that.

Regulators are, thus, concerned with the operational risk of trader behaviour less in terms of its possible impact on trader performance and firm profits, and more from a concern with malfeasance. Irrationality and the persistence of bias is not of itself a problem, but control environments that allow these biases to be used in combination with rule breaking are problematic. So if, as we discussed in Chapter 8, the upside is not managed to maximize profits this is a matter for the bank, but if a trader chases losses as Leeson did, it becomes a regulatory matter.

How could regulation be improved without imposing large burdens on trading activity? Our data point to two recommendations. The first relates to management, the second to bonuses. We deal with each in turn.

Management

Trader management is a training-free zone. In a combined 70 years of experience, the authors have never encountered so little management development in sophisticated organizations of vast resource. Trading is a complex environment with intractable principal–agent problems but managers emerge from the trading cadre with at best tacit knowledge about managing people under stress and their understanding is very uneven. In the context of the current emphasis on the establishment of effective systems for the management of operational risk (FSA, 2003) we think that there is scope for regulators to require some form of accreditation on the part of those responsible for traders, to ensure that they at least understand the existence and behavioural implications of heuristics and biases. Such accreditation might be broadened to embrace a wider range of management skills.

Bonuses

The second recommendation concerns bonus payments. The problem is fairly simply stated. The industry relies on large variable pay elements, which do not effectively align principals' interests with those of agents. They do not particularly benefit firms either but there are strong first-mover disadvantages to any firms and markets that move away from a practice so highly lucrative for traders. In Chapter 8, we indicated that a reliance on annual bonus payments is an imperfect risk control mechanism. Our recommendation here is that regulators should require firms to turn a proportion of trader bonus payments into deferred income, reclaimable on retirement from trading but retained against the possibility of malfeasance by traders.

9.6 Directions for Future Research

Finally, we turn to look at possibilities for future research. There are several broader questions raised by our findings and they have implications for work in a number of social science disciplines.

Bias and Decision-Making

The factors that underpin cognitive biases and the relationships between personality, individual psychology and the environment are already the subject of intense interest in the behavioural decision-making field. Research will continue to give us more information about what makes some people more susceptible to biases than others, and how we can screen effectively to detect this susceptibility. The trading environment is a rich context for such research given the importance of financial markets, the dominance of economics in explaining their operation, and the fact that trading environments might be regarded as bias factories in their combination of rapid decision-making, complexity, and stress.

Trader Behaviour

Within trading environments, our research has indicated the need for an integrated approach to understanding the whole constellation of regulatory, technical, and managerial controls traders experience and achieving fresh perspectives on their relationship to performance. Here, we have looked primarily at internal psychological controls and those provided by managers, but the interaction of these with, for example, controls imposed by screen based trading are of considerable interest and importance. Much of the previous work on trading, we would note, has taken place in open-outcry environments, which are increasingly rare. Another area of interest concerns trading styles and performance. We observed a number of different trading and decision-making styles to which the actors involved adhered with considerable faith, but on the basis of little supporting evidence. Research that could indicate the performance implications of different trading styles under different market contingencies would add appreciably to our understanding of how, precisely, traders make money.

Social Science and Markets

There is increasing interest in the application of a broad range of social science approaches to understanding the operation of financial markets and dialogue across disciplines has the potential to significantly enrich our understanding of markets. There are of course major obstacles in the way of this kind of work. While psychologists and sociologists may plead for a richer and more realistic picture of human behaviour and social functioning, financial economists are concerned to develop parsimonious and mathematically tractable models of market behaviour, that deliver good enough results in the aggregate. Nonetheless, the application of insights from cognitive psychology in the field of behavioural finance and the increased dialogue between financial economists and sociologists interested in markets provides grounds for optimism.

Chapter 10

APPENDIX
The Study

This appendix gives further details of our research study, our methods and the measures used.

10.1   Aims of the Study

The main objective of the study was to evaluate how the market behaviour of finance professionals is affected by individual and contextual influences, and how performance effectiveness could be enhanced by changes to management systems and controls. To achieve this aim we developed a study that used both qualitative and quantitative research methods. Interviews were designed so that the same issues were discussed with each participant (shown in Section 10.6 below), yet there were opportunities to expand areas of particular interest to the interviewees.

   We used a range of measures: both well-established measures, such as the NEO-PI-R personality inventory and new measures, the Risk Assessment Tool (RAT) and the Risk Taking Index (RTI), which we developed for the study. Together with the interviews this set of measures enabled us to develop a rich picture of the motivations, experiences, emotions, incentives, and organizational contexts that shape traders' behaviour. The measures are presented in detail in Section 10.3 below.

10.2   Participating Organizations

All the participating organizations were large, top-tier investment banks operating globally. During the data collection period only the research team knew the identification of the participating organizations. At the end of the research programme the organizations were invited to a conference at London Business School where a summary of the results and their implications were discussed. The organizations thus revealed their participation in the study. Their anonymity is, however, preserved in this book and efforts have been made to protect the identity of all the individual participants. The organizations are referred to as A, B, C, and D. Organizations A, B, and D were US headquartered banks. Organization C was a European headquartered bank.

Each organization was approached by the London Business School research team and invited to take part in the research programme. Organizations were asked to provide a sample of traders and trader managers who varied in age, experience, and areas of expertise. Participants traded in equities, fixed income, or derivatives. Participants traded a range of markets: European, US, Japan, South America, Latin America, South Africa, Australia and New Zealand, and emerging markets.

10.3   Measures

Biographical Information

Participants completed a short questionnaire that measured a set of biographical variables. The data for each organization are summarized in Table 10.A1.

In addition to the investment bank sample, a large database on personality and risk propensity has been developed at London Business School. Table 10.A2 shows the profile of the overall sample, which includes the investment bank participants.

Appendix

Table 10.A1 Investment bank sample profile

	Firm A	Firm B	Firm C	Firm D	Total sample
Sample size (*N*)	38	32	23	25	118
Senior managers interviewed	3	1	5	1	10
Age (mean years)	33.80	30.91	32.87	33.80	32.81
Mean job tenure (years)	6.18	6.11	4.74	10.08	6.71
Mean organization tenure (years)	7.18	6.67	6.57	11.30	7.80
Traders	13	22	11	11	57
Trader/managers	23	10	11	2	46
Desk managers	2	0	1	12	15
Male	38	31	22	25	116
Female	0	1	1	0	2
Education (highest qualification) (N)					
O-Level/GCSE	1	2	1	16	20
A-Level	2	4	3	5	14
HND/equivalent	1	3	2	0	6
Degree	9	13	8	3	33
Masters	16	6	6	1	29
PhD	9	4	3	0	16
Seniority: levels to CEO in the London office					
1	3	6	1	3	13
2	16	15	3	15	49
3	15	7	9	3	34
4	4	4	9	0	17
5	0	0	1	2	3
6	0	0	0	2	2
Salary, including bonus for the year end prior to the study					
£50–99k	0	3	1	0	4
£100–299k	9	13	5	14	41
£300–499k	7	6	12	9	34
>£500k	21	10	5	2	38
Not divulged	1	0	0	0	1

Table 10.A2 Personality and risk propensity sample profile

Sample size (*N*)	3,488
Age (mean years)	33.11
Job tenure (mean years)	6.18
Gender	*Frequency*
Male	2,558
Female	706
Seniority (levels to CEO)	
0	139
1	570
2	724
3	641
4	410
5	263
6	125
7	55
8	19
9	12
10	32
More than 10	10
Business type	
Manufacturing	564
Sales and retail	177
Finance	986
Professional firm	214
Arts and media	208
Public services/ military/ government	303
IT/ telecoms	324
Other services	447
Other	66
Total	3,289
Missing	199
Job function	
General management	585
Finance	1,083
Sales and marketing	382
Operations/ engineering	269
IT/ systems	125
Consulting	344
HR/ PR/ Communications	89
Other professional	303
Other	41
Total	3,221
Missing	267

Appendix

Risk Taking Index and NEO-PI-R

These measures are described in detail in Chapter 6.

Risk Assessment Tool

The RAT measured a range of cognitive biases. Most important was the illusion of control—the tendency to believe or act as if we are in control of chance events. The program informed participants that they would be asked to play a game. They were told:

> When the game starts you will see a chart, similar to the picture shown below. The vertical axis represents an index with values between −2000 and 2000. The horizontal axis shows time. The index starts at zero and every half second for 50 seconds the index is increased or decreased by some amount. Changes in the index are partly random, but three keys on the keyboard may have some effect on the index. The possible effects are to raise or lower the index by some amount to increase the size of the random movements or no effect. There is some time lag to the effects. The keys are 'Z', 'X', and 'C'. There is no advantage to pressing keys more than once in any half second. Your task is to raise the index as high as possible by the end of 50 seconds. At the end of the game the final value of the index will be added to your pool of points.

The game then ran as described. The program generated the index by overlaying a random walk onto an underlying rising trend (falling in later runs). The keys pressed by participants had no effect on the index. At the end of the 50 seconds, participants were told their score (the level reached by the index) and asked to rate their success in increasing the index by using the keys (by setting a slider bar from 1 'not at all successful' to 100 'very successful').

The game was repeated another three times. Rounds 1 and 2 were set up to guarantee that participants experienced an increase in points. In Round 3 participants lost points and in Round 4 participants' scores stayed constant (with some small random variation).

The mean illusion of control score was 46.66 (SD = 21.93, range = 0.50 to 97.00).

Performance Measures

As external researchers we did not have access to the individual performance data that organizations collect and use in their performance appraisals and bonus calculations. So we developed a set of rating scales that traders could use to rate their own performance, and managers could use to rate those traders' performance. The four aspects of performance that we measured were

- contribution to desk profits
- analytical ability
- risk management
- people skills.

Each aspect of performance was measured using percentiles. The traders were presented with four scales ranging from 0 to 100 and asked to compare themselves with others on their desk. So a rating of 60 meant that the participant considered himself or herself to be better than 60 per cent of the traders on their desk. Senior managers were asked to rate the group of participating traders and trader managers on the same scales. Table 10.A3 shows the trader self-rating data.

10.4   Semi-Structured Interviews

The final component of the data collection was an interview. The interview was a critical element in the data collection process because it enabled us to explore the key areas of interest with participants, and to hear traders' stories in their own words. The interviews ranged from 30 to 90 min in length, depending on how much time the participants were able to give to the research. The format of the interview was semi-structured: there were several key areas discussed with each interviewee and opportunities for spending more time on these areas or other relevant issues when useful and time allowed.

Each interview was recorded and transcribed. The transcripts were then processed using QSR NVIVO, a qualitative data analysis software package. This programme enabled data to be coded into categories (e.g. learning experiences). Each collection of quotes could then be analysed by the research team.

Three interview schedules were developed: one for each group of traders, senior managers and HR managers. The areas discussed are shown below.

Table 10.A3 Frequencies of self-ratings of performance

Percentile range	Contribution to desk profits	Risk management	Analytical ability	People skills
0–9	2	1	1	0
10–19	3	0	0	1
20–29	8	1	6	2
30–39	4	2	5	7
40–49	4	7	3	8
50–59	10	9	19	19
60–69	19	19	14	21
70–79	27	22	22	19
80–89	16	31	18	20
90–100	21	24	28	20
N	114	116	116	117
Missing	4	2	2	1

Interview Schedule for Traders

Role

What does your job involve?
How much risk do you take compared with others on your desk?
What is your attitude to risk?
Describe some important learning experiences.

Decision-making

Do you use heuristics?
What role does gut feeling have in your decision-making?
Are you influenced by your emotions?
Do you set stop losses and sell-point targets?
How do experiences of loss influence your decision-making?
How do experiences of gain influence your decision-making?

Organizational issues

To what extent does your team influence what you do? For example, do you discuss your decisions with your colleagues?
Is your team close?
What do you think makes a team successful in this organization?
What is your view of the management in this organization?

What happens when you make mistakes?
On what basis are you paid?
Does the annual bonus cycle affect your decision-making over the year?
What is the culture of this organization?

Interview Schedule for Senior Managers

Traders' strategies

What heuristics do traders use?
What effects do the reward systems have on traders' behaviour?
How do traders manage the stress in their job?

Trader management

What happens when a new trader starts work?
Do you think different types of traders are suitable for different types of markets?
How do you evaluate and manage their performance?
What do you do if someone you have employed does not seem suitable for the job?
How can you tell?
What do you do if a trader makes a serious error?
What are the main circumstances, if any, in which what is good for the trader is not good for the organization?
How do you manage this?

Organizational issues

What are the key aspects of the risk management system?
What informal information networks do the traders use?
What is the best and worst teamwork in this organization?

Interview Schedule for HR Managers

In Organization A, several Human Resources managers were interviewed.

Recruitment

What are you looking for when you recruit a trader?
Would risk propensity/attitude to risk be a factor you consider?

Trader management

How do you manage traders' performance?
How do you motivate the traders to achieve the organization's goals?

Appendix

Organizational issues

What is the reward system?

Do you think there is teamwork here?

What are the main issues in management of the profit and loss and operations?

References

Abolafia, M. Y. (1996). *Making Markets: Opportunism and Restraint on Wall Street*. Cambridge, MA: Harvard University Press.

—— and Kilduff, M. K. (1988). Enacting market crisis; The social construction of a speculative bubble. *Administrative Science Quarterly*, 33, 173–93.

Adams, J. (1995). *Risk*. London: Routledge.

Adler, P. A. and Adler, P. (1984). *The Social Dynamics of Financial Markets*. Greenwich, CT: JAI Press.

Allen, F. and Karjalainen, R. (1999). Using genetic algorithms to find technical trading rules. *Journal of Financial Economics*, 51, 245–71.

Alvarez, A. (1983). *The Biggest Game in Town*. New York: Houghton Mifflin.

Amihud, Y., Mendelson, H., and Lauterback, B. (1997). Market microstructure and securities values: Evidence from the Tel Aviv Stock Exchange. *Journal of Financial Economics*, 45, 365–90.

Anderson, M. J. and Sunder, S. (1995). Professional traders as intuitive Bayesians. *Organizational Behavior and Human Decision Processes*, 64(2): 185–202.

Anderson, N. R. (1992). Eight decades of employment interview research: A retrospective meta-review and prospective commentary. *European Work and Organizational Psychologist*, 2, 1–32.

Arkes, H. R. and Blumer, C. (1985). The psychology of sunk cost. *Organizational Behavior and Human Decision Processes*, 35, 124–40.

Arnold, J. and Mackenzie Davey, K. (1992). Beyond unmet expectations: A detailed analysis of graduate experiences at work during the first three years of their careers. *Personnel Review*, 21, 45–68.

Ashforth, B. E. and Tomiuk, M. A. (2000). Emotional Labour and authenticity: Views from service agents. In S. Fineman (ed.), *Emotion in Organizations*, 2nd edn. London: Sage Publications Ltd.

References

Bagnoli, M. and Watts, S. G. (2000). Chasing hot funds: The effects of relative performance on portfolio choice. *Financial Management*, 29(3): 31–50.

Baker, W. (1984*a*). The social structure of a National Securities Market. *American Journal of Sociology*, 89(4), 775–811.

—— (1984*b*). Floor trading and crowd dynamics. In P. A. Adler and P. Adler (eds), *The Social Dynamics of Financial Markets*. Greenwich, CT: JAI Press, 107–27.

—— and Iyer, A. (1992). Information networks and market behaviour. *Journal of Mathematical Sociology*, 16, 305–32.

Bandura, A. (1989). Human agency in social cognitive theory. *American Psychologist*, 44(9), 1175–84.

—— and Wood, R. (1989). Effect of perceived controllability and performance standards on self-regulation of complex decision-making. *Journal of Personality and Social Psychology*, 56, 805–14.

Bank of England (1997*a*). *A Risk Based Approach to Supervision*. Consultative paper, March. London.

—— (1997*b*). *Report to the Board of Banking Supervision; Inquiry into the Circumstances of the Collapse of Barings*. London: HMSO.

Barber, B. and Odean, T. (2001). Boys will be boys: Gender, overconfidence, and common stock investment. *Quarterly Journal of Economics*, 116(1), 261–92.

Bargh, J. A. and Chartrand, T. L. (1999). The unbearable automaticity of being. *American Psychologist*, 54, 462–79.

Barrick, M. R. and Mount, M. K. (1991). The Big Five personality dimensions and job performance: A meta-analysis. *Personnel Psychology*, 44, 1–26.

Bates, J. E. and Wachs, L. D. (eds) (1994). *Temperament: Individual Differences of the Interface of Biology and Behavior*. Washington, DC: APA Press.

Bazerman, M. (1997). *Judgement in Managerial Decision Making*, 4th edn. New York: Wiley.

—— (2001). *Judgment in Managerial Decision Making*, 5th edn. New York: Wiley.

Beatty, R. P. and Zajac, E. J. (1994). Managerial incentives, monitoring and risk-bearing. *Administrative Science Quarterly*, 39, 313–35.

Bernoulli, D. (1738). Specimen Theorae Novae de Mensura Sortis (Exposition of a new theory on the measurement of risk). Translated from the Latin by Louise Sommer (1954) in *Econometrica*, 22, 23–36.

References

Bernstein, P. L. (1996). *Against the Gods; The Remarkable Story of Risk.* New York: Wiley.

Black, F. (1986). Noise. *Journal of Finance*, 41, 529–543.

Bower, G. H. (1981). Mood and memory. *American Psychologist*, 36, 129–48.

Brehm, J. (1956). Post-decisional changes in the desirability of alternatives. *Journal of Abnormal and Social Psychology*, 52, 384–9.

Brehmer, B. and Allard, R. (1991). Dynamic decision making: The effects of complexity and feedback delay. In J. Rasmussen, B. Brehmer, and J. Leplat, *Distributed Decision Making: Cognitive Models of Cooperative Work.* Chichester: Wiley.

Broadbent, D. E. (1971). *Decision and Stress.* London: Academic Press.

Brockner, J. and Rubin, J. Z. (1992). Gambling on games of pure chance. In M. Walker (ed.) (1992), *The Psychology of Gambling.* Oxford: Butterworth-Heinemann.

Brotheridge, C. M. and Grandey, A. A. (2002). Emotional labor and burnout: Comparing two perspectives of 'people work'. *Journal of Vocational Behavior*, 60(1), 17–39.

Buss, D. M. (1991). Evolutionary personality psychology. *Annual Review of Psychology*, 42, 459–92.

Byrnes, J. P., Miller, D. C., and Schafer, W. D. (1999). Gender difference in risk taking: A meta-analysis. *Psychological Bulletin*, 125, 367–83.

Callon, M. (ed.) (1998). *The Laws of the Markets.* Oxford: Blackwell.

Calne, D. B. (1999). *Within Reason: Rationality and Human Behavior.* Toronto: Pantheon.

Cannon, D. (1995). *Making Sense of Failure: Learning or Defence?* Unpublished Ph.D. thesis, London Business School, University of London.

Cannon, D. A. and Nicholson, N. (1996). *Making Sense of Failure: Memory, Motive and Self-regulation.* London Business School: Centre for Organisational Research Working Paper.

Carver, S. C. and Scheier, M. F. (1998). *On the Self-Regulation of Behavior.* Cambridge: Cambridge University Press.

Caspi, A. (2000). The child is father of the man: Personality continuities from childhood to adulthood. *Journal of Personality and Social Psychology*, 78, 158–72.

Casserley, D. (1991). *Facing Up to the Risks.* New York: John Wiley & Sons Inc.

Chopra, N., Lakonishok, J., and Ritter, J. R. (1992). Measuring abnormal performance: Do stocks overreact. *Journal of Financial Economics*, 31, 235–68.

References

Chorafas, D. N. (1995). *Managing Derivatives Risk: Establishing Internal Systems and Controls.* Chicago: Irwin Professional Publications.

Coase, R. (1988). *The Firm, the Market and the Law.* Chicago, Ill: University of Chicago Press.

Costa, P. T. and McCrae, R. R. (1997). *NEO PI-R and NEO-FFI Professional Manual.* Odessa, FLA: Psychological Assessment Resources, Inc.

Cziko, G. (1995). *Without Miracles: Universal Selection Theory and the Second Darwinian Revolution.* Cambridge, MA: MIT Press.

Damasio, A. (2000). *The Feeling of What Happens: Body and Emotion in the Making of Consciousness.* New York: Harcourt Publishers.

Daniel, K., Hirshleifer, D., and Teoh, S. H. (2002). Investor psychology in capital markets: Evidence and policy implications. *Journal of Monetary Economics*, 49(1), 139–209.

Davis, M. H. (1996). *Empathy: A Social Psychological Approach.* Boulder, CO: Westview Press.

De Bondt, W. F. M. (1998). A portrait of the individual investor. *European Economic Review*, 42(3–5), 831–44.

—— and Thaler, R. (1985). Does the stock-market overreact? *Journal of Finance*, 40(3), 793–805.

—— and Thaler, R. H. (1987). Further evidence on investor overreaction and stock-market seasonality. *Journal of Finance*, 42(3), 557–81.

—— and Thaler, R. H. (1990). Do security analysts overreact. *American Economic Review*, 80(2), 52–7.

De Long, J. B., Schleifer, A., Summers, L., and Woldermann, R. J. (1990). Noise traders and risk in financial markets. *Journal of Political Economy*, 98(4), 703–38.

Digman, J. M. (1997). Higher-order factors of the big five. *Journal of Personality and Social Psychology*, 73(6), 1246–56.

Dormann, T. and Frese, M. (1994). Error training: Replication and the function of exploratory behavior. *International Journal of Human-Computer Interaction*, 6, 365–72.

Dow, J. and Gorton, G. (1997). Noise trading, delegated portfolio management and economic welfare. *Journal of Political Economy*, 105(5), 1024–50.

Dunbar, K. (1995). How scientists really reason: Scientific reasoning in real world laboratories. In R. J. Sternberg and J. E. Davidson (eds), *The Nature of Insight.* Cambridge, MA: MIT Press, 365–95.

Dweck, C. S. and Leggett, E. L. (1988). A social-cognitive approach to motivation and personality. *Psychological Review*, 95, 256–73.

Edmondson, A. (1996). Learning from mistakes is easier said than done: Group and organizational influences on the detection and correction of human error. *Journal of Applied Behavioral Science*, 32(1), 5–28.

Eisenhardt, K. (1989). Agency theory; an assessment and review. *Academy of Management Review*, 14, 57–74.

Elster, J. (1983). *Sour Grapes: Studies in the Subversion of Rationality.* Cambridge: Cambridge University Press.

Erickson, R. J. and Wharton, A. S. (1997). Inauthenticity and depression: assessing the consequences of interactive service work. *Symbolic Interaction*, 18, 121–44.

Fagley, N. S. and Miller, P. M. (1987). The effects of decision framing on choice of risky vs. certain options. *Organizational Behavior and Human Decision Processes*, 39, 264–77.

Fama, E. F. (1970). Efficient capital markets: a review of theory and empirical work. *Journal of Finance*, 25(2), 383–428.

—— (1991). Efficient capital markets: II. *Journal of Finance*, 46(5), 1575–1617.

—— (1998). Market efficiency, long-term returns, and behavioral finance. *Journal of Financial Economics*, 49, 283–306.

Feldman, D. C. (1988). *Managing Careers in Organizations.* Glenview, IL: Scott Foresman.

Feldman, L. and Stephenson, J. (1988). Stay small or get huge—lessons from securities trading. *Harvard Business Review*, 66(3), 116–23.

Fenton-O'Creevy, M. P., Nicholson, N., Soane, E. and Willman, P. (2003). Trading on illusions: Unrealistic perceptions of control and trading performance. *Journal of Occupational and Organisational Psychology*, 76, 53–68.

Feyerabend, P. (1970). Consolations for the specialist. In Lakatos and Musgrave (eds), *Criticism and the Growth of Knowledge.* Cambridge: Cambridge University Press, 197–230.

Fineman, S. (1996). Emotion and organizing. In S. R. Clegg, C. Hardy, and W. R. Nord (eds), *Handbook of Organization.* London: Sage, 543–64.

Finucane, M. L., Slovic, P., Mertz, C. K., Flynn, J., and Satterfield, T. A. (2000). Gender, race and perceived risk: The 'white male' effect. *Health, Risk and Society*, 2(2), 159–72.

Fischoff, B. (1982). For those condemned to study the past: Heuristics and biases in hindsight. In D. E. Kahneman, P. Slovic, and A. Tversky (eds), *Judgment Under Uncertainty: Heuristics and biases.* Cambridge: Cambridge University Press.

References

Fiske, S. and Taylor, S. (1991). *Social Cognition*, 2nd edn. Columbus, OH: McGraw Hill.

—— and Depret, E. (1998). Control, interdependence and power: Understanding social cognition in a social context. In W. Stroebe and M. Hewstone (eds), *European Review of Social Psychology*, Vol. 7. New York: Wiley.

Forgas, J. P. (1989). Mood effects on decision making strategies. *Australian Journal of Psychology*, 41, 197–214.

Frankfurter, G. M. and McGoun, E. G. (1999). Ideology and the Theory of Financial Economics. *Journal of Economic Behaviour and Organisation*, 39, 159–77.

Frese, M. (1995). Error management in training: Conceptual and empirical results. In C. Zucchermaglio, S. Bagnara, and S. U. Stucky (eds), *Organizational Learning and Technological Change*. Berlin: Springer, 112–24.

Friedland, N., Keinan, G., and Regev, Y. (1992). Controlling the uncontrollable—Effects of stress on illusory perceptions of controllability. *Journal of Personality and Social Psychology*, 63, 923–31.

Froot, K. A. and Dabora, E. M. (1999). How are stock prices affected by the location of trade? *Journal of Financial Economics*, 53(2), 189–216.

FSA (2003). Building a framework for operational risk management: the FSA's observations—Feedback on industry practice as we prepare to implement CP142: Operational risk systems and controls—Feedback on CP142. FSA Policy Statement, London.

Furnham, A. (1988). Lay *Theories*. Oxford: Pergamon.

Ganster, D. C., Fusilier, M. R., and Mayes, B. T. (1986). Role of social support in the experiences of stress at work. *Journal of Applied Psychology*, 71, 102–10.

Gasper, K. and Clore, G. L. (1998). The persistent use of negative affect by anxious individuals to estimate risk. *Journal of Personality and Social Psychology*, 74, 1350–63.

Geary, D. C. (1998). *Male, Female: The Evolution of Human Sex Differences*. Washington, DC: American Psychological Association.

Giddens, A. (1990). The *Consequences of Modernity*. Oxford: Polity.

Gigerenzer, G., Todd, P. M., and The ABC Research Group (1999). *Simple Heuristics that Make Us Smart*. Oxford: Oxford University Press.

Goleman, D., Boyatzis, R., and McKee, A. (2001). Primal leadership—the hidden driver of great performance. *Harvard Business Review*, 79(11), 42–53.

References

Gollwitzer, P. M. and Kinney, R. F. (1989). Effects of deliberative and implemental mind-sets on illusion of control. *Journal of Personality And Social Psychology*, 56(4), 531–42.

Greenspan, A. (1995). *Remarks by Alan Greenspan, Chairman, Board of Governors of the US Federal Reserve System*. Paper presented at the Annual Monetary Policy Forum, Stockholm, Sweden, 11th April.

Grefe, J. (1994). *Managementfehler und Fehlermanagement: Eine exploratieve Studie. (Management Errors and Error Management: An Exploratory Study)*. Unpublished thesis, University of Geißen, Germany.

Guidotti, T. L. (1992). Human factors in firefighting—ergonomic, cardiopulmonary, and psychogenic stress-related issues. *International Archives of Occupational and Environmental Health*, 64(1), 1–12.

Hartzmark, M. L. (1991). Luck versus forecast ability: determinants of trader performance in futures markets. *Journal of Business*, 64, 49–74.

Hayek, F. von (1945). The Use of Knowledge in Society. *American Economic Review*, 35, 519–30.

Heimbeck, D., Frese, M., Sonnentag, S., and Keith, N. (2003). Integrating errors into the training process: The function of error management instructions and the role of goal orientation. *Personnel Psychology*, 56(2), 333–61.

Hewstone, M. (ed.) (1983). *Attribution Theory; Social and Functional Extensions*. Oxford: Blackwell.

Hirshleifer, D. and Shumway, T. (2003). Good day sunshine: Stock returns and the weather. *Journal of Finance*, 58(3), 1009–32.

Hoffrage, U., Hertwig, R., and Gigerenzer, G. (2000). Learning, memory and cognition. *Journal of Experimental Psychology*, 26, 566–81.

Hogan, J. and Ones, D. S. (1997). Conscientiousness and integrity at work. In J. Johnson Hogan and S. Briggs (eds.), *Handbook of Personality Psychology* (pp 849–70). London: Academic Press.

Homer, S. and Sylla, R. (1996). *A History of Interest Rates*, 3rd edn. New Brunswick, NJ: Rutgers University Press.

Hoschchild, A. R. (1979). Emotion work, feeling rules and social structure. *American Journal of Sociology*, 85, 551–75.

—— (1983). *The Managed Heart: Commercialisation of Human Feeling*. Berkley, CA: University of California Press.

Houghton, S. M., Simon, M., Aquino, K., and Goldberg, C. B. (2000). No safety in Numbers: Persistence of biases and their effects on team risk perception and team decision making. *Group & Organization Management*, 25(4), 325–53.

References

Humphrey, N. (2002). *The Mind Made Flesh: Frontiers of Psychology and Evolution*. Oxford: Oxford University Press.

Insana, R. (1996). *Traders Tales*. New York: John Wiley.

Isen, A. M., Nygren, T. E., and Ashby, F. G. (1988). Influence of positive affect on the subjective utility of gains and losses—it's just not worth the risk. *Journal of Personality and Social Psychology*, 55(5), 710–17.

Ito, T., Lyons, R. K., and Melvin, M. T. (1998). Is there private information in the FX market; the Tokyo experiment. *Journal of Finance*, LIII(3): 1111–30.

Janis, I. (1972). *Victims of Groupthink*. Boston: Houghton Mifflin.

Jensen, M. C. and Meckling, W. H. (1976). Theory of the firm: Managerial behavior, agency costs, and ownership structure. *Journal of Financial Economics*, 3, 305–60.

Kahn, H. and Cooper, C. L. (1993). *Stress in the Dealing Room*. London: Routledge.

Kahneman, D. and Tversky, A. (1972). Subjective probability: A judgment of representativeness. *Cognitive Psychology*, 3, 430–54.

—— and —— (1973). On the psychology of prediction. *Psychological Review*, 80, 237–51.

—— and —— (1979). Prospect theory: An analysis of decision under risk. *Econometrica*, 47, 263–91.

—— and —— (1982). The psychology of preferences. *Scientific American*, 246(Febuary), 167–73.

—— and —— (1983). Extensional versus intuitive reasoning: The conjunction fallacy in probability judgement. *Psychological Review*, 439–50.

—— Knetsch, J., and Thaler, R. (1991). The endowment effect, loss aversion, and status quo bias. *Journal of Economic Perspectives*, 5, 193–206.

Karasek, R. A. and Theorell, T. (1990). *Healthy Work: Stress, Productivity And The Reconstruction Of Working Life*. New York: Basic Books.

Karoly, P. (1993). Mechanisms of self-regulation: A systems view. *Annual Review of Psychology*, 44, 23–52.

Kelley, H. H. (1967). Attribution theory in social psychology. In D. Levine (ed.), *Nebraska Symposium on Motivation*. Omaha, NE: University of Nebraska Press.

Kelsey, D. and Schepanski, A. (1991). Regret and disappointment in taxpayer reporting decisions: An experimental study. *Journal of Behavioral Decision Making*, 4, 33–53.

Keynes, J. M. (1936). *The General Theory of Unemployment and Inflation.* London: Harvest.

Kindleberger, C. P. (1978). *Manias, Panics and Crashes; A History of Financial Crises.* New York: Basic Books.

Klein, W. M. and Kunda, Z. (1994). Exaggerated self-assessments and the preference for controllable risks. *Organizational Behavior and Human Decision Processes,* 59, 410–17.

Knee, C. R. and Zuckerman, M. (1998). A non-defensive personality: Autonomy and control as moderators of defensive coping and self-handicapping. *Journal of Research in Personality,* 32(2), 115–30.

——— ——— and Kieffer, S. C. (1999). *What Individuals Believe they Can and Cannot Do: Explorations of Realistic and Unrealistic Control Beliefs.* Unpublished working paper, University of Huston.

Knorr Cetina, K. and Bruegger, U. (2002). Global microstructures; The virtual societies of financial markets. *American Journal of Sociology,* 107(4), 905–50.

Kogan, N. and Wallach, M. A. (1964). *Risk Taking: A Study in Cognition and Personality.* New York: Holt, Rhinehard and Winston.

Kowert, P. A. and Hermann, M. G. (1997). Who takes risks? Daring and caution in foreign policy making. *Journal of Conflict Resolution,* 41(5), 611–37.

Kühberger, A. (1998). The influence of framing on risky decisions: A meta-analysis. *Organizational Behavior and Human Decision Processes,* 75(1), 23–55.

Kuhl, J. (1992). A theory of self-regulation: Action versus state orientation, self-discrimination, and some application. *Applied Psychology: An International Review,* 41, 97–129.

Kwon, K. Y. and Kish, R. J. (2002). A comparative study of technical trading strategies and return predictability: An extension of using NYSE and NASDAQ indices. *The Quarterly Review of Economics and Finance,* 42(3), 611–31.

Lam, L. T. and Kirby, S. L. (2002). Is emotional intelligence an advantage? An exploration of the impact of emotional and general intelligence on individual performance. *Journal of Social Psychology,* 142(1), 133–43.

Langer, E. J. (1975). The illusion of control. *Journal of Personality and Social Psychology,* 32(2), 311–28.

Lave, J. and Wenger, E. (1991). *Situated Learning: Legitimate Peripheral Participation.* Cambridge: Cambridge University Press.

References

Lee, C. M. C. (2001). Market efficiency and accounting research: a discussion of 'capital market research in accounting' by S. P. Kothari. *Journal of Accounting and Economics*, 31, 233–53.

Leeson, N. (1996). *Rogue Trader*. London: Little, Brown and Company.

Leidner, R. (1993). *Fast Food, Fast Talk: Service Work and the Routinization of Everyday Work*. Berkeley: University of California Press.

—— (1999). Emotional labor in service work. *Annals of the American Academy of Political and Social Science*, 561, 81–95.

Lewis, M. (1989). *Liars Poker*. London: Hodder and Stoughton.

Lipson, M. L. (2003). Market microstructure and corporate finance. *Journal of Corporate Finance*, 9(4), 377–84.

Lo, A. W. and Repin, D. V. (2002). The psychophysiology of real-time financial risk processing. *Journal of Cognitive Neuroscience*, 14(3), 323–39.

Lopez, R. S. (1986). *The Shape of Medieval Monetary History*. London: Variorum Reprints.

Lord, R. G. and Levy, P. E. (1994). Moving from cognition to action: A control theory perspective. *Applied Psychology: An International Review*, 41, 97–129.

Lothian, J. R. (2002). The internationalization of money and finance and the globalization of financial markets. *Journal of International Money and Finance*, 21(6), 699–724.

Louie, T. A. (1999). Decision makers' hindsight bias after receiving favorable and unfavorable feedback. *Journal of Applied Psychology*, 84(1), 29–41.

Lyons, R. K. (1998). Profits and position control; a week of FX dealing. *Journal of International Money and Finance*, 17(1), 97–115.

MacCrimmon, K. R. and Wehrung, D. A. (1986). *Taking risks: The management of uncertainty*. New York: Free Press.

MacKenzie, D. (2002). *Mathematizing Risk: Markets Arbitrage and Crises*. Paper presented at the Workshop on Organisational Encounters with Risk, April 2002, London School of Economics.

—— and Millo, Y. (2001). *Negotiating a Market, Performing Theory; The Historical Sociology of a Financial Derivatives Exchange*, mimeo, Edinburgh University.

Macrae, C. N., Bodenhausen, G. V., and Milne, A. B. (1998). Saying no to unwanted thoughts: Self-focus and the regulation of mental life. *Journal of Personality and Social Psychology*, 74, 578–89.

Markowitz, H. M. (1952). Portfolio selection. *Journal of Finance*, 7, 77–91.

—— (1991). Foundations of portfolio theory. *Journal of Finance*, 46(2), 469–77.

Martinko, M. J. (ed.) (1995). *Attribution Theory: An Organizational Perspective*. Delray Beach, FL: St Lucie Press.

McCall, B. P., Cavanaugh, M. A., Arvey, R. D., and Taubman, P. (1997). Genetic influences on job and occupational switching. *Journal of Vocational Behavior*, 50, 60–77.

McCrae, R. R. and Costa, P. T. (1997*a*). Personality trait structure as a human universal. *American Psychologist*, 52(5), 509–16.

—— and —— (1997*b*). Conceptions and correlates of openness to experience. In J. Johnson Hogan and S. Briggs (eds.), *Handbook of Personality Psychology*. London: Academic Press, 825–47.

McNamara, G. and Bromiley, P. (1997). Decision making in an organizational setting: Cognitive and organizational influences on risk assessments in commercial lending. *Academy of Management Journal*, 40, 1063–88.

—— and —— (1999). Risk and return in organisational decision making. *Academy of Management Journal*, 42(3), 330–9.

Mehra, R. and Prescott, E. (1985). The equity premium: A puzzle. *Journal of Monetary Economics*, 15, 145–61.

Milburn, M. A. (1978). Sources of bias in the prediction of future events. *Organizational Behavior and Human Performance*, 21, 17–26.

Miller, G. (2000). *The Mating Mind*. London: Heinemann.

Mintzberg, H. (1983). *Structure in Fives*. Englewood, NJ: Prentice Hall.

Mittal, V. and Ross, W. T. Jr. (1998). The impact of positive and negative affect and issue framing on issue interpretation and risk taking. *Organizational Behavior and Human Decision Processes*, 76(3), 298–324.

Mobley, W. (1982). *Employee Turnover: Causes Consequences and Control*. Reading, MA: Addison-Wesley.

Muller-Herold, U. (2000). Risk management strategies—before hominization and after. *Journal of Risk Research*, 3, 19–30.

Nicholson, N. (1987). The transition cycle: A conceptual framework for the analysis of change and human resources management. In J. Ferris and K. M. Rowland (eds), *Personnel and Human Resources Management*, Vol. 5. Greenwich, CT: JAI Press.

—— (1998*a*). Seven deadly syndromes of management and organization: The view from evolutionary psychology. *Managerial and Decision Economics*, 19, 411–26.

—— (1998*b*). Personality and entrepreneurial leadership: A study of the heads of the UK's most successful independent companies. *European Management Journal*, 16, 529–39.

References

—— (2000). *Managing the Human Animal*. London: Texere.

—— and Cannon, D. C. (2000). Two views from the bridge. How CFOs and SME leaders perceive top team dynamics. *European Management Journal*, 18, 367–76.

—— West, M., and Cawsey, T. F. (1985). Future uncertain: Expected versus attained job mobility among managers. *Journal of Occupational Psychology*, 58, 313–20.

—— Fenton-O'Creevy, M., Soane, E., and Willman, P. (2004). Personality and domain specific risk taking. *Journal of Risk Research*, forthcoming.

Nisbett, R. E. and Ross, L. (1980). *Human Inference: Strategies and Shortcomings of Social Judgement*. Englewood cliffs, NJ: Prentice-Hall.

O'Hara, M. (1995). *Market Microstructure Theory*. Oxford: Blackwell.

Östberg, O. (1980). Risk perception and work behaviour in forestry: Implications for accident prevention policy. *Accident Analysis & Prevention*, 12, 189–200.

Pinker, S. (1997). *How the Mind Works*. New York: Norton.

—— (2002). *The Blank Slate*. New York: Viking Penguin.

Porac, J. F., Thomas, H., and Baden-Fuller, C. (1989). Competitive groups as cognitive communities: The case of Scottish knitwear manufacturers. *Journal of Management Studies*, 26(4), 397–416.

Powell, M. and Ansic, D. (1997). Gender differences in risk behaviour in financial decision making: An experiemental analysis. *Journal of Economic Psychology*, 18(6), 605–28.

Powers, W. T. (1973). *Behavior: The Control of Perception*. Chicago: Aldine.

Prechter, R. R. (2002). *The Wave Principle of Human Social Behavior and the New Science of Socionomics*. New York: New Classics Library.

Rajan, R. G. and Zingales, L. (2003). The great reversals: The politics of financial development in the twentieth century. *Journal of Financial Economics*, 69(1), 5–50.

Reber, A. S. (1989). Implicit learning and tacit knowledge. *Journal of Experimental Psychology: General*, 118, 219–35.

Riess, M. and Taylor, J. (1984). Ego-involvement and attributions for success and failure in a field setting. *Personality and Social Psychology Bulletin*, 10, 536–43.

Ross, L. (1977). The intuitive psychologist and his shortcomings: Distortions in attribution processes. In L. Berkowitz (ed.), *Advances in Experimental Psychology*, Vol. 10. New York: Academic Press.

References

Ross, S. A. (1999). Adding risks: Samuelson's fallacy of large numbers revisited. *Journal of Financial and Quantitative Analysis*, Vol. 34: 323–39.

Rude, D. (2000). *The Fallacy of Affirming the Consequent: The Logic Error that Divides Us*. Paper presented to The Society for Judgment and Decision Making Annual Conference, New Orleans.

Rutledge, R. W. (1993). The effects of group decisions and group-shifts on use of the anchoring and adjustment heuristic. *Social Behavior and Personality*, 21, 215–26.

Sabel, C. (1994). Learning by monitoring; The institutions of economic development. In Swedberg and Smelser (eds), *Handbook of Economic Sociology*. Princeton University Press, 137–66.

Salminen, S. and Heiskanen, M. (1997). Correlations between traffic, occupational, sports and home accidents. *Accident Analysis and Prevention*, 29(1), 33–36.

Sandelands, L. E., Brockner, J., and Glynn, M. A. (1988). If at first you don't succeed, try, try again: Effects of persistence performance contingencies, ego involvement, and self-esteem on task persistence. *Journal of Applied Psychology*, 73, 208–16.

Schiller, R. (1981). Do stock prices move too much to be justified by subsequent changes in dividends. *American Economic Review*, 71(3), 421–36.

Shapira, Z. (1995). *Risk Taking: A managerial perspective*. New York: Russell Sage.

—— and Venezia, I. (2001). Patterns of behavior of professionally managed and independent investors. *Journal of Banking & Finance*, 25(8), 1573–87.

Shefrin, H. (2000). *Beyond Greed and Fear; Understanding Behavioral Finance and the Psychology of Investing*. Cambridge: HBS Press.

—— and Statman, M. (1984). Explaining investor preference for cash dividends. *Journal of Financial Economics*, 13, 253–82.

Simonet, S. and Wilde, G. J. S. (1997). Risk: Perception, acceptance and homeostasis. *Applied Psychology: An International Review*, 46, 235–52.

Simonson, I. (1992). The influence of anticipating regret and responsibility on purchase decisions. *The Journal of Consumer Research*, 19(1), 105–18.

Sitkin, S. and Pablo, A. (1992). Reconceptualising the determinants of risk behaviour. *Academy of Management Review*, 17, 9–36.

References

—— and Weingart, L. R. (1995). Determinants of risky decision-making behaviour: A test of the mediating role of risk perceptions and propensity. *Academy of Management Journal*, 38(6), 1573–92.

Slovic, P. (2000). *The Perception of Risk*. London: Earthscan Publications Ltd.

Snyder, M. (1987). *Public Appearances/Private Realities: The Psychology of Self-Monitoring*. Freeman: San Francisco.

Soros, G. (1986). *Theory of Reflexivity*.

—— (1995). *Soros on Soros*. New York: Wiley.

Staw, B. M., Sandelands, L. E., and Dutton, J. E. (1981). Threat-rigidity effects in organizational behavior: A multilevel analysis. *Administrative Science Quarterly*, 26(4), 501–24.

Steinherr, A. (2000). *Derivatives: The Wild Beast of Finance*, 2nd edn. Chichester: Wiley.

Stulz, R. (2001). Why risk management is not rocket science. In J. Pickford (ed.), *Mastering Risk: Volume 1: Concepts*, Vol. 1. London: Pearson Education, 294–300.

Swedberg, R. (1994). Markets as social structures. In Swedberg and Smelser (ed.), *Handbook of Economic Sociology*. Princeton University Press, 255–83.

Taylor, S. E. and Armor, D. A. (1996). Positive illusions and coping with adversity. *Journal of Personality*, 64(4), 873–898.

—— and Brown, J. D. (1988). Illusion and well-being—A social psychological perspective on mental-health. *Psychological Bulletin*, 103(2), 193–210.

Tetlock, P. E. (1991). An alternative metaphor in the study of judgement and choice: People as politicians. *Theory and Psychology*, 1(4), 451–75.

Thaler, R. H. (1991). *Quasi-Rational Economics*. New York: Russel Sage Foundation.

—— (ed.) (1993). *Advances in Behavioral Finance*. New York: Russel Sage Foundation.

—— (1999). The end of behavioral finance? *Financial Analysts Journal*, 55, 12–17.

Tice, D. M., Bratslavsky, E., and Baumeister, R. F. (2002). Emotional distress regulation takes precedence over impulse control: If you feel bad, do it! *Journal of Personality and Social Psychology*, 80, 53–67.

Tomarken, A. J. and Kirschenbaum, D. S. (1982). Self-regulatory failure: Accentuate the positive. *Journal Of Personality And Social Psychology*, 43, 584–97.

References

Tosi, H. and Gomez-Meija, L. R. (1989). The de-coupling of CEO pay and performance; an agency theory perspective. *Administrative Science Quarterly*, 34, 169–90.

Tversky, A. and Kahneman, D. (1971). Belief in the law of small numbers. *Psychological Bulletin*, 76, 105–10.

—— and —— (1986). Rational choice and the framing of decisions. *Journal of Business*, 59, 251–78.

—— and —— (1991). Loss aversion in riskless choice: A reference dependent model. *Quarterly Journal of Economics*, 106, 1039–61.

Vancouver, J. B. and Putka, D. J. (2000). Analyzing goal-striving processes and a test of the generalizability of perceptual control theory. *Organizational Behavior and Human Decision Processes*, 82, 334–62.

Vollrath, M. and Torgersen, S. (2002). Who takes health risks? A probe into eight personality types. *Personality and Individual Differences*, 32(7), 1185–97.

Wannon, M. (1990). *Children's Control Attributions about Controllable and Uncontrollable Events: Their Relationship to Stress Resilience and Psychosocial Adjustment.* Unpublished doctoral dissertation, University of Rochester.

Warner, K. and Molotch, H. (1993). 'Information in the Marketplace; Media Explanations of the 1987 crash'. *Social Problems*, 40, 167–88.

Weber, E. U. and Milliman, R. A. (1997). Perceived risk attitudes: Relating risk perception to risky choice. *Management Science*, 43(2), 123–44.

—— Blais, A. R., and Betz, N. E. (2002). A domain-specific risk-attitude scale: Measuring risk perceptions and risk behaviors. *Journal of Behavioral Decision Making*, 15, 1–28.

Weinstein, E. and Martin, J. (1969). Generality of willingness to take risks. *Psychological Reports*, 24, 499–501.

Welch, J. (1999). Climate of fear and sexism blocks path of City women. *People Management*, 5(6), 12.

Wenger, E. (1998). *Communities of Practice. Learning, Meaning, and Identity.* Cambridge: Cambridge University Press.

West, R. and Hall, J. (1997). The role of personality and attitudes in traffic accident risk. *Applied Psychology: An International Review*, 46, 253–64.

Whiten, A. (ed.) (1991). *Natural Theories of Mind: Evolution, Development and Simulation of Everyday Mind Reading.* Oxford: Blackwell.

Whyte, G., Saks, A., and Hook, S. (1997). When success breeds failure: the role of self-efficacy in escalating commitment to a losing course of action. *Journal of Organizational Behavior*, 18, 415–32.

References

Willman, P. (1997). Appropriability of technology and internal organisation. In I. McLoughlin and M. J. Harris (eds), *Innovation, Organisational Change and Technology*. London: ITB Books.

Wiseman, R. M. and Bromiley, P. (1991). Risk return associations; paradox or artefact? An empirically tested explanation. *Strategic Management Journal*, 12, 231–42.

—— and Catanach, A. H. (1997). A longitudinal disaggregation of operational risk under changing regulations; evidence from the savings and loan industry. *Academy of Management Journal*, 40(4), 799–830.

—— and Gomez-Meija, L. R. (1998). A behavioural agency model of managerial risk taking. *Academy of Management Review*, 23(1), 133–53.

Wright-Mills, C. (1963). Situated actions and vocabularies of motive. In D. Horowitz (ed.), *Power, Politics and People*. Oxford: Oxford University Press.

Yates, J. F. and Stone, E. R. (1992). The risk construct. In J. F. Yates (ed.), *Risk taking behaviour*, 1st edn. New York: Wiley, 1–25.

Zhang, P. G. (1995). *Barings, Bankruptcy and Financial Derivatives*. Singapore: World Scientific Publishing.

Zuckerman, M. (1994). *Behavioral Expression and Biosocial Bases of Sensation Seeking*. Cambridge: Cambridge University Press.

Zuckerman, E. W. (1999). The categorical imperative: Securities analysts and the illegitimacy discount. *American Journal of Sociology*, 104(5), 1398–1438.

Zuckerman, M. and Kuhlman, D. M. (2000). Personality and risk-taking: Common biosocial factors. *Journal of Personality*, 68, 999–1029.

—— Ball, S., and Black, J. (1990). Influences on sensation seeking, gender, risk appraisal, and situational motivation on smoking. *Addictive Behaviors*, 15(3), 209–20.

—— Knee, C. R., Kieffer, S. C., Rawsthorne, L., and Bruce, L. M. (1996). Beliefs in realistic and unrealistic control—assessment and implications. *Journal of Personality*, 64(2), 435–64.

Index

Index

Index

Index

Index